中國—东盟法律评论

China—ASEAN Law Review

总第4卷 2014年 第1期（泰国法专卷）

2014 Thailand Volume

■ 主编　张晓君　纳隆·栽罕（泰国）
Chief Editors：
Zhang Xiaojun　　Narong Jaiharn (Thailand)

■ 中国法学会中国—东盟法律研究中心　主办
泰国法政大学　合办
Sponsors:
China—ASEAN Legal Research Center of China Law Society
Thammasat University of Thailand

中國—东盟法律评论

陈梓滨

Bình liền pháy liật Trung quốc—Asean.

越南—中国—东盟法律信息咨询中心主任陈大兴用越南文字为
《中国—东盟法律评论》题写刊名

Journal Undang Undang Asean-China

冯正仁

马来西亚联邦法院前大法官、第五届"中国—东盟法律合作与发展高层论坛"
组委会主席冯正仁先生以马来语为《中国—东盟法律评论》题写刊名。

柬埔寨司法部大臣昂翁·瓦塔纳用高棉语为《中国—东盟法律评论》题写刊名

中国—东盟法律研究
中心：

法学之花盛开！

任旺隆
驻东盟大使
二〇一四年二月七日

中国—东盟法律研究中心理事会人员名单

■中国

名誉理事长

陈冀平	中国法学会党组书记　中国法学会常务副会长

理事长

张鸣起	中国法学会副会长

副理事长

刘学普	重庆市委常委、市委政法委书记,重庆市法学会会长
谷昭民	中国法学会对外联络部主任
付子堂	西南政法大学校长
罗东川	最高人民法院民四庭庭长

理事（以姓氏笔画数排列）

丁丁（女）	对外经济贸易大学法学院副院长、教授
于娃宪	广西壮族自治区第十二届人民代表大会法制委员会副主任委员
万猛	中国—非洲法律研究中心秘书长,北京外国语大学法学院院长、教授
马巍	中国东南亚南亚金融及资本市场法律实务中心主任,北京大成(昆明)律师事务所主任
王玫黎（女）	西南政法大学教授
王崇敏	海南大学副校长,海南省法学会副会长、教授
邓瑞平	西南政法大学国际法学院书记、教授
王瀚	西北政法大学副校长、教授
卢代富	西南政法大学教授
许明月	西南政法大学期刊编辑部主任、教授
齐虹丽（女）	昆明理工大学法学院副院长、教授
刘晓红（女）	华东政法大学副校长、教授
刘想树	西南政法大学副校长、教授
陈云东	云南大学法学院院长、教授

沈四宝	上海大学法学院院长,上海财经大学教授
杨丽艳(女)	西南政法大学教授
陈忠林	重庆大学教授
陈咏梅(女)	西南政法大学教授
张春良	西南政法大学教授
张晓君	西南政法大学国际法学院院长、教授
陈敏	中国海商法协会秘书长
郑少华	中国—拉美法律研究中心主任,上海财经大学校长助理、教授
周杰普(女)	中国—拉美法律培训基地主任,上海财经大学法学院书记、教授
周喜梅(女)	广西民族大学东盟学院副院长、副教授
赵万一	西南政法大学民商法学院院长、教授
施文	环宇中国—东盟法律合作中心理事长,海南仲裁委主任
唐青阳	中共重庆市委党校副校长,重庆市行政学院副院长、教授
徐泉	西南政法大学科研处处长、教授
高祥	中国政法大学比较法学院院长、教授
高崇慧(女)	云南财经大学法学院院长、教授
盛学军	西南政法大学经济法学院院长、教授
曾文革	重庆大学教授
董石	司法部驻深圳办事处主任
程金华	金砖国家法律研究院常务副院长,华东政法大学教授
慕亚平	WTO 与 CEPA 法律研究中心主任,中山大学教授
谭宗泽	西南政法大学行政法学院院长、教授
潘国平	西南政法大学教授

秘书长

张晓君	西南政法大学国际法学院院长,教授

顾问委员会

■中国

1.张鸣起	中国法学会副会长
2.谷昭民	中国法学会外联部主任
3.张国林	西南政法大学党委书记
4.付子堂	西南政法大学校长
5.吴志攀	北京大学常务副校长
6.王　瀚	西北政法大学副校长
7.杨国华	清华大学法学院教授

■东盟国家

1.占·索斯威	柬埔寨司法部国务秘书
2.克拉罗·阿莱兰诺	菲律宾总检察长
3.王科林	文莱总裁协会会长
4.扎伦·叶宝赫	老挝国家社会科学院院长
5.哈利芬·东巴	印度尼西亚最高法院院长
6.麦特瑞·苏塔帕古	泰国最高法院大法官
7.冯正仁	马来西亚大法官
8.颂奇·乐派吞	泰国法政大学校长
9.温·敏特	缅甸总检察长办公室副主任

编辑委员会

主　　　编:张晓君
　　　　　纳隆·栽罕(泰国法政大学法学院院长)
本期执行编辑:徐忆斌　　王泽银
　　　　　赐米·是里坤促(泰方)　素披丽雅·乔拉易阿(泰方)

Advisory Committee

■China

Zhang Mingqi	Vice-President of the China Law Society
Gu Zhaomin	Director-General of the China Legal Exchange Center
	Director of the Department for Overseas Liaison of the China
	Law Society
Zhang Guolin	Secretary of CPC of Southwest University of Political Science
	and Law
Wu Zhipan	Vice-Chancellor of the Peking University
Fu Zitang	Chancellor of the Southwest University of Political Science
	and Law
Wang Han	Vice-Chancellor of the Northwest University of Politics
	& Law
Yang Guohua	Professor, School of Law, Tsinghua University, Beijing,
	China.

■ASEAN Countries (List in Alphabetical Order)

Chan Sotheavy	Secretary of State of the Ministry of Justice of Cambodia
Claro A. Arellano	The Prosecutor General of the Department of Justice of
	Philippines
Colin Ong	President of the Arbitration Association of Brunei Darussalam
Chaleuan Yapaoher	President of the Laos National Academy of Science in
	Humanity and Culture
Harifin A. Tumpa	President of the Supreme Court of Indonesia
Maitree Sutapakul	Justice of the Supreme Court of Thailand
Soltoni Mohdally	Senior Justice of the Supreme Court of Malaysia
Somkit Lertpaithoon	Rector of the Thammasat University of Thailand
Win Myint	Deputy Director-General of the Office of the
	Prosecutor General of Myanmar

《中国—东盟法律评论》国别法专卷系列

2013 年,中国国家主席习近平提出的共同建设"丝绸之路经济带"和"21世纪海上丝绸之路"的战略倡议得到了东盟各国的积极响应。在此背景下,加深中国与东盟国别法的相互了解,对增强互信互通,促进"一带一路"建设具有重要的现实意义。

《中国—东盟法律评论》国别法专卷系列由中国—东盟法律研究中心协同东盟国家法律、法学组织共同完成,分国别地系统介绍所属东盟国家的法律制度,旨在加强本地区各个国家法律的相互理解。

本期推出的泰国法卷为中国—东盟法律研究中心与泰国法政大学协同合作的成果。中心秘书长张晓君教授担任主编,泰国法政大学法学院院长纳隆·栽罕副教授担任合作主编,由多位资深专家、学者参与撰稿。

泰国国立法政大学是泰国最为古老的大学之一,被誉为"总理"的摇篮,培养了多名最高法院首席大法官、检察官以及优秀的律师,其主编的《法政大学法学期刊》享誉泰国法学界,为泰国一流法学期刊。

我们将继续推出国别法专卷,为"一带一路"法治建设建言献策,为本地区和平、稳定与繁荣做出积极的学术贡献。

《中国—东盟法律评论》编辑部
2014 年

China-ASEAN Law Review Special Volume of Specific Countries

In 2013, Mr. Xi Jinping, the President of People's Republic of China, raised the proposal of building "Silk Road economic belt" and "21st Century Maritime Silk Road". This proposal has received enthusiastic responses from ASEAN countries. In this background, enhancing the mutual-understanding between China laws and ASEAN laws has positive influence on the development of connectivity and establishment of "one belt one road".

China-ASEAN Law Review (special volume of specific countries) is compiled by both China-ASEAN Legal Research Center and legal institutions from ASEAN countries, aiming at introducing the legal system in specific ASEAN countries, as well as improving the mutual-understanding of laws between countries in this region.

China-ASEAN Law Review (special volume of thailand) is compiled by China-ASEAN Legal Research Center and Thammasat University. The chief editor is Professor Zhang Xiaojun, Secretary-General of China-ASEAN Legal Research Center. Associate Professor Narong Jaiharn, the Dean of Law Faculty of Thammasat University, also contributes to this publication as the co-editor. The articles are written by several senior professors.

Thammasat University is one of the eldest Universities in Thailand. It is known as the cradle of "prime minister", and also has educated several chief justices of the Supreme Court, public prosecutors and outstanding lawyers. The *Thammasat Law Journal*, which is edited by Faculty of Law of Thammasat University, enjoys great reputation among the legal professions of Thailand and is one of the first-rate law journals in Thailand. We will continue to publish "special volume of specific countries" to support the construction of legal system which ensures the establishment of "one belt one road", to contribute to the regional peace, stability and prosperity.

Editorial Board of China-ASEAN Law Review
2014

目 录

Contents

编 者 按

　　《中国—东盟法律评论》为东盟国家法律制度专刊,收录了来自中国、印度尼西亚、新加坡、马来西亚、泰国、越南、菲律宾、缅甸、老挝、柬埔寨等 10 国法律、法学界文章;而本书为其第 4 卷,为泰国专题卷,集中收录了涉及泰国民事诉讼、网络侵权、劳动法、政府与私人合作模式、泰国与东盟共同体关系等 10 篇中英文对照的文章,主要反映了泰国法律学者对本国法治发展中存在问题的反思与建议,同时表明中国学者对泰国及东盟法律制度的探索与意见。

　　在《泰国民事诉讼法中的基本规范》一文中,泰国律师协会的成员,法政大学讲师 Ueakarn Sopakdithapong 简要地介绍了泰国民事诉讼法中的 19 类基本规范。涵盖了原告起诉、管辖原则、被告答辩应诉、质证、案件审理等多个民诉法中的框架性规定。其中也包括一些和泰国现今司法现状和国情相应的弹性规定,融合了英美法系的相关规定,体现出与时俱进与改良创新的思维模式。

　　在《版权侵权案件中网络服务提供者的民事责任》一文中,泰国律师协会大律师、法政大学讲师 Chalermwut Sriporm［法政大学讲师 Dr. Jaruprapa Rakpong 翻译］通过比较研究,认为网络服务提供者的责任应属于过错责任。文章指出,一旦网络服务提供者的故意行为造成了权利人的损失,网络服务提供者则需承担相应的民事责任并对受害人进行赔偿。

　　在《泰国劳动法的基本介绍》一文中,泰国法政大学的法律教授［Wichitra (Foongladda) Vichienchom］介绍了劳动法主要是由四种相关类型的法律规范组成的,这些法律规范既适用于私营企业,也适用于国有企业,文中只对泰国劳动法中涉及的私营企业进行介绍。

　　在《PPP》一文中,泰国法政大学法学院 Anak Surasarang 和（Jaruwan Onchan）主要介绍了泰国 PPP 模式,它指通过政府与私人企业的共同合作以实现某项公共服务项目的提供,通常依赖于私人企业的资金和技术并在公共部门的监管下完成。他们还介绍了 PPP 模式的立法发展,并着重对新颁布的 PPP 法的主要内容作出说明,同时对新旧两部 PPP 法进行了简要比较。

在《老年人社会福利保障法》一文中,泰国法政大学副教授［Wichitra (Foongladda) Vichienchom］通过对泰国当前社会福利制度的研究,在比较国际和国外福利制度的基础上,找出了泰国现行法律在社会福利方面规定的不足和缺陷,并提出了一些合理的建议和解决方法。

在《泰国适合成为〈联合国全程或部分海上国际货物运输合同公约〉缔约国》一文中,泰国法政大学运输和海事法律研究所主任,法学院法律中心的主任 Pathaichit Eagjariyakorn① 教授从泰国现有的海上货物运输立法方面的现状与不足出发,引申论述加入《联合国全程或部分海上国际货物运输合同公约》的各种优点,最后提出一些对本国现有法律修改的建议,最终证明,泰国适合成为《联合国全程或部分海上国际货物运输合同公约》的缔约国。

在《泰国税制研究》一文中,泰国法政大学法学院税法教授 Sumet Sirikunchoat 简要说明了泰国的税制功能,在泰国中央税与其他税区别的前提下具体分析《税收法典》中涉及的个人所得税、企业所得税、增值税、营业税、印花税的纳税人、征税对象、税基、税率、纳税期限、纳税地点、豁免条件等,进而提出泰国税制建设需多方面优化。

在《外国国民在泰国从事商业业务的相关立法》一文中,泰国法政大学全职讲师 Ratchaneekorn Larpvanichar 博士［伦敦大学学院博士 Jaruprapa Rakpong 翻译］讨论了两个重要的相关立法,即外商经营法 B. E. 2542(1992) 和境外就业法案 B. E. 2551(2008),这两部法律相互关联且经常被引用。然而,泰国仍然保留了很多仅仅适用于本国国民的职业,因此外国投资商需要参考哪些事业类型是他们可以从事的。最后,由于商业的运作不能没有劳动力,因而又引出了外国商人的雇佣问题。

在《对泰国私人公司法的理解》一文中,泰国法政大学法学院的 Nilubol Lertnuwat 探讨了对泰国私人公司法的基本理解以及 CCC 08 修正案对泰国私人公司法的影响。他从私人公司的 6 个方面入手初步谈及对泰国私人公司的基本理解:泰国私人公司本质与形成、股份与股东、私人有限公司的管理、股东大会、股息和储备基金、资金,并穿插地谈及 CCC 08 修正案在有关泰国私

---

① Professor of Law, Director of the Transport and Maritime Law Institute and Director of the Law Center of the Faculty of Law, Thammasat University.

人公司规定上的四大修改及影响。

在《泰国与东盟共同体》一文中,西南政法大学国际法学院教授杨丽艳携中国—东盟高端法律人才培养基地研究生万强、阮氏河,在东盟共同体即将建成之际,通过对东盟共同体究竟为何物,对于泰国而言有哪些利弊和意义的阐述,引出东盟共同体的作用意义及其对亚太区域的影响等一系列问题的思考。

《中国—东盟法律评论》编辑部
2014 年

Editor's Note

China-ASEAN Law Review is the special journal for the legal system of the ASEAN countries, whose legal law articles are collected from China, Indonesia, Singapore, Malaysia, Thailand, Vietnam, the Philippines, Myanmar, Laos, Cambodia and other countries; this book(volume Ⅳ Oct. 2014) is the special subject for Thammasat University about legal law articles, which concentrates on "Basic Principles in the Law of Civil Procedure in Thailand", "Civil Liability of Website Service Providers in Cases of Copyright Infringement", "Introductory knowledge of Thai Labor Law", "PPP" etc. In addition, "Thailand and the ASEAN Community"(one of the subject results of Projcet 20120134 and Project 33113204002 in China) is also included. In total, 10 law articles are recorded. Those law articles reflect that the Thai law scholars give their own thoughts and suggestions on the problems existing in the development of the rule of law in Thailand, as well as show that Chinese legal scholars do some exploration and bring out opinions about the legal system of Thailand and the ASEAN Community.

In the article "Basic Principles in the Law of Civil Procedure in Thailand", Ueakarn Sopakdithapong, member of the Thai Bar Association, Lecturer of the Thammasat University, gives a brief explanation on the 19 steps of the law of civil procedure in Thailand, starting from the beginning of a trial until the end. It includes bringing a claim to court, jurisdiction, parties to the dispute, claim submission and so on. It includes some elastic rules about Thai current judicial status and the corresponding state as well; and integrates into Anglo-American law system, which shows the features of keeping pace with the times and innovative thinking mode.

In the article "Civil Liability of Website Service Providers in Cases of Copyright Infringement", Chalermwut Sriporm, Barrister-at-Law of the Thai Bar Association; Lecturer of the Thammasat University, by comparative studies, he finds that the civil liability of website service providers is a fault liability. It shows the two reasons for website service provider who consequently has a civil liability and must compensate the victim.

In the article "Introductory Knowledge of Thai Labor Law", Wichitra (Foongladda) Vichienchom, Professor of Law at Thammasat University, mainly tells that Thai labor law can be categorized into four types, which is suitable for both private sector and state enterprise. And this article introduces Thailand's labor law only with regard to private sector.

In the article "PPP", Anak Surasarang and Jaruwan Onchan introduce the PPPs setting, which is a form of cooperation between government and one or more private sector companies for the purpose of completing a project that will serve the public. The funding and operation of the project will be a-chieved through such partnership. And this article focuses on the explanations about the main content of PPPs law and discussions on old and new PPPs law.

In the article "The Provision of Social Welfare for Old-Aged Persons", Associate Professor Wichitra (Foongladda) Vichienchom, points out the in-sufficiency and defect of social welfare, grasps the problems, and finds solutions based on research of the administration of social welfare for old-aged persons in Thailand.

In the article "Suitability for Thailand's Becoming a State Party to the *United Nations Convention on Contracts for the International Carriage of Goods Wholly or Partly By Sea* 2009", Professor Pathaichit Eagjariyakorn[1], Director of the Transport and Maritime Law Institute and Director of the Law Center of the Faculty of Law, Thammasat University, firstly briefly introduces the status and insufficiency of legislation for the carriage of the goods by sea and then

---

[1] Professor of Law, Director of the Transport and Maritime Law Institute and Director of the Law Center of the Faculty of Law, Thammasat University.

tells about the various benefits of becoming a state party to the *United Nations Convention on Contracts for the International Carriage of Goods*, finally gives some suggestions about amending the laws and brings out strong supporting evidence.

In the article "Taxation System in Thailand", Sumet Sirikunchoat, Professor of Tax Law at the Faculty of Law, Thammasat University, introduces the function of Thai tax, and discusses the income tax, value added tax, specific business tax, and stamp duty etc. under the *Revenue Code*; and then brings out that Thailand has much work ahead before it arrives at ideal, systematic tax reforms that result in a better taxation system.

Undertaking Business in Thailand by Foreign Nationals: Related Legislation, written by Dr. Ratchaneekorn Larpvanichar, full-time Lecturer of the Faculty of Law, Thammasat University, translated by Dr. Jaruprapa Rakpong, PhD (European and International Trade Laws), of University College London, discusses two important legislations B. E. 2542(1992) and B. E. 2551(2008), which are correlative and cited inevitably. However, in the case of foreign investors, there will be additional problems compared to investors native to the country concerned. This article is limited to the study of the law concerning undertaking of businesses by foreign nationals defined in the Act and the law concerning work undertaken by foreign nationals, which affect the employment of foreign nationals to various positions within the respective business.

In the article "The Understanding of Thai Private Company Law", Nilubol Lertnuwat (Faculty of Law, Thammasat University) is intended to provide the fundamental understanding of Thai private company law and points out some significant changes in Thai private company law as a result of the amendment of the CCC in 2008. This article introduces the private company from six aspects: nature and formation of Thai private company, shares and shareholders, management of Thai private limited company, shareholders' meeting, dividends and reserve funds and capital. What's more, the author also discusses four significant changes in Thai private company law as a result of the amendment of the CCC in 2008 alternately.

"Thailand and the ASEAN Community", written by Yang Liyan,

Professor of the Southwest University of Political Science and Law, and Wan Qiang & Ruan Shihe, the graduate student of School of International Law, they introduce what is the ASEAN Community, What does it brings about for Thailand. This paper tries to discuss about such questions and even turns to the topic of ASEAN Community's significance and effects on Asian-Pacific region.

Editorial Board of China-ASEAN Law Review
2014

泰国民事诉讼法中的基本规范

Ueakarn Sopakdithapong[*]
周楠萱 译

在私法领域,当事人之间形成法律关系后,一方会出于对另一方的权利和义务的尊重而自愿履行义务。但是债务人有可能会恶意地怠于履行义务,债权人则会在法律允许的范围内想方设法实现自己的权利。在这类案例中,如果法律纵容他们实现权利的方式,势必会造成社会混乱。因此有必要创设一些规则和程序来规范他们民事实体权利的实现方式,这些规则和程序被称为民事程序法,包括民事诉讼法、法院组织法等。当一方主张实体权利时,就必须向法院起诉;要得到法院的审判,就必须遵循民事诉讼法的步骤及规则;否则权利主张将得不到法院的支持。

在泰国,各种民事纠纷可以被划分为一般纠纷、小型纠纷、确权纠纷、家庭纠纷、破产纠纷、劳工纠纷等。

下面简要地介绍一下泰国民事诉讼法中规定的从案件受理到结束的 19个步骤。

一、起诉

起诉必须遵循一定的规则,当事人适合且主动提起的诉讼才会被法院受理,一般分为两类:一是权利遭到异议;二是请求司法救济。

前者对权利本身有争议,即自己的民商法实体权利请求被否认或者被主张失效。原告对权利异议的主张即使不成立,仍有权起诉,此时法院核实后可以驳回起诉。

---

[*] LLB(Second Class Honors), member of the Thai Bar Association, Lecturer, Thammasat University.

后者期待自己权利的实现能得到司法保障,有时它需要先获得法院的确认。此类诉讼请求必须是无争议的事实且有实体法依据,否则坚持起诉也会被驳回。

二、管辖

除法律另有规定外,民事案件的审理从一审开始。

依照法院组织法,标的额不超过 300000 泰铢的由简易法院管辖,没有标的额限制或不直接涉及标的额的由其他一审法院审理。诉讼须向有管辖权的法院提起。管辖分为一般管辖和特殊管辖两类。

通常情况下,案件由被告居住地法院管辖。自然人有多处居所的,其居住地指占优势的居所。法人除章程另有规定外,其居住地通常指总公司或业务开展所在地,此外其他业务开展地及分支机构所在地也都会被视为居住地。被告无居住地,在受诉之前两年内有国内居住地的,该居住地将被视为被告居住地。

除了被告居住地的管辖原则外,因发生事故产生纠纷的,原告可以向事故发生地的法院提出诉讼。所谓事故发生地,在合同案件中指合同出现争议或者违约地,在侵权案件中指侵权行为发生地。对于其中没有争议的诉讼如宣告失踪,需要向事故发生地或者被宣告失踪人的可能失踪地、原告住所地法院提起诉讼。

特殊管辖只发生在特殊的情况下。例如不动产纠纷,需要在不动产所在地或者被告居住地提起诉讼。在泰国的轮船或者飞机上发生的纠纷,需要向泰国的法院提出诉讼。被告居住地及事故发生地均不在泰国时,如果原告是泰国人或者居住在泰国,需要向原告居住地法院或下级法院提起诉讼。对于其中没有争议的诉讼如遗产执行,需要在死亡发生地法院起诉。如果死亡不发生在国内,需要向遗产所在地法院提起诉讼。不同的诉讼请求和相关申请都只能向同一法院提起,但涉及财产执行的需要提交至有执行权的法院。

为了避免户籍所在地、争议财产所在地、事故发生地的管辖冲突,原告或被告可以基于便利原则向其中任意有管辖权的法院提起诉讼。民诉法未规定协议管辖,且该协议会因违反公序良俗原则而无效。

当原告将案件诉讼至没有管辖权的法院时,法院将裁定不予受理并向其告知或建议其向有管辖权的法院起诉,诉讼费用也将被退还。但是,如果被告坚称原告提起了错误的诉讼,法院将不予考虑案件并不予退还诉讼费用,因为在这种情况下对管辖的判决是终局。

三、诉讼参与人

泰国民诉法规定,有权起诉的自然人或法人应当具备相应的民事行为能力。未成年人、无民事行为能力人、限制民事行为能力人获得适格起诉人的书面许可的,也可以起诉。

当事人可以提起共同诉讼,共同诉讼代表人的代理权限只限于出庭、延期审理和休庭等程序利益。

当第三人有相关利益或其他正当理由时,民事诉讼法允许他参与诉讼。第三人参与诉讼的,可以独立地参与诉讼,也可以代替或者加入某一方当事人。

当事人有权委托律师或法律顾问参与诉讼。一方不愿参与诉讼时,可以委托律师、法律顾问等代表其充分行使程序权利。

四、诉讼费用的免除

通常情况下,原告需要向法院支付诉讼费用。但是满足法定条件时,诉讼费用可以免除,即有足够证据证明缺少足够的费用支付或支付费用后将出现资金危机。免除诉讼费用的请求需要由当事人在起诉或者审理阶段主动提出,法院有权裁定全部免除或部分免除,当事人在收到裁定 7 日内有权向法院申诉一次。申请免除的费用包括向法院支付的诉讼费用及向对方当事人支付的必要费用。诉讼费用的免除,不影响判决的执行。

五、提交起诉书

起诉所涉案件可以分为事实有争议和无争议两大类。法院只接受符合规定的书面起诉书,内容包括法院名称、原被告、起诉书提交时间及诉讼理由等。

起诉书必须明确案件类型和案由,并且向法院阐明相关事实及提供充分的证据,否则法院可以依法拒绝受理。起诉书不要求列明具体法规。

起诉书提交后,原告不得就同一事由向法院提起同一诉讼,即"已决事件"原则。在实践中,违反此原则的二次起诉将被法院拒绝受理,即使得到审判也不能使二次起诉行为得到合法认可。

六、向被告送达传票

原告向法院提交起诉书及副本,法院向被告送达起诉书和传票。送达文书及通知的费用由原告支付。

原告有义务要求法院在起诉书提交7天内向被告发出传票。原告也可能被要求履行一些额外的义务,如向被告送达起诉书副本。如果违反了其中的某项规定,该案件可能会被法院除名,此时原告可以在诉讼期限内再次提交起诉书。

起诉书等司法文件应当送达被告居住地。如果被告委托了律师,文件可以发往该律师的居住地或者办公地。文件派送应当在白天进行,不限于工作日。如果无法与被告取得联系,则可以送达永久居住于被告居住地附近已满20岁的公民,但是利害关系人除外。任何情况下,文件不送达居住地或办公地的一方可以说明具体情况,再予以送达或当庭送达。起诉书等司法文件也可以通过电子邮箱的方式送达。

当事人一方应接收相关文件而无正当理由拒绝接收的,法官可以请求行政长官如社区总管或警官担任证人,张贴告示以表明文件已送达。如果当事人还是拒绝接收,那起诉书及其他文件可以摆放在其面前以示合法送达。在这种情况下,必须经证人记录并签字并在事后予以记录。

如果因为被告或其代理人不在场或者不能找到而影响起诉书及其他文件的送达,原告可以请求在送达失败后15天内继续审理该案件。法院同意原告请求时,将寻求替代送达方法,如在居住地、工作地的显著位置张贴起诉书,在15天或者法院认为送达成功后,该种方式的送达被视为有效送达。

当被告居住地在国外时,传票及起诉书副本应当送达被告的居住地。如果送达方式不合法,该诉讼也会被认为是不合法的,此时被告没有应诉的义务。如果一审法院对无效送达的案件进行了审理,上诉法院有权宣布该审理无效。

七、被告答辩

被告收到法院的传票后,有义务对原告的主张进行回复,并在收到相关文件15天内向法院递交答辩状。紧急情况下,被告可以请求延期答辩,是否准许由法院决定。

答辩状应当列明被告对原告陈词认可情况的理由,以及自己对该案件结果的处理方式。如果答辩状不符合规定,法院有权拒绝并要求被告予以补正,此时被告可以该要求并非诉讼程序处理中的要求为由予以及时反馈。

被告需明确陈述接受或者拒绝原告主张,以及拒绝理由。被告没有提出合理的拒绝理由的,无权质疑相应的证据及证人证言。与此相对,原告仍享有此权利。被告给出无法辨认是接受还是拒绝的答复的,将被视为不否认或者变相接受了原告的主张。

被告除了对原告的陈述予以抗辩外,还可以提起反诉。在原告坚持自己主张的基础上,被告可以在本诉审理时提起反诉,反诉必须和之前提交的信息一致。与本诉无关的反诉、基于法院的判决而提出的附条件的反诉都被视为无效。

八、被告应诉

当事人可以向法院书面提起修正诉讼请求或者应诉的申请。该书面请求需要在和解前或质证 7 天前提交。在并没有确定和解时间及质证时间时,为避免申请提交超过期限,法院在认为有正当理由时将支持延迟申请。除了出现直接影响案件审理或者公共秩序的重大失误外,原告的申请将同样被准许。

原告请求改变诉讼标的额或者重新确定诉讼标的的价值的,应当撤诉或者调整其诉讼请求。诉讼请求的调整只能基于原有诉讼请求之上,增加新的诉讼请求是不被允许的,否则被告可以抗辩。

九、撤诉

当事人可以自愿撤诉。在被告答辩之前,原告向法院提交书面撤诉请求的,在不完全影响被告时,法院通常允许其撤诉。当被告答辩后,原告向法院提交书面撤诉请求的,法院需征求被告的意见再作决定。因原被告和解而撤诉的,法院应当允许。

撤诉将终止诉讼及相关法律程序,当事人将回到起诉前的状态。除非达成不再起诉的协议,双方当事人都可以在法定期限内再次提起诉讼,此时法院可以免除部分诉讼费用。

十、纠纷解决

收到起诉书和答辩状等相关文件后或者已过答辩期限时，法院开始对案件进行审查和复核。在特定情况下，法院可以不进行质证直接宣判。

在实践中，法院会组织当事人会面并进行庭外调解。如果双方和解，原告可以撤诉或者由法院就和解协议的内容进行宣判。如果双方不能达成和解，法院将继续审理该纠纷。解决纠纷最主要的是需要核实当事人出席法庭、陈述相关事实、质证等案件要点。

在纠纷解决当日，法院将对所有事实进行提问。对于无争议事实，主张该事实的一方免除证明义务。否认事实必须有充分理由，否则仍被视为接受该事实，但否认方无证明义务的除外。否认事实的当事人需要在7天内与法院再次商讨解决方式并提交相关证据。

如果当事人一方或多方缺席纠纷解决，法院将继续受理案件并视为缺席方已知晓该程序的进行。缺席方将丧失确认案件解决方案和相关证据的权利，但缺席符合法律规定或涉及公共秩序的除外。

十一、审理

一审法院收到原告的起诉书和被告的答辩状或者已过被告答辩时间后，法院将开始审理此案。除特殊情况外，如当事人未收到出庭通知时，当事人应当出庭。审理应当对公众开放，但涉及离婚等个人隐私的案件除外。某些案件基于当事人的申请或者法院决定可以采用简易程序，此时法院将只对个别争议点进行审理，简易程序因不包括质证环节而耗时较短。

案件可能会在必要时延期审理，延期审理的启动可以因当事人申请，也可以由法院决定。例如当出现当事人丧失民事行为能力、代理人死亡或丧失代理资格等情况时需要延期审理，法院获得该方继续审理案件的申请或者收到已经重新委托代理人、律师的通知时，才能继续审理。法院将设定期限，超过该期限时，审理程序将继续进行。

十二、质证

案件纠纷的解决需要质证，证据可以是证人、书证、物证等。

在民事案件中,法院认定某一方提出的证据有利于事实的成立,则会支持该证据。这不同于刑事案件中,法院需要质疑原告的证据直至排除被告的合理怀疑。

质证针对的事实要件包括被告权利及义务的状态及产生原因,针对的法律争议包括法律解释、法律适用和法律分析。对于常识、无须验证的史实或者被双方认可的事实,无须质证。但特定情况下,一方也可以就已被双方认可的事实提出异议,这些特定情况仅限于对案件相关证人的资格复核。

在质证环节,谁主张、谁举证。通常情况下是原告发起诉讼争取权利,所以承担相应的证明义务。如果证据不充分,原告则可能败诉。而当证据充分时,被告就可以对原告提出的证据进行质疑以削弱证据的可信度。双方也可以进行互相质证。当原告提出的证据涉及公共文件、官方证明或是被法院认可的私人文件时则无须证明,此时举证责任倒置。特殊证据将不会被采用,如无完全民事行为能力的证人、与案件无关的证据,或者可能导致审理时间过长的证据等。法院还会避免采用无可信度的传来证据,除非该证人同样能证明事实或者不能将直接证人带到法庭。通常情况下,法院对证据类型并不会限制。但相关文件成为证据时,法院将采用书面且自愿的合同作为证据。

为了顺利展开质证,当事人需要上交证据清单且对需要质证的证据进行分类。当事人在第一次质证 7 天前需要上交证据清单,在第一次质证 15 天前可以增加证据。法院可以秉着公平的原则认可没有列明的证据,法律允许庭外质证及电话远程质证。

泰国的法律体系对证人进行最大限度的保护,尤其是证人证言涉及政府机关、法律咨询、专利等机密信息时。通常当事人会向法院提供书证,如果该书证已属于对方当事人或第三人,那该方无须提供复印件就可以请求法院向该证据的持有者收回该证据。除由于不可抗力灭失等原因外,只有原始证据才会被采信。

十三、缺席判决

被告在收到传票后 15 天内仍未答辩的,原告可以请求法院缺席判决。原告未请求时,法院可以对该案件除名,也可以继续审理此案。在被告缺席判决的原因明确且不违反法律规定时,法院会同意缺席判决的请求。法院将单独对原告进行质证,当案件涉及个人身份、家庭、财产所有权、债务强制执行等情况时,法院必须在判决案件前对原告进行质证。对此被告也需要递交申请,陈述缺席判决的理由。如果被告不遵循这一步，就可能在质证环节受到限制，即被告的证据将不被质证，只可以与原告的证人进行相互质证。被告可以在法院作出准许原告缺席判决的决定的 15 日内，陈述合理的理由以及表明胜诉的可能性，以使法院撤销该决定。当有介入因素存在时，被告可以在介入因素消除后 15 天内提交该撤销申请，是否准许由法院决定。如果法院否决该请求，则被告可以对此提起上诉，上诉法院下发的判决将是终审判决。

纠纷双方都可能错过法院对质证的安排。质证对象包括事实争议和相关文件，对相关文件质证环节的缺席将被认为是已知晓且放弃了相关权利。当事人双方均缺席质证环节的，法院将终止诉讼程序。在特殊情况下，如被告要求继续审理时，法院可以继续审理。

十四、简易案件和小额诉讼

简易案件指诉讼标的额不超过 300000 泰铢或者不涉及明确货币价值的案件。简易案件适用周期短的简易程序。原告可以对此提出书面或口头的申请。书面申请中缺乏核心诉讼标的时，法院会要求补充。法院不得以事实不清楚等理由不受理此类案件，因为大部分简易案件都没有律师的帮助。

法院将确定案件审理时间并向被告发出传票。收到该传票后，被告会在 1 天内完成答辩、调解、质证等相关程序。如果调解成功，则结案。反之，被告将对原告的主张进行书面或者口头的反驳。如果法院认为被告的答辩有误，则将要求被告修正答辩并再次质证。被告不出庭或在未答辩的情况下出庭的，法院将会支持原告缺席判决的请求。被告递交答辩状却未出庭的，则是缺席质证。原告未出庭的，法院将终止审理。

简易案件是以问答式来推进案件进程的，所以法院有权引入新证据，也有权对该证据进行质证。

小额诉讼则指超过 300000 泰铢的债务强制执行。借款总额需要在书面合同中明确。原告同样可以提起加快案件审理的请求。如果法院认为该案件中不涉及疑难点，则可以适用简易案件的审理规则。如果案件需要更多的法律解释，则适用一般的民事案件审理程序。

十五、法院判决及约束力

法院的判决对当事人及权利继受者有约束力。权利继受者指如果一方当事人死亡,继受该司法程序中权利义务的人。但是判决不能约束第三人,涉及民事行为能力及所有权的情况除外。当事人可以事后另行向第三人提起诉讼。

法院判决的范围限于起诉书或者答辩状的诉讼请求范围,否则当事人可以请求撤销该判决,但涉及公序良俗的除外。

十六、向上诉法院及最高法院上诉

当事人的诉讼请求只得到法院判决的部分支持时,可以向上级法院或最高法院上诉。法律规定不能上诉的除外,如达成和解的情况。

当事人可以就事实要件和法律要件进行上诉。对事实要件上诉的,标的额需超过 50000 泰铢,案件涉及个人权利和家庭利益的不受此限。案件中不含标的额的也可以上诉,如要求返还原物。当事人不能上诉却力求上诉的需要是案件结果存在异议或能说明上诉理由的案件,获得案件一审审判长或者地区审判长同意后即可上诉。上诉的事实要件及法律要件必须是先前合法提出的。上诉人需在一审法院作出终审判决 1 个月前提起上诉并且证明自己向另一方当事人承担诉讼费用的能力。

当事人可以选择直接向最高法院提起上诉,称为"越级诉讼"。当事人向作出判决的一审法院提交的申请应限于法律要件的争议,在另一方当事人不上诉且对该上诉未提出异议时,才能实现越级诉讼。

上诉阶段不需要再进行质证。除第一审法院中已质证的证据还存在疑点外,一审法院将直接向上诉法院提交汇总的证据。一般情况下,上诉至最高法院的案件与上诉法院的案件类似,但超过 200000 泰铢的案件将诉至最高法院。

十七、判决前的临时指令

判决前的临时指令是有利于判决结果执行的程序。指令分为财产没收和临时控制。

财产的冻结和没收旨在确保财产在宣判后顺利支付给债权人。被告可以向法院提出请求,要求原告示明自身财产及其安全性。原告无必要财产的,法院将终止该案件的审理。除小额诉讼外,原告可以提出和争议相关的没收财产、冻结被告或者第三人财产的申请。指令还会禁止被告向外转移涉案财产和其他财产。法院基于必要性和合理性可以通过或者否决该申请。

如果被告胜诉,原告不再上诉,临时的指令在判决下达 7 日后失效。如果原告胜诉,那么临时指令的效力将维持至判决或指令的执行。

十八、判决结果的执行

法院作出判决后,胜诉方可以依据判决结果行使其权利。在某些情况下不存在债务的执行,例如被告胜诉或者法院不要求被告承担诉讼费用时,此时判决结果不会包含债务。

债务人恶意不履行或部分履行义务的,债权人可以在判决后 10 年内依据判决结果要求强制执行。而对判决结果的审理被看作是终审裁定。但是法律并没有对 10 年作硬性规定,即使在 10 年内不间断地执行,也不妨碍 10 年后胜诉方权利的行使。

执行可以通过执行官和第三人两种方式实现。

执行官执行时,债权人收到执行的通知后告知执行官予以执行。在涉及资金的诉讼中,执行官会在诉讼标的额内先行冻结债务人的财产以便拍卖后清偿债务。资金给付的债务,有可能会涉及物的所有权,或其他债的优先受偿权的问题。对此,有利害关系的第三方可以向法院提出申请,质疑涉案财产。财产没收冻结后,债务人将不能生成、转移、变更所涉财产和所涉案件。在拍卖前,债务人可以请求扣除拍卖中可能取得的费用。在拍卖的过程中,如执行官采取不合法的手段,如低于正常价格拍卖财产等,相关人员如投标人有权申请该拍卖无效。如果执行官执行的是没有资金给付的案件,法律规定执行官可以采取财产转移等任何有利于债权人占有该财产的措施。如果债务人抗拒执行,执行官可以上报至法院,法院将对债务人及相关人员进行逮捕。

第三人的执行指债务人需要权利登记或者其他有关法人行为的情况,还包括要求为或不为一定的行为。如果债务人不履行,则会被法院认为是动机不明,此时债权人有权请求法院进行拘留、扣押。

有执行权的法院通常指审理该案件并作出一审判决的法院。在特殊的执行中,如涉及非法拍卖等情况时,可以诉至执行法庭。所以,考虑到执行财产与执行法庭不在同一个地方,执行工作将会被移转至执行财产所在的执行法庭。而拍卖时,买方需要向执行财产所在地法院递交申请。

十九、结案

通常情况下,案件审结于法院公布审判结果并宣布执行时。在泰国法律体系中,民事案件还可以通过调解和仲裁两种方式审结。

调解由法院负责。如果法院认为当事人可以自行和解,则会要求当事人商讨相关事宜。而且,无论案件推进到哪一步,都允许法院促成双方和解。法院允许调解在私下进行,也可以委托调解人参与到纠纷解决中。调解成功后将签署调解协议,然后原告可以撤诉,或者法院依据协议进行判决。

仲裁包含庭内仲裁和庭外仲裁两类。仲裁官可以是一人或数人。他们承担和法官类似的工作,由一方当事人委托。仲裁是一种极为快捷有效的争端解决方式,尤其是在国际贸易中。仲裁的决定一般是最终的,所以可以提高效率,节约时间。

Basic Principles in the Law of Civil Procedure in Thailand

Ueakarn Sopakdithapong[*]

As an assumption in private law, a person respects the right and obligation of another and is willing to fulfill his or her obligation if there exists a legal relationship between the persons. However, it is possible that the debtor is not willing to fulfill his obligation in paying back the debt though he is capable of doing so. When such a problem takes place, the right holder will seek a channel to enforce the performance of another person as far as private law allows. In this case, if the State lets the people provoke their rights to enforce performance as they wish, social disorder will arise. The State, therefore, enacts laws to set out rules and procedures that serve the function of rights and obligations under private law. Such laws are bundles of rules called the law of "civil procedure" which involves at least the civil procedure code and law for the organization of the courts of justice. [2] When a person seeks to exercise his right under private law (substantive law), he will have to submit a claim to court. In order to receive a court judgment and enforcement thereof, the steps and rules set out in the law of civil procedure (procedural law) must be followed; [3]

---

[*] LLB(Second Class Honors), member of the Thai Bar Association, Lecturer, Thammasat University.

[2] Kanit Na-Nakorn, *Law of Civil Procedure: Book on Civil Trial*, 2nd Ed., Revision, Bangkok: Winyuchon Publishing, 2009, pp. 27~29.

[3] Sopol Rattanakorn, *The Law of Evidence*, 9th Ed., Bangkok: Nitibannakarn Publishing, 2008, p. 13.

otherwise the court may deny enforcing the right claimed by the person.

In general, disputes brought before "the civil court" are "civil disputes". These disputes arise between private parties with regards to rights and obligations under private law such as specific performance arising from a contract term and claims for damages in tort cases. In Thailand, disputes can be divided into general disputes, petty cases and small claims, family disputes, bankruptcy disputes and labor disputes.

The following is a brief explanation for the 19 steps of the law of civil procedure in Thailand, starting from the beginning of a trial until the end.

1. Bringing a claim to court

The court is in charge of reviewing cases that the party to the dispute brings to court. However, not everybody can bring a claim to court. The process that a claim is brought to court must follow certain rules. [1] Pursuant to Section 55 of the *Civil Procedure Code*, persons who have a right to bring a claim to court can be divided into two categories: (1) persons whose right has been contested and (2) persons requiring judicial protection. Persons that fall out of the scope of these two categories cannot bring a claim to court.

1.1   Contestation of rights

A case involving contestation of right is a contentious case. That is, the claiming party claims that he or she has a right over and above another party (the contesting party), while the contesting party refuses the right claimed by the claiming party, or the contesting party claims for another right which is over and above that of the claiming party. The right claimed must be a right under civil law[2] which could be found in the *Civil and Commercial Code* or other relevant laws. Although the claimant (plaintiff) might be

---

[1]   Prapon Satamarn, *Seminar on Civil Procedure*, Bangkok: Institute of Legal Education of the Thai Bar, 1975, p. 1.

[2]   Thanin Kraivichien, Explanation on the Law of Civil Procedure, Bangkok: Ramkhamhaeng University Press, 1975, p. 8.

mistaken that he has a right over and above the defendant, he still has the right to bring a claim to court. In this case, when evidence is examined and the court finds that the plaintiff has no right to bring such a claim to court, the case will be dismissed. [1]

1.2 Unilateral requirement for judicial protection

A person may have a right guaranteed by the law, but the law requires that judicial protection or measures are needed to enforce the right. In other cases, a person may need a court approval or endorsement before exercising the right. [2] In doing so, there must be substantive law that allows a person to make a non-disputed claim to court, and only persons within the scope of substantive law may make such requests. [3] The Supreme Court has explained that, if there is no law supporting the right claimed, the claimant can not successfully make a request to enforce such right. In that case, the claimant requested that the court order that he was the same person as Mr. S. The court in that case ruled that when there is no law allowing the person to make such a non-disputed claim, the court cannot accept the claim as requested. (Supreme Court Case No. 100/2524)

2. Jurisdiction

A civil case always starts at the first instance, except the law states otherwise. Pursuant to Section 25 of the *Act Promulgating the Law for the Organization of the Courts of Justice* B. E. 2543(2000), if the value of the dispute or the amount claimed is not exceeding 300,000 baht, [4] the court that has jurisdiction over the claim is the Summary Court. Other courts of

---

① Jakrapong Leksakulchai, *Explanation on the Civil Procedure Code*, 11th Ed., Bangkok: Nitidhama Publishing, 2010, p. 3.

② Manoch Joramart, *Explanation on the Civil Procedure Code* 1, 2nd Ed., Bangkok: Bannakom Publishing, 1979, p. 257.

③ Thanin Kraivichien, p. 515.

④ See the *Act Promulgating the Law for the Organization of the Courts of Justice* B. E. 2543, Section 25.

first instance have jurisdiction over cases with no limit to the amount claimed and cases with no monetary claim. [1]

For civil cases, the *Civil Procedure Code* requires that the claimant bring his claim to court that has jurisdiction. Jurisdiction can be divided into two categories: general jurisdiction and specific jurisdiction. [2]

2.1 General jurisdiction

For a disputed claim, general jurisdiction means cases under Section 4 (1)of the *Civil Procedure Code*. In general, it is the court situated in the place of domicile of the defendant. For a natural(non-juristic)person, a place of domicile usually refers to the dominant place of residence of the person. There may be more than one place of domicile. For a juristic person, it refers to a place where the head office or the main place of business is situated, otherwise it can be a special domicile or a domicile specified in the constitution of the company. In cases where there is more than one place of business and there are also branches, each place of business or branch is deemed to be domicile for part of the place where the business is operated. Pursuant to Section 3(1)of the *Civil Procedure Code*, if it appears that the defendant is not domiciled in the country but used to have domestic domicile within two years before the plaintiff makes a claim; such a place is deemed to be the defendant's domicile. In cases where the defendant operates or has operated business in whole or in part in the country, whether by himself, his representative or his agent, the place where the business is operated is deemed to be the domicile of the defendant(if the plaintiff makes a claim within two years of the defendant's business operation).

Besides the place of domicile, the claimant may also bring a claim to court situated in the place where the cause of action arises. A "cause of action" means a cause which is a basis for the contestation of right giving rise to the claimant's right of claim. Other places include related places

---

[1]　See the *Act Promulgating the Law for the Organization of the Courts of Justice B.E. 2543*, Section 18 and Section 19.

[2]　Khanit Na-Nakorn, p. 72.

(Supreme Court Case No. 2437/2540). In cases of contract claims, it means the place where the contract at issue is concluded or the place where the contract is dishonored. [①] In cases of torts, it means the place where the tortuous act is committed. Although an insurance company may pay compensation for the damage and subsequently gains a right to recourse against the defendant, the claim must be brought to court where the tortuous act takes place, not the place where the insurance compensation is paid.

For the non-disputed claim such as a petition filed to have a court order that someone is a permanently missing person, generally Section 4(2) of the *Civil Procedure Code* requires that the petitions submit to the court in the jurisdiction where the cause of action takes place, for example, the place where the person is suspected to be missing or the place where the petitioner is domiciled.

2. 2　Specific jurisdiction

Specific jurisdiction arises in certain circumstances. Pursuant to Section 4*bis*, a non-disputed claim such as a claim regarding immovable property (such as mortgage enforcement) must be brought to court where the property is situated or the place of the defendant's domicile. In cases involving disputes taking place on a Thai vessel or a Thai aircraft located outside of Thailand, Section 3 requires that the claim be brought to the civil court in Thailand. In cases where the defendant is not domiciled in Thailand and the cause of action does not take place in Thailand, Section 4*ter* requires that, if the claimant is a Thai national or domiciled in Thailand, a claim must be brought to the civil court or the court in the jurisdiction where the claimant is domiciled.

For non-disputed claims including a petition requesting for an appointment of an estate executor, Section 4 *quarter* requires that the petition be submitted to the court in the jurisdiction where the deceased is domiciled. However, if the deceased is not domiciled in the country, the

----

① Jakrapong Leksakulchai, p. 25.

petition should be submitted to the court in the jurisdiction where the inherited property is situated. In addition, any claim regarding a juristic person, Section 4 *quiquies* requires that the claim be submitted to the court in the jurisdiction where the head office of the juristic person is situated.

Moreover, any claim or petition submitted to the court at a later date which is to be brought to the court previously accepted the claim or petition in accordance with Section 7, such as petitions related to an execution of judgment, the petition must be brought to the court that has the power to execute the judgment under Section 302(i. e. the court that issues the notice of execution).

In cases where several courts concurrently have jurisdiction due to multiple qualified place of domicile, location of the disputed property, the place where the cause of action takes place, or wrong doing, Section 5 states that the plaintiff or claimant may bring a claim or petition to any court that has jurisdiction in order to make it convenient for the plaintiff or claimant.

According to the *Civil Procedure Code*, there is no provision that allows the parties to the dispute to make a prior agreement upon the court jurisdiction. The agreement to do so is contrary to the public order and morale. As a result, such a contract provision is null and void, pursuant to Section 150 of the *Civil and Commercial Code*.

If the claimant brings a case to a court that does not have jurisdiction, Section 18 allows the court to return the claim to the party and may suggest him or her to resubmit the claim to a court that has jurisdiction. A paid court fee may be refunded, pursuant to Section 151. However, if the defendant alleges that the claimant brings the case to a wrong court, the court may dismiss the claim and order that the court fee is non-refundable pursuant to Section 151 because the judgment given on the issue of jurisdiction is considered a final review for the case. [1]

3. Parties to the dispute

Pursuant to the *Civil Procedure Code*, both natural persons and juristic persons have a right of claim in civil cases. That is, an entity that is not qualified as a natural or juristic person such as a group and a department, does not have a right of claim,[2] whether or not such an entity is a Thai national.

The person that wishes to bring a claim to court or litigate must be a person with competence. However, this does not mean that the lack of competence will prevent a person from bringing a claim to court. Rules on competence of person under civil procedure are consistent with the rules on competence set out in the *Civil and Commercial Code* and other relevant laws. In cases that a natural person has limited competence such as being a minor, legally incompetent, or quasi-incompetent, Section 56 of the *Civil Procedure Code* allows him to bring a claim to court on condition that there

---

[1] Supreme Court Case No. 8947/2547: The plaintiff claims that the cause of action arises within the jurisdiction of the court, making the court of first instance understand that the plaintiff has lawfully submitted the claim to the court of first instance. As a result, the court of first instance accepts the plaintiff's claim. When the defendant submits its answer and raises the issue regarding the court jurisdiction, the court of first instance, therefore, has to review the issue of jurisdiction and examine the facts and evidence brought in by the plaintiff and the defendant. As the facts cannot establish that the cause of action takes place in the jurisdiction of the court of first instance as argued by the plaintiff, the court may dismiss the plaintiff's claim and not refund the court fee to the plaintiff because the first paragraph of Section 151 of the *Civil and Commercial Code* provides that the court fee is fully refunded only in the case that the court does not accept the plaintiff's claim without reviewing the issue of the case. Therefore, the order of the court of first instance to exempt the court cost is lawful.

[2] Jakrapong Leksakulchai, p. 14.

is written consent from a person specified by law. [1]

Section 59 of the *Civil Procedure Code* allows joinder of parties to make the same claim. A joinder is allowed in cases where the co-parties share common interests in the claim. For example, co-parties may be heirs claiming for the same inherited property. (Supreme Court Case No. 443/2511) Although the parties are on the same side, each of them cannot litigate on behalf of the others[2] except that the issue is on an inseparable debt repayment such as cases for co-debtors. In such cases, the only procedure that can be run by one party on behalf of the other is hearing at trial(except a trial that may adversely affect reputation of the other parties) and postponement or recess of a trial.

In cases where a third party is interested in joining the case, or there is a cause to call upon a third party to join the case, Section 57 of the *Civil Procedure Code* allows case intervening. The intervening may be done in several ways. The third party (intervener) may act independently as an intervener at trial or in the execution of judgment process. It may join or replace one of the parties to the dispute, or enter the case upon call by one of the parties when such a party wants to exercise a right to recourse against the intervener.

4. Exemption of a court fee

Pursuant to Section 60, either the plaintiff or the defendant(and/or the intervener) has a right to litigate without appointing a lawyer or a legal

---

[1]   Luang Jamroon-nethisart, *Explanation on the Law of Civil Procedure*, 3rd Ed., Bangkok: Winyuchon Publishing, 2010,pp. 26~27.

[2]   Supreme Court Case No. 1680/2523: Although the fifth and the first plaintiff are co-parties in the same case, the cause of action is not based on an inseparable debt as each plaintiff may have different interests. As the fifth plaintiff submits a petition to the court, it could be considered that the fifth plaintiff undertakes the proceeding on behalf of the first plaintiff pursuant to Section 59 of the *Civil Procedure Code*. As the first plaintiff is not the party that submits the petition, the first plaintiff does not have the right to appeal such petition to the Supreme Court.

counselor. However, if any party does not want to run the case, a lawyer, a legal counselor or a representative may be appointed to follow certain procedures on its behalf. In any event, a representative does not have the full right to litigate as lawyers. Therefore, a representative may appoint a lawyer to litigate.

In general, when a party submits a claim, it is responsible to pay a court fee. However, it can request for an exemption if it satisfies the conditions under Section 156/1. That is, the party must have an insufficient fund to pay for the court fee, or can demonstrate that if an exemption is not granted, it will suffer from distress. Pursuant to Section 156, the party generally has to submit a request for an exemption along with the claim or the answer. If the party becomes incapable of paying the court fee later on, it should submit a request to the court after such constraint takes place. The court has discretion to allow an exemption in whole or in part. The party may appeal against the court order within 7 days from the date of the order, pursuant to Section 156/1. The order of an appellate court is final. The amount exempted is the court fee payable to the court under Section 18 and a court cost payable to another party under Section 229. However, the exemption does not lift security that has to be placed in accordance with Section 234 and a fee for stay of execution under Section 231.

5. Claim submission

Pursuant to Section 1(3), a claim means a claim in a disputed case, and in a non-disputed case. A claim has to be in writing, composed of information specified in Section 67, including the name of the court, names of the parties to the dispute, the date of claim submission and a detailed summary of the cause of action. Failure to state the required information is a ground for the court to return the claim to the claimant for a correction, or the court might deny the claim pursuant to Section 18.

A claim must clearly demonstrate the nature of claim and the ground for which the claim is caused to arise. The claim must describe relevant facts and circumstances for the court to be able to understand. Unclear statement of claim is considered a disjunctive allegation pursuant to Section 172. The court may dismiss a disjunctive allegation as it is difficult for the defendant to argue the case. (Supreme Court Case No. 255/2484) The description of the cause of action does not have to specify the law or legal provision which is a source of liability because the court itself is responsible for applying legal analysis to the case. [1]

After a claim has been submitted, the claimant can no longer submit the same claim on the same issue against the same party to the same court or a different court. This principle is called *res judicata*, preventing the party to make double claims on the same issue against the same party, pursuant to Section 173(1). In practice, the court's may dismiss the second claim. Even if the second claim has already been decided, i. e. has been ruled by the final decision of the court, the submission of the second claim remains prohibited and unlawful. (Supreme Court Case No. 7188/2553)

6. Serving claim and notices to the defendant

After the plaintiff brings a claim to court, the plaintiff must make a copy(copies)of the claim equal to the number of the defendant(s)and provide them for the court officer along with the submission of claim, pursuant to Section 69. After the court accepts the claim, the court will order that the copy of the claim be delivered to the defendant along with a notice to answer. The documents will be delivered by the court officer. The plaintiff is responsible for the delivery fee. For other notices, the same rule applies. (Section 70)

The plaintiff has a duty to make a request to the court officer to serve a notice to answer to the defendant in 7 days from the date when the claim is

---

[1] Supreme Court Case No. 974/2492: In civil cases, the law does not require the plaintiff to choose to pursue either a tortuous action or a contractual action. The plaintiff's claim may simply describe facts and demand compensation. The court is responsible for the application of law and determination of whether the law allows compensation to the plaintiff's claim.

submitted. The plaintiff may be ordered by the court to have additional duties such as delivering a copy of claim to the defendant. A violation against the court's order constitutes neglect under Section 174(2) and the court may strike the case out of the case list. However, in such a case the plaintiff may resubmit the claim within the prescription period under Section 176.[①]

The claim or other documents must be delivered at the place of domicile of the defendant. If the defendant has appointed a lawyer for the case, they can be delivered to the lawyer(Section 75)at the place of domicile or the office of the lawyer. Delivery must be done during the daytime, but not necessary during the government office hours. If the defendant is not present or nowhere to be found, the documents may be delivered to any person with the age above 20 years old residing permanently in the defendant's residence, pursuant to Section 76. Delivery to a counter-party is prohibited. For example, in a divorce case, documents cannot be delivered to a divorcing spouse who still lives in the same residence.[②] In any event, delivery outside of the place of domicile or office of another party or the person specified in the claim or documents is allowed under Section 77 if such a party to which the documents are delivered accepts delivery or delivery is done in court. The claim or related documents may also be sent by mail, pursuant to Section 73*bis*.

If a party or a person who is legally qualified to accept delivery of claim or related documents denies delivery without a reasonable ground (as specified by law), the court officer may attach a notice in accordance with Section 78 by requesting an administrative officer such as the sub-district headman or a police officer to witness the delivery. If the party or the person stated above remains in refusal of delivery, the claim or documents may be placed before such person and by doing so the documents are deemed to be lawfully received. In such a case, a placement of notice must be recorded

---

① Jakrapong Leksakulchai, p. 125.

② Jakrapong Leksakulchai, p. 127

and signed by a witness (administrative officer). Such delivery of notice must be recorded in a report thereafter.

If it is impossible to deliver the claim and other related documents because the defendant or his representative is absent or the defendant's domicile cannot be found, the claimant must request to proceed with the case within 15 days from the date of failed delivery. If the claimant fails to request, the case will be considered neglected and the court may strike the case out of the case list. If the claimant requests, the court may order an alternative delivery method in accordance with Section 79, such as posting the pleading in a conspicuous place like the place of domicile or office of another party. Delivery with such methods becomes effective after the 15-day period has passed, or as *the court sees appropriate*.

In cases where the place of domicile of the defendant is outside of the country, a notice and copy of claim must be delivered at the place of domicile or office of the defendant abroad, pursuant to Section 83*bis*. The claimant has a duty to submit a request for the serving of notice within 7 days, pursuant to Section 83*bis*.

If the method of document delivery is unlawful, for example, posting a notice without the presence of an administrative officer as a witness, the claim is also considered unlawful. As a result, the accused does not have a legal duty to answer. If the court of first instance rules the case involving an unlawful delivery of document, the appellate court may overrule.

7. The defendant's answer

After the court accepts the claim and the defendant has been served a notice to answer, he has a duty to answer or make a statement to defend against the plaintiff's allegation(s), pursuant to Section 1(4).

Pursuant to Section 177, the defendant must answer in writing and submit it to the court along with a copy (copies) of the answer to be delivered to every plaintiff within 15 days from the date when the defendant is served with the claim. The counting of days follows the rules set forth in the *Civil and Commercial Code*. The defendant may request for an extension to answer in case of emergency, pursuant to Section 23 of the *Civil Procedure Code*. The court may allow or disallow an extension and set the extended duration at its discretion.

The answer must state clearly whether the defendant accepts or denies the plaintiff's allegation in whole or in part, and for what reason, pursuant to the second paragraph of Section 177. The answer must also state the defendant's disposition to the result of the case, for example, the case should be dismissed. If the defendant fails to do so, the court will not rule the case and return the answer to the defendant for correction or deny the answer, pursuant to Section 18. In cases where the court denies the answer, the defendant may appeal the order immediately because such an order is not an interlocutory order under Section 226. The appeal must be done in 1 month from the date of the court order under the second paragraph of Section 228.

"Clear answer" means that the defendant states clearly whether he accepts or denies the plaintiff's allegation, along with reasons in case of denial. If the defendant does not explicitly deny, he is deemed to accept the allegation. As a result, the plaintiff does not have to examine witnesses or evidence to prove his allegation. In cases where the defendant denies the allegation without a reasonable ground(so called "denial on the basis of in-sufficient information")[1], such as denying the debt claimed by the plaintiff for an amount of 20,000 baht without stating a reason. In such cases, the defendant will not have a right to examine witnesses or evidence but the plaintiff still has such a right. (Supreme Court Case No. 1498-1499/2508) In cases that the defendant gives an ambiguous answer that cannot be discerned whether he accepts or denies the allegation, it implies that he or she does not deny, or in fact accepts the plaintiff's allegation.[2] In certain cases, the

---

[1]　Sopol Rattanakorn, pp. 118~122.

[2]　Supreme Court Case No. 218/2488: The plaintiff brings a legal action to divorce the defendant. The defendant denies the marriage but does not deny the cause of divorce. The denial of the marital status cannot be considered denial of a ground to divorce. As such, the ground to divorce is not an issue in this case. The plaintiff does not prove it.

defendant may lose the case even though the plaintiff lacks the right to examine witnesses or evidence because the defendant fails to provide sufficient answer. (Supreme Court Case No. 652/2541)

Besides giving answer to the allegations made against him, the defendant may also submit a counterclaim imposing a different claim against the plaintiff. As a result, the defendant becomes a plaintiff in the counterclaim. The counterclaim must be submitted with the answer or a petition to correct the answer previously submitted. [Section 177, Supreme Court Case No. 629/2524(General Meeting)] Counterclaim must be related to the plaintiff's claim, such as a counterclaim on the issue of contract which is the cause of action in the plaintiff's allegation. A counterclaim unrelated to the previous claim is invalid. [1] Also, a counterclaim can only be made when the plaintiff asserts his allegation. A conditional counterclaim, such as a counterclaim stating that it is conditional upon the court's ruling against the defendant, is invalid. (Supreme Court Case No. 153/2512) The counterclaim must be submitted to the court that hears the plaintiff's case, pursuant to Section 7(1). After the defendant submits his counterclaim, the plaintiff then has a duty to answer against the defendant's counterclaim.

8. Amendment to the plaintiff's claim and the defendant's answer

The party to the dispute may amend or adjust the claim or answer that

---

[1] Supreme Court Case No. 1613/2513: The plaintiff brings an eviction claim, arguing that the defendant has defaulted on the rental agreement. The defendant argues that P. sold and delivered the rented building to the plaintiff. P. and the plaintiff agreed that the plaintiff will pay the defendant the moving expenses but the plaintiff has not made a payment. Therefore, the defendant may occupy the building until the plaintiff fulfills his obligation. The defendant's counterclaim that the plaintiff has to pay the moving expenses is not related to the previous claim on the defendant's default. (The counterclaim is irrelevant to the previous claim and refers to P. who is a third party not involving in the claim.)

has been submitted to the court by filing a petition under Section 180. The petition must be filed before the date for the issue settlement is set[①]or at least 7 days before the date of evidence examination. In cases where the rule does not require that the date for issue settlement be set(such as cases involving labor disputes), and before the court rules if there is no date set for issue settlement and evidence examination, in cases where the party files the petition after the due date(either the issue settlement date, the witness examination date or after the court has rendered its judgment, as the case may be), the court may order the petition to be dismissed, except that there is a reasonable cause for late filing or the amendment is made to an insignificant error which is not a major issue that directly affects the case or an issue regarding public order such as an issue of jurisdiction of the court. (An issue regarding prescription periods is not an issue regarding public order.)[②]

Pursuant to Section 179, if the plaintiff requests for an increase or decrease in the amount claimed or resets the value of the property in dispute, but not adding another property to the claim(Supreme Court Case No. 2124/2518), or he cancels certain claims or adjusts the existing claim, in any event, it is prohibited to make an additional claim to the existing claim. (Supreme Court Case No. 966/2512) The amendment must be related to the previously submitted claim, pursuant to the last paragraph of Section 179. The defendant. may raise any argument against the claim though the argument is not necessarily related to the previously submitted answer. However, if the newly raised argument is in conflict with the previously asserted statement, he or she has to renounce the previously asserted statement, or the court may disallow an assertion of the new statement which may not be beneficial to the defendant. (Supreme Court Case No. 2236/2545)

---

① Supreme Court Case No. 3642/2555: Both defendants submit a petition to amend their answers on September 3, 2010 before the court of first instance settles the issues on September 6, 2010. It is deemed that the defendants have lawfully submitted the petition before the date of issue settlement, pursuant to Section 180 of the *Civil Procedure Code*.

② Jakrapong Leksakulchai, pp. 153~156.

9. Withdrawal of claim

The party that submits a claim may withdraw such a claim if he or she no longer wishes to continue the case process. The withdrawal, if taking place before the defendant answers under the first paragraph of Section 175, the plaintiff must submit it to the court in writing demonstrating his attention to withdraw the claim. The court usually allows withdrawal as requested if it does not adversely affect the defendant. If the defendant has already answered to the claim under (1) of the second paragraph of Section 175, the plaintiff must file a petition to withdraw the claim without having to state the reasons. If the court sees that the withdrawal should be allowed, the court has to hear the defendant's opinion before doing so. The court may exercise its discretion to allow or disallow the withdrawal in such a case. (Supreme Court Case No. 771/2510) In cases where the plaintiff withdraws the claim due to a contract of compromise under (2) of the second paragraph of Section 175, the court has a legal duty to allow withdrawal.

The withdrawal under Section 176 results in cancellation of claim and any judicial procedure associated with the claim. The parties return to the same position as if the claim has not been submitted.

The plaintiff may resubmit the claim within the prescription period specified by law, except for the cases that the plaintiff makes an agreement with the defendant before the court that he or she will not resubmit the claim against the defendant. In such a case, the plaintiff no longer has a right of claim on the same issue against the defendant. For the court fee, the court may order that the fee is partially refunded in accordance with Section 151 and the regulations on the Judiciary No. 7. [1]

---

[1] Jakrapong Leksakulchai, p. 167.

10. Settlement of issues

After the claim and associating answer are submitted to the court, or the period in which the answer has to be submitted ends, the court then begins the process of reviewing the claim and the answer together. In certain cases, the court may rule without examining evidence or witnesses.

In practice, the court usually makes an appointment with both parties to engage in an agreement of compromise in accordance with Section 19. If the parties reach an agreement of compromise, the plaintiff has to withdraw the claim pursuant to Section 175(2) or the court may rule according to the agreement of compromise pursuant to Section 138.

If an agreement of compromise is not reached, the court will proceed to the issue settlement process. The main objectives of issue settlement are to have the parties appear before the court and clarify facts on the disputed issues, settle the issues to be examined, and specify the burden of the proof according to the claim that needs to be verified. Finally, the court will resolve the disputed issues.

On the day of issue settlement, the court may ask the parties whether there is any factual issue that both parties do not accept. The accepted factual issues will no longer be disputable, meaning that the party raising the facts does not have the burden to prove them. The court will admit the facts that both parties accept. For example, in cases that the plaintiff brings a tortuous claim against the defendant's employee, if the defendant accepts that the wrongdoer is the defendant's employee and has committed a tortuous act that causes damages to the plaintiff within the scope of employment, such facts will no longer be disputed and the party will not have to provide any evidence for the facts. Other issues that the defendant does not accept, such as whether his employee has been negligent, will have to be proven.[①] The burden of proof usually falls on the party that raises the

---

① Sopol Rattanakorn, p. 124.

issues, pursuant to Section 84. In any event, the denial of facts will have to be explainable with an unequivocal cause, otherwise the denying party is deemed to accept the facts, pursuant to the second paragraph of Section 183, except that he is not in a position to demonstrate the cause, pursuant to the third paragraph of Section 183. The party has a right to contest the issue settlement or the burden of proof set by the court either verbally or by submitting a petition to the court within 7 days.

If one or both parties to the dispute are absent on the date of issue settlement pursuant to Section 183*bis*, the court may proceed with the issue settlement and the absent party is deemed to have acknowledged the procedure on that day. The absent party does not have a right to contest the issue settled and the burden of proof that the court has established, except that the reason for being absent is based on the ground of necessity as prescribed by law, or the contest involves a public order issue. [1]

11. Trial

After the court of first instance accepts the plaintiff's claim and the defendant has answered or the period that the defendant may give an answer ends, at this point the court starts a trial which is a hearing on argumentations of the parties to the dispute. In general, both parties must be present in the hearing in order to allow each party to argue its case, pursuant to Section 103, except certain cases where the court may hear the case without the presence of the party such as the case that one party is missing the court appointment. Moreover, pursuant to Section 36, a hearing must be accessible to the general public, except certain cases where hearing should be done in private such as divorce cases. In certain cases, the court might give a preliminary final ruling over certain legal issues, pursuant to Section 24, rendering the entire case or certain issues to be decided. In such cases, the hearing process will be shortened because witness and evidence

---

[1] Jakrapong Leksakulchai, pp. 172~173.

examination is not undertaken. The shortened procedure may be requested by one of the parties or the court allows at its discretion. ①

The court may postpone hearing at its discretion on the ground of necessity pursuant to Section 40, or by law(due to death of a party to the dispute, pursuant to Section 42). In cases of death of the party to the dispute, when the court is informed that a party passes away, the court has to order a postponement of a hearing until an heir, executor, or protector of the deceased's estate continues the case proceeding on behalf of the deceased. The persons stated above may voluntarily file a petition to become a party to the dispute on behalf of the deceased or the court serves them a notice upon request of another party to the dispute, pursuant to Section 44. In another case, hearing may be postponed because a party to the dispute becomes legally incompetent pursuant to Section 45. That is, the party to the dispute is alive but becomes legally incompetent after submitting the claim to the court, including the case that the party's representative dies or no longer has an authority to undertake the legal action on behalf of the party. The court may postpone the hearing until the person asks for the court's permission to proceed with the case by himself or inform the court that a new representative or lawyer has been appointed. The court will set a certain period of time for the person to inform the court. Beyond that period, the court may order a re-hearing. ②

In any proceeding during the course of trial, if a party is of an opinion that it cannot undertake certain procedure within the period specified, it may file a petition requesting for an extension of the deadline, pursuant to Section 23.

12. Evidence or witness examination

In ruling over the issues that have been settled at the beginning of the

---

① Jakrapong Leksakulchai, pp. 174~180.
② Jakrapong Leksakulchai, pp. 181~195.

case, relevant facts have to be proven. The process of proving requires examination of evidence. Evidence could be persons, documents and materials.

In civil cases, Section 104 states that if the court sees that evidence of any party is more probable to prove facts, the court may rule in favor of that party. This is different from criminal cases whereby the court has to examine the plaintiff's evidence until it establishes the defendant's guilt beyond reasonable doubt. If it is not proven beyond reasonable doubt, the court may dismiss the claim. [1]

Evidence examination takes place for the dispute on factual issues on whether the defendant has committed an act or omission that gives rise to liability. The involving facts are situations or causes of the defendant's rights and obligations. On the other hand, legal issues are issues involving legal interpretation and interpretation of contract terms, application of legal provisions to relevant facts, and analysis on how the parties' action gives a legal result. The application of law is the sole responsibility of the court, not the parties to the dispute. [2] Factual issues, if known by the general public such as the fact that the sun rises in the east, or uncontestable facts such as historical information, or facts accepted by both parties, [3] Section 84 provides that such facts are exempted from examination. In case facts are accepted by both parties, there is a special rule on challenges which allows a party to accept facts raised by the other party upon certain conditions. Such conditions are limited to those related to the case proceeding such as swearing or witnesses' testifying. If the conditions are fulfilled, the other party has to accept the facts raised by the opponent. [4] For example, a party challenges the other party to let the first party win if the executing officer surveys the land at issue and finds that it is situated within the area where the court orders a sale by auction. (Supreme Court Case No. 379/2509)

In the process of examining evidence and witnesses, Section 84/1 states

---

[1]   Sopol Rattanakorn, p. 17.
[2]   Sopol Rattanakorn, pp. 49~52.
[3]   Sopol Rattanakorn, p. 85.
[4]   Sopol Rattanakorn, pp. 131~132.

that the party that raises facts has burden to prove such facts. Consequently, that party has to bring forward evidence and witnesses for an examination. Usually, the plaintiff has a burden of proof because the plaintiff raises a claim against the defendant that the defendant interferes with the plaintiff's right. If the proof is unsatisfaltory, the plaintiff may lose the case. On the contrary, if the proof is satisfaltory, then the defendant may examine evidence and witnesses to undermine the probability and accountability of the plaintiff's evidence and witnesses, pursuant to Section 89. The defendant may also cross-examine the plaintiff's witnesses to prove that the plaintiff's witnesses are unreliable. [1]

In any event, Section 84/1 states that if the plaintiff benefits from a legal presumption[2], for example, when a party refers to a public document issued and certified by a competent government official, or a private document certified true document by the court, it can be presumed that the documents are authentic and true. In such cases, the burden of proof is shifted to the other party to prove that the document is unauthentic and false. [3]

In the process of examining evidence, certain evidence is inadmissible, meaning that it cannot be included in the examination process. Examples include witnesses who are incapable of understanding or answering questions pursuant to Section 95 (1), evidence irrelevant to the issue of the case making the examination fall outside the scope of claim or answer (in this case, the court may exercise its discretion to decide whether the evidence is relevant to the issues pursuant to Section 104), overly excessive evidence or evidence that may cause delay to the hearing at trial pursuant to Section 86, and hearsay (which is the message a person who does not see, hear or know testified directly). The second paragraph of Section 95/1 prohibits admissibility of hearsay as such, except in cases where it is probable that the

---

[1] Sopol Rattanakorn, pp. 61~64.

[2] Sopol Rattanakorn, pp. 140~149.

[3] Sopol Rattanakorn, pp. 465~467.

hearsay witness may prove the facts, or it is impossible to bring the witness who directly sees or knows the event to testify[1]

In general, the law does not limit the types of evidence that the parties may bring forward. However, in cases where the law requires that the party bring or demonstrate a document as proof, such as cases where the law provides a condition that a contract be done in writing or the transaction is void or unenforceable (as in the case of the borrowing of money exceeding 2,000 baht in accordance with Section 653), for example, Section 94 prohibits the examination of a witness instead of a document, and also prohibits the examination of a witness in order to add, delete or change any message in the document, except that the examination of a witness is done to prove veracity, accuracy or authenticity of the document, or to prove that the contract or the underlying debt is invalid and void, or to prove that another party has interpreted the message in the document incorrectly (in that the message could be interpreted in several ways). [2]

In order to bring evidence or witnesses for the examination, the party must submit an evidence list in accordance with Section 87 (2) and the list must specify the items of evidence or witnesses that the party wants to examine. The list must be submitted at least 7 days before the first examination takes place. The party may also submit an additional list of evidence or witnesses later on but it has to be done within 15 days from the date of first examination. In any event, the court may admit the items that are not specified in the evidence list if they finds that such evidence is necessary for preservation of justice. In certain cases, the court may allow out-of-court examination, pursuant to Section 102. The party may request to have a witness examination through a teleconference, pursuant to Section 120/4.

The Thai legal system provides protection for witnesses to a great extent. Section 92 allows immunity to witnesses who are not willing to testify

---

[1] Sopol Rattanakorn, p. 193.
[2] Sopol Rattanakorn, pp. 237~265.

if they could disclose confidential information of the government units, [1] legal counseling, invented materials, models or other creativity such as patented innovation. [2]

For documentary evidence, Section 90 in general requires that the party submit a copy of the document to the court and the other party. However, if the document is already in possession of the other party or a third party, the party proving it does not have to provide a copy and may request the court to recall the original document from the possessor. In general, only original documents are admissible, except for cases under Section 93 such as documents that have been destroyed due to force majeure.

Pursuant to Section 103/2, the party may request the court to examine evidence as agreed by both parties. The court may allow it if appropriate.

13. Default judgment

13.1　Failure to answer

In cases where the defendant fails to submit answer within 15 days, he or she is missing the due date. Section 198 requires that the plaintiff request a default judgment from the court. If the plaintiff fails to request as such within 15 days from the date when the defendant has to submit his answer, the court may strike the case out of the case list, pursuant to Section 132 (2). In cases where the plaintiff never misses any court's date, it can be inferred that he wishes to continue the proceeding. In such cases, even if the plaintiff does not request the court to render a default judgment in favor of the plaintiff, the court is unlikely to dismiss the case. (Supreme Court Case No. 1065/2533)

If the plaintiff requests for a default judgment, Section 198*bis* states that the court may rule in favor of the plaintiff only when the cause of action exists and is not contrary to the law. The court may proceed with an

---

[1]　For more details, see Section 56 of the *Constitution and the Government Information Act* B.E. 2540(1997).

[2]　Ibid. p. 377.

examination of evidence of the plaintiff alone. For cases involving personal status, family, ownership in property, debt enforcement in money term, the court must examine evidence on the side of the plaintiff alone before ruling, pursuant to Section 199. The defendant may submit a petition to the court explaining that he does not intend to miss the court's appointment. Excuses could be traveling on a business trip to a southern province preventing him to know about the lawsuit (Supreme Court Case No. 422/2525), or having to attend the military drafting process. [1] If the defendant does not follow this step, he will be subject to limitation on arguing the case, that is, he may not examine evidence that he brought forward, but may cross-examine the plaintiff's witnesses only. [2] If the court renders a default judgment in favor of the plaintiff under Section 199 quarter, the defendant may submit a petition to request for a withdrawal of such judgment by demonstrating the reasons that he does not intend to miss the court hearing, or having other reasonable causes. Besides that, he also has to establish that he might have a chance to win the case if the case continues on. The petition must be submitted within 15 days from the date when the court delivers the default judgment. However, if there is an intervening event that prevents the defendant from submitting the petition such as floods, [3] he may make a submission within 15 days from the date when the event ends. The court may or may not allow as per the defendant's request. If the court allows in accordance with Section 199*quiquies*, the default judgment and the previous proceeding are effectively withdrawn. A new hearing will commence from the date when the defendant misses the court's appointment. If the court disallows, the defendant has a right to appeal. The decision of the appellate court is final.

13.2 Missing the court's appointment

The parties to the dispute, either the plaintiff or the defendant, may

---

[1] Jakrapong Leksakulchai, p. 215.

[2] This does not mean that the defendant will always lose the case. (Supreme Court Case No. 9676/2539)

[3] Jakrapong Leksakulchai, p. 230.

miss the court's appointment for evidence examination. Pursuant to Section 200, it is the situation where the party is absent from the court on the first appointment to examine the evidence, or comes late to the court. (Supreme Court Case No. 3388/2545) The examination must involve issues in dispute, not the examination for the subsequent petition. (Supreme Court Case No. 440/2539) If a party is absent from any subsequent evidence examination, the party is deemed to have known about the proceeding and waived his right to proceed with the case only for that portion of the proceeding from which he is absent. Such a case is not considered missing the court appointment. (Supreme Court Case No. 767/2535)

If both the plaintiff and the defendant are absent, Section 201 states that the court may order the case to be struck out of the case list. If the plaintiff is absent in accordance with Section 202, the court may also strike the case out of the case list unless the defendant requests for continuation. If it is the defendant that is absent in accordance with Section 204, the court may unilaterally render a final judgment and the plaintiff may not make the same request. The party that misses the court hearing is usually subject to similar limitations applicable to missing the court's due date to answer. The party may make a request to the court in the same nature, whether the request is done before or after the court rules the case. [1]

14. Petty cases and small claims

Pursuant to Section 189, petty cases involve claims not exceeding 300,000 baht in value and also cases without monetary value such as cases involving eviction of a tenant with monthly rental not exceeding 30,000 baht. The law requires a concise and short proceeding in order to finish a case in an expedite manner. Pursuant to Section 191, the plaintiff may submit a claim in writing or verbally to the court. In cases of written submission, if the court finds that the claim lacks the main objective, it may

---

[1] For more details, see Section 206 and Section 297 of the Civil Procedure Code.

order the plaintiff to amend the claim. The court will not dismiss the claim on the ground of disjunctive allegation under Section 172 because most petty cases are not run by a lawyer. Therefore, it is normal that the claim might not be as well-written as cases represented by a lawyer. [1] The plaintiff may submit a petty claim to the district court.

The plaintiff is responsible for a court fee of 200 baht. Next, the court will set a hearing date and serve the defendant the notice to appear, pursuant to Section 190 quarter and Section 193.

Upon receiving the notice, the defendant may appear in court to answer, mediate the issues, and examine evidence all in one day. If the mediation succeeds, the case terminates. On the contrary, if the mediation fails, the defendant may submit a written or verbal answer against the plaintiff's allegation. In cases where the court finds the defendant's answer incorrect, it might order the defendant to amend or clarify it and examine evidence later on.

If the defendant does not appear in court, or makes appearance without having answered and still gives no answer whatsoever, Section 193 allows the court to order that the defendant miss the court appointment and give a default judgment in favor of the plaintiff. In cases where the defendant has submitted an answer but does not appear in court, he is deemed to miss the evidence examination appointment. If the plaintiff does not appear in court, Section 193*bis* provides that the plaintiff no longer wishes to continue the proceeding and the court may strike the case out of the case list.

In petty cases, the proceeding is done on an inquisitorial basis. As such, the court has the power to call upon any evidence or witnesses in the examination, whether or not the evidence or witnesses are brought forward by the parties. The court also has the power to examine witnesses regarding the facts relating to the case though the parties do not raise them. [2]

Small claims, pursuant to Section 196, are claims which involve

---

[1]   Jakrapong Leksakulchai, p. 261.
[2]   Jakrapong Leksakulchai, p. 265.

monetary value exceeding 300,000 baht with regard to enforcement on a debt repayment. The amount of debt must be certain as specified in a written contract, such as an amount written on a cheque. The plaintiff submits a claim the same way as he would do for other civil claims, together with a petition requesting that the case be expedited. If the court finds that there is no complicated issue at hand, it will apply rules on petty cases to the claim. But if the court finds the contrary, such as cases involving further interpretation, it will apply general rules on civil procedure to the claim.

15. Court judgment and its binding effect

Court judgment, pursuant to Section 145, is generally binding the parties to the dispute and persons to whom the right is transferred, such as the party to the dispute dies and the right from the judicial proceeding is transferred to his heir. However, the judgment is not binding a third person, except the case involving competence of person, ownership of a property(which is beneficial to a party). The party could raise the latter cases against a third person not involving in. In order to render a judgment pursuant to Section 142, the court is bound to rule on the issues in dispute stated in the claim or the answer. The court cannot rule over and beyond the issues set out in the claim,[1] except for certain cases such as ruling on an issue of public order and morale including the charging of interests exceeding the rate prescribed by law. (Supreme Court Case No. 708/2548) Even if a case doesn't have an issue in dispute, the court may render a judgment as well. Ruling above and beyond the issues in dispute makes the judgment un-

---

[1] Supreme Court Case No. 5403/2537: When both defendants miss the due date to give answer, the issues in dispute must have arisen from the plaintiff's claim on the cause of action whether both defendants owed the plaintiff an amount of money under the overdraft and guarantee contract. The issue was not whether the plaintiff has agreed not to charge any interest. The ruling of the Appeal Court Region II that the plaintiff has agreed not to charge interest is a judgment outside the scope of claim. Such ruling is invalid.

lawful. In that case, the party may request that the judgment be with-drawn. [1]

After the court has ruled, in cases where the plaintiff or the defendant brings the claim to court on the issues that have already been decided, the new procedure is considered duplicated. This is prohibited under Section 144. In cases where the court judgment is final pursuant to Section 147 (i. e. resubmit the claim after 1 month from the date when the court renders a judgment), not only is it a repeated procedure, but also a repeated claim submission pursuant to Section 148. Both cases are prohibitive. The reason why the court disallows the duplication is to save time and reduce the number of cases brought to the court. [2]

16. Appeals to the appeal court and the Supreme Court

If either the plaintiff or the defendant loses at trial or wins with distress (for example, the plaintiff who wins the case but does not receive full com-pensation as requested), the party has a right to appeal to the appeal court or the Supreme Court, as the case may be. In certain cases such as compromise cases in court under Section 138 or other cases as prescribed by law, the party cannot appeal.

The party may appeal on both issues of facts and law. However, an appeal on facts is limited to cases with value in dispute exceeding 50,000 baht, pursuant to Section 224. Cases involving rights of a person and rights of a family, even if the value in dispute is not exceeding 50,000 baht, the party still has the right to appeal. Cases with no monetary objective, such as a claim for a borrowed thing to be returned to the owner, which the party may not gain any tangible property, can also be appealed. While cases on eviction of a tenant living in a rental property with rent not exceeding 5,000

---

[1] Supreme Court Case No. 5403/2537: The question whether the court has rules above and beyond the claim is a legal issue involving public order. Even if the defendant does not raise the issue in his appeal, it is still able to raise it at the Supreme Court level.

[2] Jakrapong Leksakulchai, p. 307.

baht per month cannot be appealed. Cases that are not appealable but the party wishes to appeal must be cases in which the trial judge has made a dissenting opinion, or where the party requests an affirmation that there is a reasonable cause to appeal. The party may appeal upon receiving a permission to appeal from the chief judge of the court of first instance, or the chief judge of the region. The factual or legal issues subject to appeal must be the issues that have been raised lawfully at trial. If the issues have not been raised at trial, they cannot be appealed except that they involve public order under Section 229. The appellant must submit his appeal to the court of first instance that renders a judgment on the case within 1 month from the date when it has the final judgment, and place the court fee that he has to pay for another party. Pursuant to Section 229*bis*, the party may elect to appeal directly to the Supreme Court according to the legal theory called "leap of frog procedure". [1]

This is limited to an appeal in legal issues only and the appeal must be submitted to the court of first instance that renders the judgment. If the other party is not appealing and is not contesting the appeal, the party may proceed with an appeal to the Supreme Court.

An appeal does not function as staying in execution. This is based on the same underlying principle in common law, but different from civil law in some jurisdictions such as European countries and Japan. [2] That is, when a party loses the case at the trial level, the creditor by judgment will pursue an execution including seizure of property and sale by auction. Proceeds from the sale will be used to pay off the debt. However, the losing party who wants to appeal may also request the appellate court at any time before it renders judgment, and provide the court with reasons why the execution should be stayed. The appellate court may allow it without any condition or with conditions such as the appellant must provide security or collateral to

---

[1]　Jakrapong Leksakulchai, p. 351.

[2]　Wanchai Boonbamroong, *The Civil Procedure Code: Reference Version*, 4th Ed., Bangkok: Winyuchon Publishing, 2011, p. 657.

the court. The court's order to stay an execution cannot be appealed. (Order No. 1676/2547)

Unique procedure at the appeal level is that there is no witness examination. This is because witness examination which has been undertaken during trial should not be done with duplication and delay. The appellate court reviews evidence from what the court of first instance has summarized and submitted to it, except for the case where the appellate court is of an opinion that it should re-examine witnesses because the court of first instance does not review the case clearly. [1]

Cases appealed to the Supreme Court in general are similar to those appealed to the appellate court. The difference is on the value of claim. Section 248 requires that the value exceed 200,000 baht for cases appealed to the Supreme Court. Cases with no monetary value such as eviction of a rental property must involve a rent exceeding 10,000 baht per month. [2]

17. Temporary orders before judgment

Temporary orders before judgment is the procedure that facilitates the execution of judgment. There are two forms of orders: seizure of property or placement of property, and temporary restraining order. An order to seize or place property aims to protect and maintain the property in dispute or money which has to be paid to the party following the court judgment. Without a temporary restraining order, the losing party may transfer property elsewhere before judgment, making the execution of judgment difficult. [3]Section 253 provides that the defendant may request the court to order the plaintiff to place property or security with the court. If it is apparent that the plaintiff is not domiciled or does not have an office in the country and does not have any property that can be executed in the country,

---

[1]   Jakrapong Leksakulchai, pp. 330~331.

[2]   For more details, see Section 247 to Section 252 of the *Civil Procedure Code*.

[3]   Somchai Julaniti, *Explanation on Civil Procedure*, *Region* Ⅳ, Bangkok: The Institute of Legal Education, the Thai Bar Association, 2014, p. 1.

or it can be reasonably believed that if the plaintiff loses the case, he might avoid paying the court fee and cost; the court may remove the case out of the court list once the plaintiff fails to comply with the court order. (Request at the appellate court and Supreme Court level follow the rules under Section 253*bis*.) If the plaintiff makes a request, it must follow the rules under Section 254, that is, the request can be brought forward only for cases which are not petty cases. The request must be related to the issues in dispute only and it could ask for seizure of property in dispute or the defendant's property(usually money in practice)or stay of money or property of a third person which is due to be repaid to the plaintiff(for debt owed to the defendant by the third party). [1] In addition, the order may prohibit the defendant from transferring or disposing property in dispute or any other property owned by the defendant as well. The court grants an order on the ground of necessity and reasonableness pursuant to Section 255. Moreover, the plaintiff may request the court to expedite the steps taken under the order, pursuant to Section 266 and Section 267 and the court may grant it on the basis of necessity and reasonableness.

Temporary restraining orders are granted for disputes in property, and not disputes in money. The claim must be direct to the property itself. For example, disputes to part a joint ownership, aiming to split ownership in the property without having any monetary objective. Temporary restraining orders may also provide the party temporary protection by establishing certain legal status during a certain period of time in order to lessen damages to the party [2] such as ordering a legally incompetent person to be under care of a third person. In either case, the party may make a request in accordance with Section 264.

If the defendant wins the case, the applicable temporary order is no longer effective after 7 days from the date of judgment or order, except in

---

[1] Somchai Julaniti, *Explanation on Civil Procedure*, Region Ⅳ, Bangkok: The Institute of Legal Education, the Thai Bar Association, 2014, p. 13.

[2] Hiroshi Oda, *Japanese Law*, 2nd Ed., Butterworths, London, 1999, pp. 400~401.

the case where the plaintiff appeals. If the plaintiff wins the case, the temporary order remains effective as long as it is necessary to continue its effect for compliance to the court judgment or order.

18. Execution of judgment

After the court renders judgment, the winning parties is able to enforce its right upon the debt of another parties through an execution of judgment. The party that may legally request for an execution is the wining party(i. e. creditor by judgment). This does not include other party such as a transferee of debt by judgment in accordance with Section 306 of the *Civil and Commercial Code*. However, transfers occur by law, for example, the transfer under the *Emergency Degree on the Reform of Financial Institutions B. E.* 2540 (1997) is allowed during the execution period. [1] In certain cases, there is a debt by judgment. In the case where the defendant wins the case and the court orders that the defendant be not responsible for the court cost (or both the plaintiff and the defendant have to pay for the court cost), then there is no debt by judgment.

Once all elements above are satisfied but the debtor by judgment fails to comply with the judgment in whole or in part, the creditor by judgment may submit a petition to have the judgment executed within 10 years from the date of judgment or order. The Supreme Court has decided that the judgment being executed has to be final. (Supreme Court Case No. 3193/2553) [2] In any event, the law does not set out a timeframe that a requested execution must be completed in a 10-year period. Although the execution has been carried on continuously over 10 years, the execution remains lawful and is not expired after 10 years. (Supreme Court Case No. 5546/2556)

The execution of judgment can be exercised in two ways. One is exercised by an executing officer and the other is exercised by other persons.

---

[1]   Somchai Julaniti, pp. 80~83.

[2]   Some authors oppose this idea. See Somchai Julaniti, pp. 72~77.

For the execution by an executing officer, after the court issues a notice of execution, the credit by judgment has to inform an executing officer regarding the notice issued, pursuant to Section 276, and affirm with the executing officer to proceed with an execution. In the case of monetary debt, the executing officer will seize property owned by the debtor by judgment or stay any claim of the debtor against a third party in order to sell the property in auction. The executing officer cannot seize or stay property with a value exceeding the debt by judgment. This method is also applied to an execution in order to separate joint ownership in a property which is partly owned by the debtor by judgment. In the case of monetary debt, there might be possibility that seizure involves property of a third person such as seizure of property of a person who claims that the debtor by judgment does not have an ownership in the property, or seizure of property owned by the debtor by judgment but his creditor has a right of preference to the property. [1] Section 287 to 291 require that the third party having the right associated with the seized property submits a petition to contest the seizure or stay of property or requests for debt repayment, as the case may be. [2]

After the seizure or stay takes place, the debtor by judgment is ceased from establishing, transferring, or changing the right in the property or right of claim. The next execution steps is to sell the seized property in auction. Proceeds from the sale by auction will be repaid to the creditor by judgment. Before the sale, the debtor by judgment may request for an exemption of execution by referring to Section 293 in deducting the sale proceeds from the debt owed to the creditor by judgment. During the process of sale by auction, if the executing officer has undertaken any unlawful steps such as selling the property at a price lower than the reasonable price, the person at stake such as the bidder[3] may request for the sale to be revoked, pursuant to Section 296 and 309 *bis*.

---

[1] See the *Civil and Commercial Code* on preference right(Section 251 to 276).

[2] Hiroshi Oda, pp. 410~411.

[3] Somchai Julaniti, p. 184.

For the execution undertaken by an executing officer which does not involve monetary debt(such as eviction cases against the debtor by judgment and his related persons under Section 296 *bis* to Section 296 *quarter* and cases of removal of construction from land under Section 296 *bis* to Section 296 *quiqies*),Section 296 *bis* requires that the executing officer may undertake any steps as necessary in order to allow the creditor by judgment to occupy the underlying property. The steps may include removal and evacuation of items situated in the property. In the case where the debtor by judgment does not comply with the execution rules, the executing officer may report to the court and the court may order an arrest. The debtor by judgment and his related persons may be arrested as such, pursuant to Section 296 *quarter*.

Executions of judgment by other persons other than the executing officer include cases where the debtor by judgment is required to register the right or juristic act for the creditor by judgment. If the debtor by judgment does not comply, the court judgment shall be taken as an intention of the debtor by judgment, pursuant to Section 213. Other cases is when judgment that orders the debtor by judgment to perform or not to perform (besides eviction and removal of property). If the debtor by judgment does not comply, the creditor by judgment may request the court to order that the debtor by judgment be arrested and detained, pursuant to Section 297 and Section 300.

The court that has general jurisdiction for an execution, pursuant to the first paragraph of Section 302 is the court that hears the case and renders the final judgment in the first instance. Certain executions such as the claim to revoke an unlawful sale by auction can be submitted to the executing court (this is the case where the executed property is outside jurisdiction of the court that hears the case, therefore a request for an execution has to be submitted to an executing court instead). Therefore, in the case where the property subject to an execution is located outside the executing court's jurisdiction, the execution has to be transferred to the court where the property is located. In the case of sale by auction, the purchaser must submit a petition to the court in the jurisdiction where the property being executed is situated, pursuant to Section 309 ter.

19. Case termination

In general, a case ends when the court renders a final judgment and orders an execution of the judgment. In the Thai legal system, civil cases may also terminate by the following procedures: mediation and arbitration. A mediation can be done by the court. If the court sees that the parties may negotiate to reach an agreement of compromise in accordance with Section 19, the court will order the parties to appear in court(but Thai lawyers do not usually encourage mediation based on an assumption that they might earn less compensation for the dispute settlement[①]). Moreover, no matter how far a case has been proceeded, Section 20 allows the court to pursue parties' mediation. Pursuant to Section 20 *bis*, the court may order that the mediation be held in private or appoint a mediator or a group of mediators in the dispute resolution process. Mediation must follow the *Rules of the Civil Court on Mediation for Agreement of Compromise B. E.* 2537 (1994). After the parties successfully mediate, the next step is to enter into an agreement of compromise. The plaintiff may withdraw his claim in accordance with Section 175 (2), or the parties may ask the court to rule according to the agreement of compromise in accordance with Section 138. In civil cases, successful mediation is said to be the summit of justice because the parties' agreement means both parties are satisfied with the outcome of dispute settlement while no one loses. It is the win-win situation which is different from litigation that ends with a loser. [②]As Sun Tzu says, "The best troop leader wins without a fight. "[③]

---

① Moreover, it is usual for Thai lawyers to charge their clients more than what they would appropriately charge. See Sawang Boonchalermwipas, *Compilation on the Principles of the Legal Profession*, 9th Ed., Bangkok: Winyuchon Publishing, 2009, p. 290.

② Jakrapong Leksakulchai, p. 166.

③ Sawang Boonchalermwipas, p. 291.

An arbitration can be an in-court arbitration under Section 210 or out-of-court arbitration under Section 221 and the *Arbitration Act B. E.* 2545 (2002). An arbitrator(s)can be just one person or a group. However, they must not be sitting as a judge. The parties appoint an arbitrator(s)to decide the issues at hand. Arbitration is a famous dispute resolution method, especially in international trade cases, as it saves time for the dispute to be settled. An arbitration award(judgment)is generally, final, therefore, the time spent on appeal is eliminated. However, arbitration is quite costly to date. [1]

References

Thai Sources

Kanit Na-Nakorn, *Law of Civil Procedure : Book on Civil Trial*, 2nd Ed. , Revision,Bangkok:Winyuchon Publishing, 2009.

Jakrapong Leksakulchai, *Explanation on the Civil Procedure Code*, 11th Ed. , Bangkok: Nitidhama Publishing, 2010.

Thanin Kraivichien, *Explanation on the Law of Civil Procedure*, Bangkok: Ramkhamhaeng University Press, 1975.

Prapol Sataman, *Civil Procedure Seminar*, Bangkok: *The Institute of Legal Education*, the Thai Bar Association, 1972.

Manoch Joramart, *Explanation on the Civil Procedure Code 1*, 2nd Ed. , Bangkok: Bannakom Publishing, 1979.

Wanchai Boonbamroong, *The Civil Procedure Code: Reference Version*, 4th Ed. , Bangkok: Winyuchon Publishing, 2011.

Somchai Julaniti, *Explanation on Civil Procedure*, *Region* IV, Bangkok: The Institute of Legal Education, The Thai Bar Association, 2014.

Sawang Boonchalermwipas, *Compilation on the Principles of the Legal Profession*, 9th Ed. , Bangkok: Winyuchon Publishing, 2009.

---

[1]　Jakrapong Leksakulchai, pp. 270~272.

Sopol Rattanakorn，*The Law of Evidence*，9th Ed.，Bangkok：Niti-bannakarn Publishing，2008.

Luang Jamroon-nethisart，*Explanation on the Law of Civil Procedure*，3rd Ed.，Bangkok：Winyuchon Publishing，2010.

English Sources

Hiroshi Oda. *Japanese Law*，2nd.，Butterworths，London，1999.

版权侵权案件中网络服务提供者的民事责任

Article written by Chalermwut Sriporm[*]
Translated by Dr. Jaruprapa Rakpong[*]

徐 浪 译

摘要 近年来,网络版权侵权成为一个重要问题。具体来说,有通过视频分享网站诸如 YouTube 上传资源的方式侵犯他人版权。版权人很难通过起诉直接侵权人(用户)来保护自己并获得补偿。且调查侵权行为的过程也极其复杂和困难。据此,由网络服务提供者来履行替代义务是一个很好的选择,因其具备营利性、足够的资金和固定的经营场所。但问题是,版权侵权引申出网络服务提供者的何种民事责任?

通过比较研究,作者认为网络服务提供者的责任应属于过错责任。文章指出,一旦网络服务提供者的故意行为造成了权利人的损失,网络服务提供者则需承担相应的民事责任并对受害人进行赔偿。这是因为,通过审核是资源发布在网上的前提:

第一,如果网络服务提供者明知或应知用户在网上发布并传播的资源侵犯他人版权,那么根据泰国 1994 年《版权法》第 32 条第 2 款的规定,网络服务提供者将承担第二次侵权的责任,类似于将他人版权作品向公众发布并牟利的行为。

第二,如果侵权人发布的版权侵权资源是通过自动程序生成的,根据泰国《民商法典》第 432 条之规定,网络服务提供者在明知或应知版权侵权行为已经发生的情况下,未在合理时间内删除或阻止该非法资源的生成,则可认为是故意扩散或支持版权侵权的行为。网络服务提供者因此将承担连带的侵权责任。

一、引言

网络版权侵权现象越发严重,而确定直接侵权人(用户)的过程烦琐,且花费较大,然而,网络服务提供者具备营利目的、充足的资金和固定的经营场所三大特征,因此作者认为追究网络服务提供者的民事责任是一个很好的解决办法。

关于本文的写作目的,作者一是希望为被侵权人提供帮助,二是警醒网络服务提供者转变营利模式,并抑制如今泛滥的网络版权侵权行为。

本文作者对中泰两国的法律做了对比研究,中国在解决网络争端特别是网络服务提供者的法律责任方面有着特殊的立法,作者期望通过分析研究进而为泰国法律提供修订意见。

二、泰国法律下网络服务提供者的民事责任

原则上,侵权责任应根据泰国《民商法典》第420条至第425条之总则来判断。不过,侵权责任也通过一些特别法进行规制,如泰国1992年《危险物质法》关于危险物质造成损失的民事责任的规定,或是泰国1994年《版权法》关于版权侵权的民事责任的规定。

解决版权侵权问题通常适用两类法律:一是1994年《版权法》,二是泰国《民商法典》。具体规定如下:

(一)泰国1994年《版权法》

对版权物的财产权是版权人的排他性权利,未经版权所有人允许或许可,不得被他人使用,否则即造成侵权。根据泰国1994年《版权法》之规定,版权侵权行为可以分为直接侵权和间接侵权两类。不过,本文中作者仅讨论关于间接侵权的法律规定。

法律规定,间接侵权又称为第二次侵权,即"行为人明知或应知某作品是通过侵犯他人版权的方式创作的,则对该作品任何以营利为目的的行为都将被视为侵权",包括:

(1)销售,许诺销售;出租,许诺出租;分期付款购买,许诺分期付款购买;

(2)向公众发布;

(3)通过可能造成版权所有人损失的方式传播;

(4)引入本国。

时至今日,泰国1994年《版权法》第31条在司法实践中并无相关判例。据此情况,一旦网络服务提供者被诉,泰国律师普遍认为如果上传作品并非他人的版权物,则无须在第31条项下考虑责任。一部分泰国律师认为,即使网络服务提供者明知或应知该作品是通过版权侵权的方式创作的,如果他们没有以营利为目的,则不必根据第31条追究责任。另一部分泰国律师认为,网络服务提供者根本不属于第31条规制的行为人主体,因此无须承担责任。

(二)泰国《民商法典》

侵权责任的基础建立在泰国《民商法典》第432条关于连带责任的规定上。根据泰国《民商法典》第432条之规定,如果一个行为组织共同侵犯他人权利,造成他人损失,则行为组织中的每一个人都应当承担连带责任。该规定也适用于集团案件中无法确定侵权人的共同侵权行为。而且,唆使或支持侵权行为的人也将承担连带责任。除非法官有其他判断,承担赔偿责任的行为人都承担同等的责任。

第432条对于侵权责任之规定,可以分为两种情况:

(1)多人实施侵权行为。关键因素是侵权行为发生时的"共同故意",而非"共同过失",后者通常是个人的过失造成他人损失。

(2)教唆或支持侵权行为。教唆是指使他人产生犯意,无论是直接行为(诸如利用,雇佣,迫使,威胁)还是间接行为(诸如劝说,刺激,引起犯意的欺骗)等。而支持指强化他人的犯意,在刑事案件中属于共犯,在民事案件中将承担连带责任。无论是教唆还是支持侵权行为,都仅限于故意,不存在过失教唆或过失支持。

时至今日,在泰国《民商法典》第432条项下并没有直接的判例。一些泰国律师认为,根据该法条,网络服务提供者将承担连带责任,如果:(1)允许其用户通过传播侵权资源的方式侵犯他人版权;(2)允许侵权发生,并且没有删除侵权信息。

三、中国法律关于网络服务提供者的民事责任之规定

对于网络服务提供者的侵权责任,中国法律的适用可以分为两类:直接侵权和间接侵权。

(一)直接侵权

2001 年修订的《中华人民共和国著作权法》第 10 条第 12 款规定,"信息网络传播权"是著作权人的专属权利,由著作权法保护。任何人未经著作权所有人允许而使用该权利的视为对著作权的直接侵犯。

"信息网络传播权"即以有线或者无线方式向公众提供作品,使公众可以在其个人选定的时间和地点获得作品的权利。这赋予著作权人通过网络上传和使用其原创作品,包括许可或禁止他人使用其作品的排他性权利。如果用户擅自上传了著作权人所有的一段视频,则构成著作权的直接侵权,该用户也将对侵权行为负责。

但紧接着的问题是:视频分享网站的网络服务提供者是否应承担直接责任?一方面,一些中国律师认为,如果网站设立了审核团队对视频先行审核,而视频仍然侵权,则网络服务提供者应该担责。在这种情况下,该网络服务提供者和审核团队有责任判定是否给予视频审核通过,即使他们不是明知侵权,但由于未尽到合理注意的义务,网络服务提供者应视为直接侵犯了著作权人的信息网络传播权。

然而,2010 年 7 月 1 日生效的《中华人民共和国侵权责任法》第四章第 36 条第 1 款规定,如果网络用户、网络服务提供者利用网络侵害他人民事权益,应当承担侵权责任。该条第 2 款"民事权益"的定义中也包括著作权。

(二)间接侵权

1.《中华人民共和国民法通则》(1987 年)

民法通则第 130 条规定:二人以上共同侵权造成他人损害的,应当承担连带责任。除此之外,最高人民法院在关于 2000 年网络版权争端的听证会上对法条的具体应用作出了司法解释,并于 2006 年进行修订。该司法解释第 4 条规定:网络服务提供者与他人共同支持或鼓励第三方网络侵权,法院应该根据《中华人民共和国民法通则》第 130 条之规定,适用共同侵权的连带责任。该司法解释第 5 条规定:如果网络服务提供者明知用户侵权或者权利人以确凿证据告知其侵权,网络服务提供者却仍没有删除侵权资源或者未阻止侵权行为的继续,则法院可根据《中华人民共和国民法通则》第 130 条之规定,适用共同侵权的连带责任。"网络服务提供者"一词指代:(1)网络服务的提供方,(2)网络内容的提供方,(3)涉及网络服务提供的中间人。

总之,根据中华人民共和国 1987 年颁布的民法通则第 130 条以及 2000

年最高人民法院司法解释的第 4 条之规定,如果网络服务提供者与他人共同支持或鼓励第三方侵权,即被视为共同侵权而承担连带责任。

又或者,如果网络服务提供者明知用户侵权或者被权利人以确凿证据告知侵权,却仍没有删除侵权资源或者未阻止侵权的继续进行,则法院可根据《中华人民共和国民法通则》第 130 条和 2000 年最高人民法院的司法解释第 5 条之规定,适用共同侵权的连带责任。

2.《中华人民共和国侵权责任法》(2010 年)

2010 年颁布的侵权责任法是关于侵权规定的特别法,提供了侵权责任机制和救济机制,与民法原则、普通法和中国的国情共同作用。该法分为 12 章,关于网络服务提供者的侵权责任在第 4 章"关于责任主体的特殊规定"中提到。第 36 条规定了网络服务提供者的侵权责任,其中第 1 段规定了直接侵权的责任,作者已经在前文进行了讨论。

第 36 条第 2 段规定:网络用户利用网络服务实施侵权行为的,被侵权人有权通知网络服务提供者采取删除、屏蔽、断开链接等必要措施。网络服务提供者接到通知后未及时采取必要措施的,对损害的扩大部分与该网络用户承担连带责任。

第 36 条第 3 段规定:网络服务提供者知道网络用户利用其网络服务侵害他人民事权益,未采取必要措施的,与该网络用户承担连带责任。

该法第 36 条第 2 段和第 3 段以 1987 年民法通则为基础,对网络侵权进行了具体规定:无论是否侵犯了知识产权或其他类型的民事权利,也无论何种类型的网络服务提供者,结果都是承担连带责任。

不过,该法第 36 条第 2 段的规定限于"损害的扩大部分"。而在第 3 段,即明知侵权却未采取必要措施的规定中,网络服务提供者为全部损害担责,而不仅是扩大的损害。

基于上述中国法律规定,视频分享网站的网络服务提供者的民事责任基于其"明知或应知"网络版权的侵权行为,但怠于采取删除或阻止侵权信息传播的必要措施的事实,因而网络服务提供者应承担连带责任,且属于直接侵权,应对受害人提供赔偿。

四、审核环节

在审核环节,作者基于视频分享网站网络服务提供者的信息传播形式,将审核分为两类。

（一）有先行审核义务的网络服务提供者的责任

如果网络服务提供者已经设立了审核团队对上传信息进行审核并由此决定是否传播，那么如果网络用户上传的资源涉及侵权，则是否需要网络服务提供者承担责任？如何承担责任？

关于这个问题，中国律师认为：如果视频分享网站设立了审核团队对视频先行审核，在明知或应知侵权的情况下，通过了视频审核，则视为对权利人的直接侵权。

而根据泰国法律，根据1994年《版权法》第31条第2款之规定，审核的主要问题是考虑向公众传播的侵权作品是否来自"以营利为目的"的网络服务提供者。

关于这个问题，作者认为网络服务提供者以营利为目的传播侵权作品的途径如下：第一，网络服务提供者通常是靠经商获利的商人，如Clipmass网站（泰国某视频分享网站）即在国家商务部门登记注册；第二，网络服务提供者主要通过出租商品或服务的广告位来获利，如Clipmass网站的网络服务提供者在网上公布其电话及电子邮箱，以方便广告商联系。并且，Clipmass网站还发布招商广告以吸引潜在的客户，比如在主页、插件甚至支付窗口发布。第三，视频内容的传播和浏览量是网络服务提供者吸引广告商投放广告的主要手段。Clipmass网络服务提供者会评估网页、插件等的月浏览数据，从而将广告发布在用户最容易看到且观看时间最长的地方。

因此，视频服务提供者通过用户浏览数据这一因素吸引广告商的广告投放，并收取相应的广告费。如果没有视频分享，网络服务提供者就失去了赚取广告费的基础。所以，向公众传播视频的网络服务提供者应该被视为以营利为目的，且实际上是从视频传播中直接获益的主体。

不过，根据泰国《版权法》第31条第2款"明知或应知他人侵犯第三方的版权"的规定，网络服务提供者也可以承担间接侵权责任。即如果网络服务提供者以营利为目的将侵权作品传播至公众领域，该网络服务提供者"明知或应知侵权"而承担责任。

（二）无先行审核义务的网络服务提供者的责任

网络服务提供者通常使用一种"用户生成"的视频分享网络系统，即网络服务提供者仅仅为用户的视频传播提供渠道。用户在互联网创作和传播中起着关键作用，因此，该系统是一个自动系统，不需要审核团队对视频传播先行审核。

首先,根据1994年《版权法》的规定,网络服务提供者不承担第二次/第三次侵权的责任,因为公开发布和传播是用户行为造成的直接结果,与网络服务提供者无关。而且,发布和传播是依靠自动生成系统,根据1994年《版权法》,网络服务提供者没有任何传播行为。

其次,根据泰国《民商法典》第432条之规定,网络服务提供者是否因支持或鼓励传播侵权作品而承担连带责任?作者认为如果满足以下两点,则应该承担连带责任:(1)有支持侵权的行为,(2)造成了故意支持侵权的效果。

第一点又被称为行为的外部要素,即网络服务提供者实施了促进或支持侵权的行为。作者认为,如果视频传播网站的运行机制是通过审核的,就可以认为他们支持或鼓励侵权行为,因为网络服务提供者已经为侵权作品的发布和传播提供了运行机制。如果这种运行机制不存在,用户根本不能公开上传及发布侵权视频。因此,将传播放在技术角度来看,网络服务提供者有"行为"去支持或促使网络用户进行版权侵权行为。

第二点也被称为行为的内部要素,侵权责任实际上是过错责任,因而这一点很重要。如果没有过错,网络服务提供者即使产生了支持侵权的效果,也不用承担连带责任。过错仅指故意支持或促使侵权,而过失行为按道理说是不能产生责任的。

作者因此想通过审核两类因素来判断网络服务提供者是否是故意支持或鼓励侵权行为的:

1. 明知侵权行为

当网络服务提供者明知用户通过其网络上传并传播侵犯他人版权的视频,但服务提供者怠于限制或阻止传播,则被视为故意支持侵犯版权的行为。在这种情况下,根据泰国《民商法典》第432条之规定,网络服务提供者将承担连带责任。

关于"明知"的定义,作者认为:权利人已经"通知"或"告知",并有足够证据证明自己是真正的权利人且该传播作品确实侵权。

中国法律规定:如果权利人已经通过确凿的证据告知网络服务提供者侵权,那么该网络服务提供者就已"明知"。最高人民法院在2005年处理了环球唱片公司诉济宁之窗信息有限公司一案,并适用该规定。

涉及通知的形式,作者认为权利人必须直接告知网络服务提供者其传播的作品已经侵权。且通知必须是书面形式,可以通过邮件或电邮传递文件、信件,并有证据证明通知已经送达网络服务提供者。网络服务提供者的地址等信息通常发布在网上公众所知的地方,并且网络服务提供者往往为版权侵权的投诉开辟了专门渠道,便于权利人告知侵权信息。

至于通知的内容,作者认为必须合理、清楚、明确、可信。权利人需确保以下内容:

(1)如果权利人涉及多种作品被侵权,他需要准备侵权清单。

(2)必须提供充足的信息,以便网络服务提供者找到侵权的具体方位,从而删除或清除侵权信息。

(3)必须提供充足的联系信息,如地址或者联系方式,以确保情况紧急之时网络服务提供者能够联系。

(4)保证传播的信息确实侵犯了权利人的版权。

(5)保证一切信息都真实可信,且告知人确实是权利人。

(6)签字人已经获得权利人的授权,代表权利人的利益。

通知包含上述细节信息,作者认为其好处在于,国家授权网络服务提供者进行相关核实,比如在知识产权部门处理的案子中,权利人向知识产权部门提供版权信息,以便网络服务提供者清楚地获知版权侵权情况。

2. 应知侵权行为

问题的关键在于"应知"的范围。一方面,网络服务提供者明知或应知其服务可能包含版权侵权信息,即使其并不清楚哪部分的侵权是故意的。如此,鉴于如今过滤系统的先进程度,无论是通过身份信息过滤还是文字过滤,网络服务提供者都应当知道侵权行为。而且,事实上,视频分享网站涉及版权侵权一事众人皆知,因而网络服务提供者应当知道。这种观点认为"应知"的范围很广,即无须网络服务提供者知道侵权的具体位置或者具体来源,只需大致了解其服务平台上存在侵权,即可认为是故意支持版权侵权。第432条站在保护权利人的角度解释这种情况,由此使得权利人追究网络服务提供者的民事责任变得更简单。

但是,有人提出异议,认为视频分享网站的用户可能是合法使用其视频,比如在YouTube上以个人经济目的或个人版权所有的方式传播私人视频片段、家庭视频片段。然而,网络服务提供者仅靠自己去获悉用户是否合法利用视频是不合理的。就比如,除非有人告知或者房东自己发现,否则房东无法获悉租客正非法使用其租赁物。

正因为有争议,作者认为"应知"的范围应当明确下来,而不应对网络服务提供者适用类似于严格责任的责任。因此,作者认为"应知"应该是对侵权行为的"故意"支持，即前提必须是有事实表明版权侵权是显而易见的。换言之，即使网络服务提供者因为没有接到权利人的告知而未明确获知侵权情况，但如果网络服务提供者作为一个完全民事行为能力人应该知道该内容不是由权利人上传的，那么也可认为网络服务提供者"应知"。比如，上传新上映的电影、著名电影片段等都可被认为是侵权。北京市高级人民法院在 2010 年 5 月发布了第 166 号指导性案例，指出如果视频涉及的是新上映的电影或电视剧，而该视频被发布至网站的主页或重要页面，或者发布在网站负责人容易发现的位置，又或者该视频已经得到评价，或者已经被分类至"电影或电视剧"，在这些情况下，作者认为可以适用该指导案例。

进一步说，即使网络服务提供者自己没有发现侵权，但有来自第三方完全民事行为人的侵权告知，则视为网络服务提供者"应知"侵权。

因此，根据泰国《民商法典》第 432 条之规定，网络服务提供者在不明知但应知侵权的情况下，未在合理时间内采取删除或阻止侵权信息传播的必要措施，则该服务提供者被视为故意支持用户侵权，将承担连带侵权责任。

五、总结

通过作者上述的分析和建议，总结如下：首先，有先行审核义务的网络服务提供者在明知或应知上传作品侵犯第三方版权的情况下，仍然以营利为目的，通过审核并使侵权作品向公共领域传播，根据泰国 1994 年《版权法》第 31 条第 2 款之规定，网络服务提供者应当承担第二次侵权的责任。

其次，无先行审核义务的网络服务提供者，由于上传的作品是通过自动评估传播的，无须审核团队先行审核，根据泰国《民商法典》第 432 条之规定，网络服务提供者因下述行为而承担侵权连带责任：(1)支持侵权的行为，(2)造成了故意支持侵权的效果。

因此，如果网络服务提供者明知或应知侵权行为却没有在合理时间内采取删除或阻止传播的必要措施，而为侵权提供传播机制，根据泰国《民商法典》第 432 条之规定，视为网络服务提供者故意支持用户对版权的侵权，应当承担侵权的连带责任。

该规定除了适用于视频分享网站的网络服务提供者，也可适用于允许用户编辑或创造内容的其他"用户生成内容服务"网站。即用户创造信息，而网络服务提供者只是构建存储或传播信息的运行机制，比如 Facebook 网站或 Pantip 论坛。

　　总之,作者提出的所有建议的初衷在于:为因版权作品的非授权传播而遭受损失的权利人提供救济。作者主张网络服务提供者承担民事责任,将提醒网络服务提供者注意自己的所作所为,否则可能要承担民事责任,这也使网络服务提供者真正意识到必须抑制日益泛滥的互联网版权侵权行为。

Civil Liability of Website Service Providers in Cases of Copyright Infringement

Article written by Chalermwut Sriporm[*]
Translated by Dr. Jaruprapa Rakpong[**]

Abstract In this day and age copyright infringement over the Internet is a significant problem, in particular copyright infringement by uploading material to video sharing websites such as YouTube, which infringes another person's copyright. It may be difficult for copyright holders to protect themselves and seek remedy through prosecution of the service users who are directly infringing the copyright. The process of finding the person infringing the copyright is difficult and complicated. Because of this, requiring website service providers to accept liability is a good alternative since in principle website service providers are generally profit-seeking enterprises, and are certain to have capital and a definite place of residence. Consequently, there is a problematic issue of what website providers' civil liability is from copyright infringement committed by their service users.

From comparative studies, it has been found that the civil liability of video sharing website service providers is liability based on fault. This states that when a loss arises from the intentional actions of a website service provider, that website service provider consequently has civil liability and

---

   *   * 949547088 * LLB(2nd Class Honors), Thammasat University; Barrister-at-law, the Thai Bar Association; LLM(Private Law), Thammasat University; Lecturer, Thammasat University.

   **   LLB(1st Class Honors), King's College London; LLM(2nd Class Honors), University of Cambridge; PhD (European and International Trade Laws), University College London, Lecturer, Thammasat University.

must compensate the victim. This is because, from examination of the material made available on the website, it is found that:

Firstly, if the website service provider selects the material that the service user reproduces on the Internet and disseminates that work in the knowledge of or with reasonable suspicion that it infringes another person's copyright, the service provider shall be liable for secondary copyright infringement in accordance with Article 31(2)of the *Copyright Act B. E.* 2537(1994), as the service provider has acted to release another person's copyrighted work into the public domain and to seek profit from that work.

Secondly, if the dissemination of copyright infringed material that the service user reproduces on the Internet is through an automated process on the website, the website service provider may be jointly liable for the infringement with the service user in accordance with Article 432 of the *Civil and Commercial Code* for intentionally aiding and supporting the copyright infringement if they were clearly aware of or had reasonable grounds to suspect copyright infringement from the facts or circumstances that the copyright infringement obviously occurred and did not delete or block access to the illegal material within a reasonable period of time.

1. Introduction

In this day and age, copyright infringement over the Internet is a significant problem, in particular copyright infringement by uploaidng material to video sharing websites, for example the You Tube website, which infringes another person's copyright. In cases such as these, if the copyright holder were to sue the website service user, he would be likely to encounter obstacles due to the difficulty, complexity and potentially considerable cost in the process of locating and identifying the person who infringed the copyright. Therefore, claiming against the website service providers may be a good solution. This is because in principle, website service providers are profit-seeking enterprises, and are certain to have capital and a definite place of residence.

Consequently, there is a legal issue of what the civil liability of video sharing website providers is for copyright infringement by their service users. The answer to this question is one means for copyright holders of seeking remedy for the loss. It is also a means of stimulating website service providers to turn and cooperate to restrain and suppress the extensive infringement of copyright over the Internet today.

In this article, the author undertakes a comparative study between the legal principles of Thai law and that of Chinese law. This is because China introduced interesting legislation to use in disputes that arise over the Internet, in particular the legal liability of Internet service providers. In conclusion, the author analyzes and proposes a method of amending current Thai law.

2. Civil liability of website service providers under Thai law

In principle, the liability for tort is in accordance with the general principles prescribed in the *Civil and Commercial Code*, from Articles 420 to 452. However, liability for tort may be specifically prescribed under special legislation, for example, the civil liability for losses arising from hazardous substances is prescribed under the *Hazardous Substances Act B. E.* 2535(1992) or liability for copyright infringement is provided under the *Copyright Act B. E.* 2537(1994).

The legal principles that could be considered for application in such problems can be divided into the examination of special legislation namely the *Copyright Act B. E.* 2537(1994) and that of general law under the *Civil and Commercial Code*, details of which are shown as below.

2.1 *Copyright Act B. E.* 2537(1994)

The economic right to copyright material[①] is the exclusive right of the copyright holder. If a person uses copyright material without the permission or acknowledgement of the copyright holder, it is a clear infringement of the copyright. The *Copyright Act B. E.* 2537 (1994) prescribes the rules

---

① Article 15 of the *Copyright Act B. E.* 2537(1994).

concerning infringement of copyright in Section 1, Sub-Section 5. Infringement of copyright can be divided into two categories: direct and indirect copyright infringement. However, in this article the author only discusses the legal principles concerning the indirect infringement of copyright.

The indirect infringement of copyright or referred to by some Thai legal professionals as secondary infringement[①] is prescribed in Article 31 of the *Copyright Act B. E.* 2537(1994) which lays down the principle that "A person who is aware of or has reasonable grounds to suspect that a work created through the infringement of another person's copyright, any act on that work in search of profit by that person shall be construed as infringement of copyright, if he acts as follows:

(1)Sell, possess to sell, offer to sell, rent out, offer to rent out, hire-purchase or offer to hire-purchase;

(2)Release into the public domain;

(3)Distribute in a means that may cause losses to the copyright holder;

(4)Bring or order into the kingdom. "

To date, no court judgment has emerged from Thailand regarding liability under Article 31 of the *Copyright Act B. E.* 2537(1994). In cases where website service providers were sued, the shared opinions amongst the Thai lawyers involved could be summarized as if the work uploaded onto that website is not the copyright material of another person, it is not necessary to consider liability under Article 31 of the *Copyright Act B. E.* 2537(1994)at all. [②] In cases where work is created through infringement of copyright, some Thai lawyers consider that even if website service providers are aware or have reasonable grounds to suspect that the work infringes copyright, website service providers do not have any liability under Article 31, On

---

① Was Tingsmitr, *Copyright: Text and Observations of the Articles and Supreme Court Judgments*, 4th Printing, Bangkok: Nittitham Press, B. E. 2551,2008, p. 26.

② Cheewin Mallikamal, "Liability of Websites that Offer Torrent Downloading Services", http://legal-informatics. org/file/cheewin. htm, accessed 30 December 2013.

condition that they do not have the objective of seeking profit. [1] Other lawyers are of the opinion that website service providers have not acted within the scope of Article 31 at all and therefore are not liable for indirect infringement of copyright. [2]

2.2 Civil and Commercial Code

The basis of liability for tort under the *Civil and Commercial Code* that may be considered applicable to this problem is joint liability for tort under Article 432.

Article 432 states that: "If a group of persons cause a loss to another person through jointly committing a tort, those persons shall jointly be responsible for compensating for that loss. This clause shall also be used in cases where it is not possible to ascertain which person within the group is the person that committed the tort.

Furthermore, persons who instigate or support the tort can also be held to have jointly committed the tort.

Amongst these persons who are liable for compensation, they are equally liable, unless the court judges the behavior to be otherwise. "

The provisions of Article 432 are for cases of joint liability for committing a tort, which may arise under two circumstances, namely, [3]

(1) Several persons participate in committing a tort. The key criterion is that if there was a joint intention at the time when the tort was committed, there is joint liability. There may not be a joint negligent committing of the

---

[1] Kessaraporn Sa-ngiem, "Civil Liability of Internet Service Providers", Master's Thesis, Faculty of Law, Thammasat University B. E. 2551, 2008, pp. 87 ~ 89; and Chaichana Issarawit, "Legal Measures Relating to Civil Liability of Internet Service Providers", Personal Academic Work, College of Justice, Judicial Training Institute, Office of the Courts of Justice, B. E. 2552,2009, pp. 44~45.

[2] Phansiam Huaykaew, "Liability for Infringement of Copyright of Internet Service Providers", Master's Thesis, Department of Law, Faculty of Law, Chulalongkorn University, B. E. 2550,2007, p. 97.

[3] Sanankorn(Champee) Sodthiphan, *Explanation of the Characteristics of Tort, Management of Affairs without Mandate and Undue Enrichment*, 4th Printing, Bangkok: Winnyachon, B. E. 2555,2012, pp. 120~121.

tort, in which case this depends on each person's negligence in committing the tort towards another person. ①

(2) Among a group of people, even if some people do not actually commit the tort, the law still considers them to have jointly committed the tort in cases where they have instigated or supported the committing of that wrong. It means that instigating others to commit an offence is considering causing others to commit an offence, irrespective of whether it is directly encouraging such as through using, paying, asking, threatening or indirectly encouraging such as through urging, provoking anger, deceiving in order to induce the committing of an offence. ② As for supporting, it is facilitating others to commit an offence. In criminal cases this is an accomplice, but in civil cases this is treated as jointly committing a tort. ③

The instigation or the supporting of an act of committing a tort is only limited to cases with intent, because reckless instigation or support does not exist. ④

To date, there has been no direct court judgment regarding liability under Article 432 of the *Civil and Commercial Code*. Some Thai lawyers consider that website service providers may be jointly liable for tort if they allow users of the work to infringe another person's copyright on their website. It means that if that website is a forum which invites the widespread infringement of copyright, for example, a torrent website, they may be liable for supporting the tortuous act. Or if website service providers allow information which infringes the copyright to appear, and remain indifferent and do not delete or remove that information, they are considered to have promoted or supported the act of infringement under the second

---

① Prajak Buddhisombat, The *Civil and Commercial Code*, *Categories of Tort and Management of Affairs without Mandate*, 4th Printing, Bangkok: Meesombat Co. Ltd., B. E. 2548,2005, p. 146.

② Prajak Buddhisombat, p. 148.

③ Prajak Buddhisombat, 146.

④ Prajak Buddhisombat, p. 149.

paragraph of Article 432. [1]

3. Civil liability of website service providers under Chinese law

    The basis of Chinese law that can be applied to the liability of video sharing website service providers can be divided into legal principles in the case of direct infringement and in the case of indirect infringement.

3.1 Direct infringement

    Chinese copyright law, amended in 2001 in Article 10(12)[2] guarantees that the "right of communication through information networks" is the exclusive right of the copyright holder, which is protected by copyright law. If any person uses this right without receiving permission from the copyright holder, they are considered to have directly infringed copyright.

    "Right of communication through information networks" means the right to enable the public to access the work through a wired or wireless network, whereby the public are able to access at a time and from a place of their own choice. This is the exclusive right of the copyright holder to upload and use his own creative work over the Internet, including the right to permit or forbid others from doing likewise. [3]

---

    [1]   Cheewin Mallikamal, supra note 3; Phansiam Huaykaew, supra note 5, pp. 97～98; Kessaraporn Sa-ngiem, supra note 4, p. 95; Chaichana Issarawit, supra note 4, p. 48 and Thida Siripisitsak, "Civil Liability for Secondary Infringement of Copyright," Thesis of Master of Laws in Business Laws (English Program), Faculty of Law, Thammasat University, Bangkok, 2011, p. 80.

    [2]   Article 10: "Copyright includes the following personal rights and property rights: (12) the right of communication through information network, that is, the right to make a work available to the public by wire or by wireless means, so that people may have access to the work from a place and at a time individually chosen by them. "

    [3]   Fuping Gao, "A Legal Framework for the Development of the Content Industry in the People's Republic of China," In: Brian Fitzgarald, Fuping Gao, Damien O'Brien and Sampsung Xiaoxiang Shi, Eds. , *Copyright Law*, *Digital Content and the Internet in the Asia-Pacific*, Sydeny: Sydney University Press, 2008, p. 37.

The uploading of works, such as songs and videos, to a website space on the Internet, is considered to be allowing the public to access works over a computer network. Therefore, if a website user uploads a video clip without permission of the copyright holder, the communication over an information network is considered to be a direct infringement of copyright and that person is liable for infringement of copyright. [①] But there is a subsequent problem of whether or not the video sharing website service provider is liable for direct copyright infringement for the uploading of copyrighted works onto the system.

On this point, some Chinese lawyers are of the opinion that the video sharing website service provider is liable for direct copyright infringement once a review team has been set up to examine video uploads. In such cases, the website service provider and the review team have the responsibility to decide whether or not to disseminate it on the website. If the review team decides to disseminate a video upload which infringes another person's copyright, even if the team is unaware, in such cases the website service provider will be considered as having directly infringed the copyright holder's copyright in the communication over an information network. [②]

Nevertheless, it has been observed that since 1 July, 2010, there has been legislation named the *Tort Law of the People's Republic of China* of 2010 [③] which has come into force. Section 1 of Article 36 of the aforementioned act prescribes that "if an Internet service user or service provider infringes upon the civil rights or interests of another person over Internet networks, they are considered to assume liability in tort." [④] The term "civil rights" or "interests" is a concept that the law offers protection

---

① Qian Wang, "The New Right of Communication through the Information Network in the People's Republic of China", In: Brian Fitzgarald, Fuping Gao, Damien O'Brien and Sampsung Xiaoxiang Shi, Eds. , *Copyright Law*, *Digital Content and the Internet in the Asia-Pacific*, sydney: Sydney University Press, 2008, p. 278.

② Qian Wang, p. 278.

③ Subsequently referred to in this article as "Law of Tort, 2010."

④ Subsequently referred to in this article as "Law of Tort, 2010." Article 36.

by means of a definition in Article 2 which also includes copyright. ①

3.2 Indirect infringement

Details of the legal principles concerned are as follows.

3.2.1 *General Principles of Civil Law of the People's Republic of China* of 1987②

The principle of Chinese civil law that the court can apply is the *General Principles of Civil Law* of 1987, Article 130 states: "If a group of two or more persons jointly infringe the copyright of another person and cause that person to suffer a loss, they shall bear joint liability." ③

Besides this, the Chinese Supreme People's Court issued the Interpretations of the Supreme People's Court on Certain Issues Concerning the Application of Laws in the Hearing of Cases relating to Computer Network Copyright Disputes of 2000, amended in 2006. ④ In Clause 4, "In cases where the Internet service provider cooperates with another person, supports or encourages another person to infringe a copyright over an Internet network, the court shall proceed with the case in accordance with the *General Principles of Civil Law of the People's Republic of China*, Article 130 because he has jointly acted in tort with that other person". (author's own emphasis) In Clause 5, "In cases where the Internet service provider is providing the content in clear knowledge that an Internet service user is infringed another person's copyright over an Internet network or is informed as such along with credible evidence from the copyright holder and does not act to delete the copyright infringed material or eradicate the act of

---

① "Civil rights and interests" used in this law shall include the right of life, health, the right of name, reputation, honor, the right of self-image, privacy, marital autonomy, guardianship, ownership, usufruct, security interest, copyright, patent right, exclusive right to use a trademark, the right of discovery, equities, succession, and other personal and property rights and interests.

② Subsequently referred to in this article as "General Principles of Civil Law, 1987. "

③ Subsequently referred to in this article as "General Principles of Civil Law, 1987. " Article 130.

④ Subsequently referred to in this article as "Interpretations of the Supreme People's Court, 2000. "

tort that has arisen, the court shall proceed with the case in accordance with the *General Principles of Civil Law of the People's Republic of China*, Article 130 because he has jointly acted in tort with that other person. " (author's own emphasis)[①] The term "Internet service provider" may refer to (1) the Internet service provider, (2) the content provider or, (3) a person who is involved in the provision of an Internet service. [②] In summary, if an Internet service provider cooperates with another person, supports or encourages another person to infringe a copyright, he is considered to be liable because he has jointly committed an offence under Article 130 of the *General Principles of Civil Law of* 1987, as well as Clause 4 of the *Interpretations of the Supreme People's Court of* 2000.

Alternatively, in cases where the content service provider has had clear knowledge about the copyright infringement or has been warned along with credible evidence and does not act to delete or eradicate the material which infringes copyright, he shall be considered to be liable because he has jointly acted in tort under Article 130 of the *General Principles of Civil Law* of 1987, as well as Clause 5 of the *Interpretations of the Supreme People's Court* of 2000.

3.2.2 *Tort Law of the People's Republic of China of* 2010

The Tort Law of 2010 is the law which is used for acts of tort in particular and has a mechanism covering liability and remedy, and combines the concepts of civil law, common law and the state of Chinese society. [③] It is divided into 12 parts. The contents relating to tort liability of the Internet service provider are in the 4th part concerning "Special Provisions on Tort

---

① Qian Wang, supra note 14, pp. 199~200.

② Zhipei Jiang CJ, "The Judicial Protection of Copyright on the Internet in the People's Republic of China", In: Brian Fitzgarald, Fuping Gao, Damien O'Brien and Sampsung Xiaoxiang Shi, Eds. , *Copyright Law*, *Digital Content and the Internet in the Asia-Pacific*, Sydney: Sydney University Press, 2008, p. 22.

③ Mo Zhang, "Tort Liabilities and Torts Law: The New Frontier of Chinese Legal Horizon," *Richmond Journal of Global Law and Business*, Vol. 10, Issue 4(Fall 2011), p. 145.

Favors. " This prescribes the tort liability of the Internet service provider in particular in Article 36, the first paragraph as the liability arising from direct tort, as the author has already previously discussed. Article 36, the second paragraph provides that, "In cases where the Internet service user has committed a tort through an Internet network, the victim of that wrong has the right to notify the service provider to arrange necessary measures, such as deletion, blocking or disconnection. If after receiving the aforementioned notification, the service provider fails to provide any necessary measures within a reasonable period of time, the service provider shall be jointly and severally liable for the additional harm with the Internet service user. " (author's own emphasis)

In the third paragraph, "in cases where the Internet service provider is aware of the infringement of the civil rights and interests of another person by a service user through their own Internet network and the service provider fails to put in place any necessary measures, the service provider is jointly and severally liable for the additional harm with the Internet service user. "(author's own emphasis)[1]

These provisions in Article 36, Paragraphs 2 and 3 are based on the *General Principles of Civil Law* of 1987, and specifically provide details concerning committing tort on an online system. Regardless of whether it is an infringement of the intellectual property or other types of civil rights, the consequence is irrespective of the types of Internet service providers,[2] they are jointly and severally liable with the person who committed the tort. Nevertheless, the liability of the Internet service provider under Article 36,

---

[1] Article 36, SubSection 2 and 3, "Where a network user commits a tort through the network services, the victim of the tort shall be entitled to notify the network service provider to take such necessary measures as deletion, block or disconnection. If, after being notified, the network service provider fails to take necessary measures in a timely manner, it shall be jointly and severally liable for any additional harm with the network user. "

[2] Qian Tao, "The Knowledge Standard for the Internet Intermediary Liability in China," *International Journal Law of Information Technology*, Vol. 20 (1) (Spring 2012), p. 2.

Paragraph 2 is limited to "the additional harm." In cases under Article 36, Paragraph 3, if the Internet service provider is aware of the tort and neglects to put any necessary measures in place, such as deletion, blocking or disconnection, the Internet service provider may be liable for the entire loss, not only the additional harm. [①]

Based on all of the above Chinese legal principles, the civil liability of a video sharing website service provider arises on the grounds that the website service provider is aware of the unlawful or copyright infringed content but does not immediately eradicate or suppress access to the content or delays the eradication or suppression of access to the content. In other words, it is a knowledge-based liability which may have arisen from being informed of the infringement of copyright or having reasonable grounds to know about the clear infringement. This causes the website service provider to be jointly liable with the service user that has directly committed the tort in compensating the victim for the loss. [②]

Where a network service provider knows that a network user is infringing upon a civil right or interest of another person through the network services, and fails to take necessary measures, he shall be jointly and severally liable for any additional harm with the network user".

4. Review

In the review to summarize the problem at hand, the author divides the examination into two parts, based on the form of dissemination of the content by the video sharing website service provider.

4.1 Website service provider liability where the works have been reviewed prior to dissemination

In the case where the service user has uploaded a work which infringes

---

① Mo Zhang, supra note 24, pp. 457~458.

② Qian Tao, "Intermediary Liability of Website Operators in Privacy Cases in China," *Masaryk University Journal of Law and Technology*, Vol. 5, Issue 1(Summer 2011), p. 109.

the copyright of another person by the systems of the website service provider, if the service provider has set up a review team to examine the work on the system of the service user before deciding to disseminate it on his website, there is the problem whether or not and how the website service provider is liable for the copyright infringement.

On this point, Chinese lawyers are of the opinion that if the video sharing website service provider has set up a review team responsible for exa mining the video uploaded by a website user and if the review team decides to disseminate the video in the knowledge that it infringes the copyright of another person, or if they are not aware of this fact as they do not exercise reasonable care, it may be considered that the website service provider has directly infringed the copyright of the copyright holder in the communication through an information network.

Under Thai law, if this aspect is examined under the *Copyright Act B. E.* 2537(1994)Article 31(2), the main point to consider first is whether or not the dissemination to the public of a work that infringes copyright has been done by the website service provider in search of profit.

On this point, the author considers that the website service provider has disseminated a work that infringes copyright in search of profit for the reasons beneath. Firstly, website service providers are generally often busi-nesspersons who are seeking profit from undertaking a business, for example, the service provider of the website Clipmass, which is a video sharing website in Thailand, is commercially registered with the Department of Business Development, Ministry of Commerce undertaking name of S2P Media Co. Ltd. [1]

Secondly, the primary method for website service providers to seek an income is renting space on the website for advertising goods and services, for example,the service provider of the Clipmass website display his telephone number and e-mail address on the website so that anyone looking for

---

[1] The Department of Business Development (no date) [online], http://www.s2pmedia. com, accessed on 21 October, 2014.

advertising goods or services can contact them. Furthermore, they display the form of an advertisement for examination by prospective customers. For example, it states that they offer services positioning advertisements on the homepage, positioning advertisements on website clip viewing pages, including charges. [①]

Thirdly, dissemination of the video contents and the number of viewers are the main factors that website service providers use to attract people to advertise. For example, the providers of the Clipmass website display statistics on monthly number of websites hits, website members and video clips or uses inviting messages stating if you place advertisements on the website pages for viewing video clips, it would be the position closest to the viewers and where they would view the advertsements longest. [②]

For the above reasons, generally it can be seen that the provision of video sharing services is undertaken for seeking profit, namely, the number of video clips and viewers is a key factor to attract those interested in selling goods and services to decide to place advertisements on the website space, with the website service provider receiving fees for placing the advertisements in return. If there is no video sharing, the service provider is unlikely to be able to seek income from advertising goods and services in that fashion. Therefore, the dissemination of video contents by website service providers to the general public must be regarded as being done to seek profit from video contents and indeed is the direct seeking of profit from such contents.

Nevertheless, the website service provider shall be liable for indirectly infringing copyright under Article 31(2)of the *Copyright Act B. E.* 2537, if he knows or should have known that his actions infringed another person's copyright. That is, if the service provider releases infringing work on the system into the public domain, with the intention of seeking profit from that

---

① Clipmass(no date)[online], http://adserv. clipmass. com/dev. php, accessed 31 December 2013.

② Clipmass(no date)[online], http://adserv. clipmass. com/dev. php, accessed 31 December 2013.

work, the service provider shall be liable if that work was released in the knowledge of or on reasonable grounds to suspect that it infringed copyright.

4. 2   The website service provider's liability when the works have not been reviewed prior to dissemination

The website service provider generally uses a user generated video sharing website system in which The service provider only facilitates the dissemination of the service user's videos.

Service users play an important part in the creation or dissemination of their own content on websites. Therefore, the system of videos dissemination is an automatic website mechanism that does not pass or examine by people or teams from the service provider before dissemination. [①]

At first glance, the author holds the opinion that the website service provider is not liable for either primary or secondary infringement of copyright according to the *Copyright Act B. E.* 2537(1994)as the replication and release of the works to the public domain are the direct result of an action by the service user in which the website service provider has no involvement. Furthermore, the procedure of replicating and releasing follows an automated website procedure. The website service provider does not undertake an action of releasing the works into the public domain which would fit the elements of the *Copyright the works Act B. E.* 2537(1994).

The next point to consider is whether or not the website service provider is jointly liable for the infringement as providing support or encouragement according to Article 432 of the *Civil and Commercial Code*.

The author considers that the website service provider has a civil liability as encouraging the infringement under Article 432 of the *Civil and Commercial Code*, if he satisfies two elements of the law, namely,

(1)there is an action of promoting or supporting the infringement；

---

① 32. Wikipedia(no date)[online], http://en. wikipedia. org/wiki/List_of_video_hosting_services,a Accessed on 26 December, 2013.

(2)there has to be an intentional promotion or support of the infringement.

The first element may be called an external element in the sense of the action, namely the website service provider undertakes an action of promoting or supporting the infringement.

The author holds the opinion that if the mechanisms of video sharing websites are examined, it may be considered that they have facilitated or encouraged an infringement because the website service provider provides a mechanism in his system to facilitate the replication and release of the works into the public domain through a website page. If no such system existed, the service user could not upload and release a video which is a work of infringement into the public domain. For this reason, regarding the action of facilitation in the technical sense, it can be therefore considered that the video sharing website service provider has acted to promote or support the copyright infringement by the service user.

The second element is called an internal element and is an important element in determining the liability of the website service provider as it is a liability in tort which in principle is a liability based on fault. If there is no fault, then even if there is support in committing the tort, the website service provider is not jointly liable. Fault in this case only refers to the intentional promotion or support in committing the tort. A careless action, by definition, cannot amount to committing a tort.

The author would therefore like to propose a measure to examine whether or not a service provider intentionally supports or encourages copyright infringement by examining two mental elements:

The first element: the website senice provider should have clear knowledge that there is a copyright infringement on his own website.

When a website service provider clearly knows that a video currently being disseminated through his system is a work infringing another person's copyright, but he neglects to restrain or suppress the dissemination, it can be considered that the service provider intentionally encourages the copyright infringement. In such cases, the website service provider must be jointly liable as the joint party committing a tort on the basis of encouraging copyright infringement by service users according to Article 432 of the *Civil and Commercial Code*.

As for the criterion that the website service provider is considered to "have clear knowledge" that the content infringes copyright, the author proposes that it has to arise from "notification" from the copyright holder, and must be accompanied by reasonably credible evidence for the website service provider that the person is the genuine copyright holder and the work disseminated through the system infringes copyright.

As regards Chinese law, it clearly lays down the principle that if the website service provider is informed about the copyright infringement along with credible evidence, the website service provider is aware of the copyright infringement. [1] This principle has been laid down by the Supreme People's Court in the case of Universal Music Group vs. Jining's Window Information Ltd. (2005).

Regarding the method of notification, the author proposes that the copyright holder must directly notify the website service provider that a work that infringes copyright is being disseminated. The notification should be in written form, be it a document or letter sent by post or e-mail, so that there would be evidence demonstrating that the notification has already been made to the service provider. The address of the website service provider is usually made available to the general public on his website. Furthermore, the website service provider often provides a specific channel for lodging complaints about infringement of copyright. Therefore, the copyright holder is able to conveniently notify the website service provider through the channel provided.

As for the content of the notification, the author believes they must have reasonable clarity, certainty and credibility, with the copyright holder

---

[1] Legal interpretation of the Supreme People's Court 2000, Item 5.

specifying the following:[①]

(1) If the copyright holder's multiple works'copyrights are infringed, they should prepare a list.

(2) The contents of infringement must be deleted or blocked, along with sufficient information that the service provider can identify the location of that content.

(3) Sufficient information is a must to contact the notifying person, for example, an address or telephone number that a person is able to contact in case of urgency.

(4) Confirming that the notifying person has acted in good faith belief that the content has been disseminated through infringement of copyright.

(5) Confirming that all the information is correct and that the notifying person really holds the copyright of the work in question.

(6) Containing the signature of the copyright holder or person who has been authorized to act on behalf of the copyright holder.

The benefit of a notification with sufficiently clear details as in the example provided by the author is that the service provider is able to verify his accuracy with state authorities, for example, the Intellectual Property Department in cases where the copyright holder has lodged copyright information with the Intellectual Property Department, which would allow the service provider to clearly know about copyright infringement on their system.

The second element: the website provider should know that there is a copyright infringement on his own website.

There is the problem of how wide the scope of the term "should know" is.

On one side, there may be the opinion that the website service provider has an idea or should know that his service may contain infringement of

---

① The author refers to the provisions of the Clause 512(c)(3)(A) of the *United States Digital Millennium Copyright Act* of 1998(DMCA) concerning the elements of a notification to make the Internet service provider aware of a copyright infringement on their system.

copyright, even if the service provider does not clearly know which part of the tort is intentional. In such a case, the website service provider has reasonable grounds to know about the tortuous act as today's filtering systems are more modern, be it the Content-ID filtering program or a word filtering program. The service provider is able to apply these to his own system. Furthermore, the fact that there are copyright infringements on video sharing websites nowadays is widely known. Therefore, the service provider has reasonable grounds of knowing about this.

This view is an interpretation that the term "have reasonable grounds to know" has a broad definition, namely that the website service provider need not know where the infringement occurred or arose from which part of the service provided. He only need to be broadly aware that there are infringements on his service platform. This can be construed as already intentionally encouraging copyright infringement. An interpretation in this manner protects the copyright holder because it makes it easier to argue for the service provider to bear civil liability under Article 432.

However, those disputing this may argue that it is possible to lawfully use video sharing website service, for example, disseminating personal video clips, family video clips, video clips for one's own business purposes or one's own copyrighted works on the YouTube website. ① Therefore there cannot be reasonable grounds for the service provider to know whether or not a service user is using the service legally if it is not clearly apparent to the service provider. For example, a landlord may not know whether or not the tenant will use the leased property in an illegal manner until someone notifies him or he observes it himself.

On this point, the author therefore proposes that the interpretation of "have reasonable grounds to know" must have a reasonably clear scope. It should not be broadly interpreted as imposing a liability on the service provider similar to that of a strict liability. Therefore, the author's view is

---

① Blognone(no date) [online], http://www. blognone. com/node/36682, http://www. blognone. com/node/35873, accessed on 26 December, 2013.

that "have reasonable grounds to know" should be regarded as the intentional encouragement of copyright infringement. There must be reasonable grounds of knowing from the facts or circumstances that a copyright infringement is clearly apparent. In other words, even when there is no explicit awareness or knowledge because there is no notification from the copyright holder, if the website service provider encounters content then as a reasonable person[①], he should know that the content has not been uploaded by the copyright holder. For example, a clip of an entire film, a newly-released film, a famous film or other videos which should be known are copyrighted works of another person. The Higher People's Court of Beijing issued Guideline No. 166 in May, 2010 providing observations of which cases shall be held that the video sharing should have been known as an infringement of copyright. That is, if the video is a film or a television drama which has been released recently or not that long ago, and the video has been displayed on the main page or an important page of the website, or in a location that the person controlling the website can easily find, or the video has received recommendations, or fallen into the category of "film or drama series"[②], the author considers that the interpretations in the Guideline can also be adopted.

Furthermore, even if the service provider does not encounter it himself, if any content receives notification of a third-party copyright infringement, when the service provider has verified in the opinion of a reasonable man, that the content is a third-party copyright infringement, it is considered that the website service provider has reasonable grounds of knowing. This is con-

---

① Chinese courts use the standard of a reasonable person to determine "constructive knowledge." Refer to Qian Tao, "The Knowledge Standard for the Internet Intermediary Liability in China", *International Journal Law of Information Technology*, Vol. 20(1) (Spring 2012), p. 10.

② Chinese courts use the standard of a reasonable person to determine "constructive knowledge." Refer to Qian Tao, "The Knowledge Standard for the Internet Intermediary Liability in China", *International Journal Law of Information Technology*, Vol. 20(1) (Spring 2012), p. 12.

sidered to be intentional encouragement of copyright infringement if he neglects to delete or block access to the content within a reasonable period of time. Therefore, even if the website service provider does not have express knowledge but has reasonable grounds to know of a third-party copyright infringement, and does not take steps to block access or delete the content from the system within a reasonable period of time, it is considered that the service provider has intentionally encouraged the service user to infringe copyright. He has joint liability for the infringement under Article 432 of the *Civil and Commercial Code* for encouraging copyright infringement by the service user.

5. Summary

According to author's review and suggestions of ways of addressing the problems outlined in Section 4, it can be summarized as follows:

The first case is when the website service provider verifies the work before the service user uploads it, for example, the service user uploads a video or a copyrighted song onto a system of the video sharing website without the copyright holder's permission. In this case, the website service provider has a team to verify and examine the work before releasing it into the public domain. The author's proposal in the first case is if the website service provider already knows or has reasonable grounds to know that the work is a third-party copyright infringement, the service provider is liable for secondary infringement according to Article 31(2) of the *Copyright Act B. E.* 2537 (1994) as the service provider has acted to release another person's copyrighted work into the public domain and has acted in search of profit. The second case is when the website service provider does not verify the work before it is disseminated. The release of the work into the public domain is through an automated system of the website service provider, without assembling a team to examine and verify the uploaded work before it is disseminated. When the service user has uploaded a work onto the system, the mechanism of the website service provider automatically instantly evaluates and disseminates the work on the Internet.

The author proposes in this case that the website service provider has joint civil liability with the service user on the basis of encouraging copyright infringement under Article 432 of the *Civil and Commercial Code*, if it can be demonstrated as the following two elements are present:

(1) There is an action to promote or support the infringement.

(2) The promotion or support of the infringement has to be intentional.

Therefore, if the website service provider who facilitates or provides a mechanism for the infringement, who has explicit knowledge of or reasonable grounds to know that it is dissemination of another person's copyrighted work, but neglects to take action to delete or block access to the content within a reasonable period of time, it means that the service provider has intentionally encouraged the copyright infringement by the service user and has civil liability on the basis of joint infringement with the service user under Article 432 of *Civil and Commercial Code*.

The above proposals, apart from being able to be modified to use in the case of civil liability of the video sharing website service provider, can also be used for civil liability of the website service provider for other types of user-generated content(UGC) services on his system that allow the service user to write or create content on the website. The service user brings in content or information, whilst the website service provider only facilitates the mechanism of information storing and disseminating, for example, the website Facebook or the forum Pantip.

In summary, all of the author's above proposals can be adopted as an option in remedying the damage that the copyright holder suffers from the dissemination of unauthorized works on a website. He is able to claim that the website service provider has civil liability. It can also be a stimulus for the website service provider to recognize that his service can also result in civil liability so that all website service providers should cooperate to suppress today's excessive online copyright infringement.

泰国劳动法的
基本介绍

Wichitra(Foongladda)Vichienchom*
邹 茜 译

　　摘要　泰国并没有编撰劳动法典,其劳动法是由多个相关的法律规范组成的,主要包括以下四种类型:(1)劳动合同法;(2)劳动保护法;(3)劳动关系法;(4)劳动诉讼法。这些法律规范既适用于私营企业,也适用于国有企业,但自从 B.E.2534(1991)文件的出台,国营与私营企业在劳动保护法和与劳动相关法律规范的适用上逐渐产生差别。新出台的旨在规制劳动者保护的《关于就业状况最低标准的劳工联盟宣言》(B.E.2549 2006)以及规制劳动关系的《国有企业劳动关系法》(B.E.2543 2000)都只适用于国有企业。

　　但在劳动合同法和劳动诉讼程序领域,私营企业和国有企业都适用于同一法律规范。具体包括《民商法典》(B.E.2535 1992)和《建立劳动法庭和劳动诉讼程序法》(B.E.2522 1997)。因此,当雇佣劳动者时,无论是私营企业还是国有企业都要受《民商法典》第六章第三节关于服务雇佣条款的约束。根据法律,各方当事人必须订立雇佣合同(如劳动合同、就业协议),订立形式可以是书面形式或者口头形式。如果劳动合同中关于权利和义务的方面发生争议,双方当事人都有权依据《建立劳动法庭和劳动诉讼程序法》诉诸劳动法庭。本文只对泰国劳动法中涉及的私营部门进行介绍。

　　* Professor of Law at Thammasat University. (LLB Thammasat University, LLM Chulalongkorn University, Docteur en droit Université de Paris Ⅱ) This article is translated from Thai to English by Thitirat Thipsamritkul, Lecturer of Law at Thammasat University.

一、劳动合同法

泰国的劳动合同分为两种,即固定期限合同和无固定期限合同。劳动合同可以通过多种形式订立,并且在合同履行过程中以及合同终止之后为各当事人规定权利和义务。合同可通过一般方式或者特殊方式终止。此外,合同中的一些权利义务的法律关系可以发生转移。

(一)合同的订立(劳动合同)

合同的订立主要有三种方式。第一种是明确订立,当劳动者提供劳动,雇主接受并且同意对劳动者的劳动给予相应薪酬,视为合同已订立;第二种是通过事实推定合同订立,在不能认为该劳动是无偿的情况下视为已订立劳动合同;第三种是通过法律推定订立,如果劳动者在约定的期限截止之后仍继续提供劳动,雇主知道并没有表示反对,则法律推定双方在相同的条款下订立了新的劳动合同,但该合同是无固定期限合同。

(二)劳动合同中各方的权利义务

1.劳动者的权利义务

作为劳动合同一方的劳动者的首要义务是谨慎小心地向雇主提供自身劳动。并且该劳动是劳动者通过明示或暗示方式承诺履行的。同时,劳动者有义务遵循雇主的合理要求,如诚实守信义务、保密义务和竞业限制义务等。劳动者还需依照《社会保障法》(B. E. 2533 1990[3])向社会保障基金缴纳一定款项。

劳动者的主要权利是收取劳动报酬,包括加班工资、休假工资、节假日加班工资。同时劳动者还享有劳动时的安全保护权、获得法律或劳动合同条款中提供的福利权利、公平待遇权、获得工作资历证明权利、来自于其他地区而享有的回家差旅费权利等。并且劳动法和其他相关法律规范也对劳动者的其他权利进行保护,如《社会保障法案》中劳动者享有获得福利和补贴的权利。

2.雇主的权利义务

雇主的主要义务是向劳动者提供的劳动支付相应报酬。并且依照《劳动保护法》(B. E. 2541 1998[4])第 90 节第 1 条规定,雇主向劳动者支付的报酬不得低于最低工资标准。因此,如果雇主支付的报酬低于最低工资标准,则雇主对劳动者未履行的低于最低标准的差额,应依照《劳动保护法》第 9 节第 1 条规定的每年 15％ 的利息予以支付。如果雇主无合理理由未支付工资,则应自支付的合理日期截止后 7 日起算,以每 7 天未支付工资的 15％ 支付额外费用给劳动者。

同时,雇主有义务向劳动者提供安全卫生的工作环境,有义务为劳动者提供福利,有义务平等对待劳动者,有义务向劳动者提供工作资质证明,有义务为来自其他地区的劳动者提供回家差旅费,以及履行在劳动法和其他相关法律规范项下规定的其他义务。然而,如果劳动者在劳动期间对第三人造成损害,雇主应承担连带责任。雇主承担赔偿责任后有权要求劳动者偿还。

雇主的主要权利是获得服务或工作收益。如果劳动者工作时未尽谨慎小心的义务或者没有维护雇主的利益而造成损失,雇主有权要求劳动者对不符合劳动合同中的行为所造成的损失进行赔偿,并可能包含劳动者因正常劳动而造成损失的补偿。

(三)劳动合同关系的转移

劳动合同权利的转移指,在声明权利是可转移的情况下,劳动者可将获取报酬的权利转移给第三人。雇主也可以在劳动者同意的情况下将权利转移给第三人。

劳动合同义务的转移在雇主同意的前提下,劳动者可将工作交由第三人履行。雇主也可以通过相关债务文件将支付报酬的义务转移给第三人。

劳动合同关系转移还包括劳务派遣。合法的劳务派遣行为应满足以下条件:劳动者同意;不得低于原劳动条件;原雇主享有的一切权利义务都转移给新雇主;连续计算经验。

(四)劳动合同的终止

劳动合同的终止有两种方式,即一般的合同终止和特殊的合同终止。

1.一般的劳动合同终止

固定期限劳动合同可能因固定期限到期、雇用条款或时间条款的条件得到满足、合同双方合意终止合同等情况而终止;无固定期限劳动合同可能因完成零散工作、合同双方合意终止合同、进行下次工资支付之前有终止合同的通知等情况而终止。

2.特殊的劳动合同终止

第一种是劳动合同在双方都无过错的情况下终止。包括当事方的死亡,特别是劳动者的死亡。但是雇主的死亡只有在劳动合同依附于雇主的人格特性时，才能使得合同终止；对于劳动者来说，无法完成工作；对于雇主来说，无法提供工作的必备条件。

第二种是在一方有过错的情况下终止。劳动者的过错包括基于劳动者的责任，工作不能得到交付；劳动者明示或暗示保证在自己工作的领域拥有特殊技术，但并没有该项技术；劳动者在未经雇主同意的情况下将工作交予第三人履行；劳动者任意地违背或习惯性忽视雇主的合法要求，缺勤、旷工或进行与适当忠诚地履行法定义务不相符的行为。雇主的过错包括基于雇主不能提供工作的条件而使劳动者无法完成工作；雇主未经劳动者同意擅自将承担的权利转移给第三人；雇主强迫劳动者辞职；雇主进行了严重的不道德行为，如未支付工资、身体虐待等相当于犯罪的行为。

（五）劳动雇佣和劳务雇佣的区别

一些经营者为避免成为劳动合同项下的"雇主"，而选择与之有相似劳动和支付形式的劳务合同方式。这两种合同由以下四种理论进行区分：

典型性理论注重对劳动或劳务回报的计算。劳动合同中的工作报酬以劳动时间计算，而劳务合同中的报酬以工作数量或质量来计算。

合同目标理论中，劳动合同的目标指向劳动，因此工资报酬是对劳动本身的支付，即使指定的工作没有完成，仍应为付出的劳动支付报酬。而劳务合同的目标指向工作，工作完成才能获取报酬。

控制力理论中，劳动合同雇主对劳动者拥有一定的指挥控制权力，而劳务合同雇主没有。

综合测试理论中，如果一项工作是经营的主要部分，并且该项工作遵循劳动合同，则不管经营者对该项工作予以承揽还是以散工为基础，该经营者都被视为劳动合同项下的雇主。而劳务合同项下的工作被视为一种附属的工作。

二、劳动保护法

基于《民商法典》对劳动者保护的不足，泰国对劳动者的保护进行了专项立法。不论在经济理论还是实践情况下，劳动者相对于雇主通常处于不利的地位，雇主在劳动合同中享有优势。因此《劳动保护法》通过强制执行力设定最低待遇标准是必要的。雇主必须遵循《劳动保护法》与劳动者签订合同。该法被视为一种公共秩序，以刑事处罚为后盾。

(一)一般劳动保护

1. 工作时间

雇主设定的工作时间一天不超过 8 小时,一周不超过 48 小时。对可能造成劳动者健康损害和人身危险的工作,工作时间一天不应超过 7 小时,一周不超过 42 小时。

2. 休息时间

雇主应在工作当天或在工作时提供给劳动者不低于 1 小时的休息时间。休息时间不算为工作时间,除非每天总休息时间超过 2 小时。超过 2 小时的休息时间应计入工作时间。对于正常工作时间结束后的加班工作,若加班时间超过 2 小时,雇主应在开始加班工作前给劳动者提供至少 20 分钟的休息时间。

3. 休息日和请假事由

雇主应提供给劳动者一周一天的休息日;劳动者有权要求一年不超过 13 天的传统节假日,包括劳动节;连续工作满一年的劳动者有权要求不少于 6 天的带薪年假。

请假事由为以下六种:

(1)病假(sickness leave)——劳动者有权在生病期间享有病假;

(2)绝育假(sterilization leave)——劳动者有权享有绝育假,且依据科学证明能在该时间内康复;

(3)事假(business leave)——依据工作规程劳动者有权享有的事假;

(4)兵役假(military leave)——当军队需要为视察调动部队、进行军事化训练、进行警报测验等行动招募兵役的,劳动者有权享有兵役假;

(5)培训假期(training leave)——劳动者依据部门规章和程序,享有知识培训和技能发展的假期;

(6)产假(parturition leave)——怀孕的女性劳动者有权享有不超过 90 天的产假。

4. 薪酬

劳动者薪酬包括劳动工资、加班工资、法定节假日加班工资和休息日加班工资。

劳动者的工资不应低于最低工资水平。最低工资水平主要有两种,一是全国最低工资为每天 300 泰铢;二是拥有技术标准工作的工资不应低于全国最低工资。

一般加班工资指在雇主要求劳动者加班的情况下，雇主应支付劳动者不低于每小时 1.5 倍于工资基数的加班工资。

如果雇主要求劳动者在法定节假日加班，则雇主必须支付劳动者不低于每小时 3 倍于工资基数的加班工资。

如果雇主要求劳动者在休息日工作，雇主应支付劳动者不低于每小时 2 倍于工资基数的加班工资。

5. 福利

雇主应依法提供给劳动者必要的福利。如应提供涉及健康方面的热饮、公共厕所、急救、医疗保健等，涉及安全方面的紧急出口，依据特殊工作的危害性质给予个人安全保护设备等。同时，雇主应依照劳动合同或关于劳动条件的协议提供相应的福利。

6. 工作的安全性

雇主应使职业安全、职业卫生以及职业环境与《职业安全卫生和环境法》规定的标准相符合。该特殊法律建立了安全监管模式，以确保法律对劳动者的保护。同时该法也建立了旨在提高职业安全性的职业安全卫生和环境发展协会，通过制定相应标准以提高职业的安全性，并通过研究调查发展人力资源和相关领域。

7. 赔偿

即使工作场所具备相应的安全措施，但当劳动者因工遭受危险或者因工患病，则有权依据《劳动者赔偿法》要求赔偿。赔偿包括医药费、护理费、丧葬费或与案件有关的损害赔偿。

8. 遣散费

如果劳动者连续工作超过 120 天且无法律规定的特殊情况，在合同终止时有权要求雇主支付遣散费。遣散费有以下 5 种类型：

(1)工作时间超过 120 天不足 1 年的情况，遣散费以 30 天日薪计算；

(2)工作时间超过 2 年不足 3 年，遣散费以 90 天日薪计算；

(3)工作时间超过 3 年不足 6 年，遣散费以 180 天日薪计算；

(4)工作时间超过 6 年不足 10 年，遣散费以 240 天日薪计算；

(5)工作时间超过 10 年，遣散费以 300 天日薪计算。

特殊遣散费包含两种情况。一种是工作场所迁移——即雇主迁移工作场所，并且该迁移会对劳动者或家人的生活造成不利影响。雇主首先应在搬迁前 30 日告知劳动者搬迁事宜，如果劳动者不想继续从事该工作，劳动者有权终止劳动合同并要求雇主支付特殊遣散费。该特殊遣散费不应低于一般合同终止所产生的遣散费。另一种是裁员——在机器化和技术的发展导致对劳动者需求减少的情况下,企业为了寻求企业或产品重组、资源有效分配、生产线升级而不得不终止部分劳动合同。雇主应在合同终止日期前至少 60 天通知相关劳动者的合同终止日期、终止原因和终止人员名单。如果劳动者在该企业连续工作满 6 年,雇主应在一般遣散费之外给予特殊遣散费。该特殊遣散费不应低于每年 15 天的工资薪酬,但总的特殊遣散费不应超过 360 天的工资薪酬。

9.劳动的管理控制权

法律规定拥有 10 人及以上劳动者的雇主必须准备以下四种文件以进行劳动监察:工作规章、劳动者名单或登记信息、关于工资报酬的文件和关于雇佣条件的文件。

10.请求支付金钱的权利

如果雇主违背或不符合《劳动保护法》关于金钱支付的条款,劳动者有权提起劳动争议诉讼。若劳动者不想起诉,可请求有能力的行政人员依据《劳动保护法》采取措施,或请求劳动监察部门进行调查并作出裁决。如果当事方一方没有依照劳动监察的裁决进行执行,另一方可在知道该裁决之日起 30 日内向劳动法庭起诉。

11.劳动者福利基金

依据《劳动保护法》规定,当劳动者所在企业规模在 10 人及以上的情况下,应享有劳动者福利基金,并和雇主一同支付相同比例的数额,但雇主支付的数额不应超过月工资的 5%。该基金用于支付劳动者的遣散费或丧葬费。但是泰国至今并没有对筹集这笔资金做好准备,因为它同时覆盖了劳动者在《社会保障法》中享有的伤残救济金、无效合同救济金、生育救济金、死亡救济金、抚养救济金、赡养救济金以及失业救济金这 7 种福利基金。

(二)对女性劳动者的保护

1.限制性工作

雇主不得要求女性劳动者从事用肩扛抬、拖拉物品超过 25 公斤的高强度劳动。不得要求女性采矿或其他在地下、水下、洞穴、隧道或火山口等地方工作,但基于工作性质不会对女性身体和安全带来危害的除外;不得在超过 10 米及以上的脚手架上工作;不得生产运输易燃易爆物品,但对女性身体安全无危害的工作除外。

2.晚间工作

当雇主要求女性劳动者在凌晨 0 点到 6 点进行工作,若劳动监察人员认为该工作可能对女性身体和安全造成危害,则该劳动监察者可向劳动福利部门或劳动保护部门的负责人报告,并由该部门要求雇主改变工作时间或者减少女性的工作时间。

3.怀孕的女性劳动者

除以上对女性劳动者的保护措施外,《劳动保护法》还针对怀孕的女性劳动者提供特殊保护。雇主不应要求劳动者进行以下工作:与震动的机器或引擎相关的工作;与驾驶、航行等任何交通工具相关的工作;与拖拉、抬举等负重超过 15 公斤相关的工作;在船上的工作。

雇主不得要求怀孕的女性从事 22 点到凌晨 6 点的工作、不得加班、不得在休假日工作。但是如果怀孕的女性员工处于管理职位,或从事研究工作、行政工作,或与金融会计相关的工作,在不影响怀孕女性健康且女性员工同意的情况下,雇主可以允许怀孕的员工在工作日加班。

如果怀孕的员工有一流医生给出的诊断书证明她不能再从事当前的工作,该女性员工有权要求雇主在她分娩前后临时改变她的职务。

女性劳动者有权享有不超过 90 天的产假。并在产假期间享有不超过 45 天的同等于正常工资的报酬。在怀孕期间雇主不得终止劳动合同。

(三)对未成年工的保护

1.年龄限制
雇主不得聘用低于 15 周岁的儿童作为劳动力。

2.雇主对未成年工的义务
劳动合同的通知义务,即雇主必须在未成年工开始工作之日起 15 天之内,将该未成年工的劳动合同报告给劳动监察部门。

工作情况记录义务,即雇主应对未成年工进行工作情况记录,并将记录文件置于工作场所,以便劳动监察者的巡查。

合同终止的通知义务,即雇主应在未成年工离职 7 日之内通知劳动监察部门未成年工的劳动合同终止情况。

3.休息时间
雇主应提供给未成年工在连续工作不超过 4 小时的情况下,至少 1 小时的休息时间。雇主不得要求未成年工在 22 点到凌晨 6 点区间工作,除非有来自劳动福利部门或劳动保护部门的责任人的书面允许文件。雇主可以要求未成年工在此时间区间从事电影表演、戏剧表演以及其他类似的工作,但应提供未成年工合理的休息时间。雇主不得要求未成年工从事工作日加班工作和休假日加班工作。

4.高强度工作

女性未成年工不得从事超过 20 公斤强度的工作;男性未成年工不得从事超过 25 公斤强度的工作。

5.有害的工作

雇主不得要求未成年工从事以下对其健康和安全有危害的工作:与金属冶炼、金属制造、金属滚压等相关的工作;与五金冲压相关的工作;处于非正常水平的高温、低温、振动、噪音、光线等环境下可能对未成年工造成伤害的相关工作;与可能造成伤害的化学物质相关的工作;与有毒的微生物如病毒、细菌、真菌或其他微生物相关的工作;与有毒物质或易燃易爆物质相关的工作,燃料加油站除外;驾驶或控制叉车以升降卡车或起重机;使用电锯的工作;从事地下或水下工作,或在岩洞、隧道、火山口工作;与放射性物质有关的工作;对运行中的机器或引擎的清洗工作。

6.禁止的工作场所

未成年工不得在屠宰场、赌场、娱乐场所进行工作。

7.工资和保证金

雇主应支付未成年工工资,不得向未成年工收取任何形式的保证金。

8.技能培训权利

为了提高未成年工生活质量和工作能力,未成年工有权参加由教育机构、劳动福利和保护部门同意的国有或私有企业举办的会议、研讨班、培训或其他课程。该未成年工申请参加培训需要给予雇主相关活动的证明材料。如果可能,应提前告知雇主,雇主在培训期间应给予未成年工不多于 30 天的工资待遇。

三、劳动关系法

劳动关系法旨在重视和保护劳动组织的自由联合,通过关注劳动双方的友好关系以使劳动组织在雇主和劳动者之间加强话语权,同时法律保护劳动者免受雇主虐待。

(一)劳动组织

法律认可并保护形成劳动组织的自由,并有以下三个等级:工会、劳工联盟、泰国劳工代表大会。雇主的组织有雇主协会、雇主联盟、泰国雇主联盟。

(二)《关于劳动雇佣条件和劳动争议解决的协议》

《关于劳动雇佣条件和劳动争议解决的协议》指关于雇主和劳动者之间、雇主或雇主联盟与工会之间涉及的劳动雇佣条件的协议。《关于劳动雇佣条件和劳动争议解决的协议》必须包含以下方面:工作环境、工作时间、工资、福利、劳动合同终止、劳动者投诉、该协议的修订。

1.关于劳动雇佣条件协议的种类

第一种是必须依法订立该协议,当雇主有 20 名及以上的雇员则必须提供劳动雇佣条件协议,并且必须采用书面形式。第二种是被法律视为订立了该协议,雇主依照《劳动保护法》形成的工作规章可被视为《劳动关系法》中的关于劳动雇佣条件的协议。第三种是通过默示或者习惯而订立的该协议,该种协议不经劳动者同意而是通过雇主单方面行为形成,依习惯而被人遵循。第四种是依双方需求而订立协议,该协议可依需求以书面形式订立。双方参与协议修改并达成新劳动雇佣条件协议。

2.《关于劳动雇佣条件和劳动争议解决协议》的程序问题

在不违背维护平等劳动关系的基础之上,劳动双方都有权提出订立或修改该协议。主要有以下四个步骤:提出需求、谈判协商、调解仲裁和劳动争端解决。

(三)援用合法权利对劳动者进行保护

1.在订立或修改《关于劳动雇佣条件协议》过程中的保护

若在谈判、争端解决或是仲裁过程中产生了订立或修改该协议的需求,雇主不得随意解雇任何员工、员工的代理人、与该需求有关的劳工成员、劳动联盟成员等,除非解雇的对象有以下不法行为:该成员不诚信履行义务或故意对雇主实施犯罪行为;该成员故意对雇主造成损失;该成员在雇主给出书面警告或注意的情况下仍违背工作规章或雇主的合法要求。

2.不公平措施

不公平措施指雇主对劳动者采取的不合理待遇,包括虐待、利用或阻止劳动者援用法律权利等。对不公平措施的保护性措施主要表现为雇主不应有下行为:因劳动者或工会组织集会、提起诉讼等而终止劳动合同或采取其他使劳动者无法继续工作的行为;因劳动者是工会的成员,而终止劳动合同或采取其他使劳动者无法继续工作的行为;阻碍劳动者成为工会成员、使劳动者从工会中离职、给予工会人员金钱以使其拒绝劳动者的申请等;阻碍工会或劳工联盟的运行、阻碍劳动者申请加入工会等;非法干预工会或劳工联盟的运行。

同时任何人不得直接或间接地强迫或威胁劳动者,使其成为工会一员或从工会离职;不得有导致雇主违背《劳动关系法》的行为。

其次,诉讼程序包含一审和上诉程序。一审中,不公平措施的受害者有权自违反者实施违反行为之日起 60 日内向劳动关系委员会提出控告。劳动关系委员会自收到控告之日起 90 日内作出判决裁定。委员会有权要求雇主重聘劳动者,支付赔偿金等。如果一方当事人对判决裁定不满,有权上诉。劳动者可针对劳动关系委员会的判决向劳动法庭提起上诉,但上诉必须在一审判决下达之后,且必须符合上诉程序。

四、劳动诉讼法

《劳动诉讼法》旨在将劳动法庭作为特殊的法庭,包括最高劳动法庭、省级劳动法庭和区域性劳动法庭。劳动法庭中应有 3 名工作人员——一名文职人员,一名针对雇主的法官,一名针对劳动者的法官。这三种法庭都可进行一审,并可在作出判决的 15 日内针对法律问题提起上诉,上诉机构是最高法院的劳动庭。

(一)劳动争端类型

1.针对劳动合同中的权利义务产生的纠纷;

2.依据《劳动保护法》《劳动关系法》《国有企业劳动关系法》《社会保障法》《劳动者损害赔偿法》等与劳动相关的法律中的权利义务产生的纠纷;

3.依据《劳动保护法》《劳动关系法》《国有企业劳动关系法》中必须通过法院才能行使的权利纠纷;

4.对行政部门依据《劳动保护法》、劳动关系委员会依据《劳动关系法》、国有企业劳动关系委员会依据《国有企业劳动关系法》、上诉委员会依据《社会保障法》、赔偿基金委员会依据《劳动者损害赔偿法》所作出的判决,可进行上诉;

5.雇主和劳动者在执行劳动合同时,因不当行为所引起的纠纷;

6.劳动部门要求劳动法庭依据《劳动关系法》或《国有企业劳动关系法》或《就业安排和求职者保护法》进行判决所产生的纠纷;

7.基于劳动法庭的管辖权产生的纠纷。

在诉诸法院之前,应该保证当事人已经用尽上述提到的一切救济手段及救济程序。

(二)劳动争端解决的基本原则

劳动争端解决的基本原则主要包括成本效益原则、便利原则、公平原则、公平对待双方原则、救济覆盖原则以及不公正辞退案中恢复劳动者同等工资水平原则。

(三)不公平的解雇

1.不公平解雇的特点

不公平的解雇一般是无理由解雇或未依据《民事法典》中的程序进行解雇,其解雇行为违反《劳动保护法》、《劳动关系法》,并违反了诚实信用原则和有约必守原则。

2.不公平解雇的结果

如果劳动法庭认定解雇行为是不公平的,法庭有权要求雇主恢复劳动者在被解雇时的同等工作地位。但是如果劳动法庭认为劳动双方无法在一起工作,法庭可要求雇主提供相应的损害赔偿以替代工作的恢复。损害赔偿金额需要考虑到劳动者的年龄、工作期限及劳动者在被解雇时受的苦难等因素,使劳动者获得应有的补偿。

Introductory Knowledge of Thai Labor Law

Wichitra(Foongladda)Vichienchom *

1. Introduction

In Thailand, there is no codified labor code. Thai labor law is a combination of many legislations, which can be categorized into four types: (1)employment contract law; (2)labor protection law; (3)labor relations law; and (4)labor procedure. The same set of legislation used to applied for both private entities and state enterprises, but since B. E. 2534(1991) the distinction has been drawn in the area of labor protection law and labor relations law. The new established legislations applied only for state enterprises are the *Announcement of Labor Federation Concerning Minimum Standard of Employment Conditions B. E.* 2549 (2006) which governs labor protection, and the *State Enterprise Labor Relations Act B. E.* 2543(2000) which governs labor relations.

However, in the area of employment contract law and labor procedure, both private sector and state enterprise are subject to the same legislations, which are the *Civil and Commercial Code B. E.* 2535(1992)[2] and the *Act on Establishing Labor Courts and Labor Procedure B. E.* 2522 (1997).

---

* Professor of Law at Thammasat University. (LLB Thammasat University, LLM Chulalongkorn University, Docteur en droit Université de Paris II) This article is translated from Thai to English by Thitirat Thipsamritkul, Lecturer of Law at Thammasat University.

② Hereinafter referred to as *"Civil and Commercial Code."*

Therefore, when hiring a person for service, the employer—either private or state enterprise—is subject to the provisions concerning "Hire of Services" in Book Ⅲ, Chapter Ⅳ of the *Civil and Commercial Code B. E.* 2535 (1992). According to the law, both parties must conclude a contract of hire (i. e. employment contract, employment agreement), which can be in written or verbal form. If there is dispute concerning the rights and duties under employment contract, both parties shall have rights to bring their case to the Labor Court, following the provisions of the *Act on Establishing Labor Courts and Labor Procedure B. E.* 2522(1997). This article introduces Thailand's labor law only with regard to private sector.

2. Employment contract law

There are two types of employment contract; contract with fixed period of hire and contract without fixed period of hire. The contract, which can be concluded in many forms, can provide both parties the rights and duties during the time of contract and also after the contract has terminated. Employment contract may terminate in general or special ways. Moreover, some contractual relationship is transferable.

1. 1 The conclusion of employment contract(contract of hire)

There are three ways to conclude employment contract.

1. 1. 1 Explicit conclusion

Employment contract is concluded when the "employee" offers services and the "employer" accepts and agrees to pay a renumeration for the services of the employee. (*Civil and Commercial Code*, Section 575)

1. 1. 2 Conclusion implied by fact

Employment contract is implied to be concluded, under the circumstances it cannot be expected that the services are to be rendered gratuitously. (*Civil and Commercial Code*, Section 576)

1. 1. 3 Conclusion implied by law

In the case that the employee continues to render services even after the end of the agreed period and the employer knowing thereof does not object, the law presumes that the parties have made a new employment contract on the same terms, but in the form of a contract without fixed period of hire. (*Civil and Commercial Code*, Section 581)

1.2　The rights and duties of parties in employment contract

The employment contract gives rise to the rights and duties between both contracting parties as described below.

1.2.1　Employee

The employee who is a party to the employment contract has rights and duties as follows:

(1)Duties of employee

The primary duty of employee is to render services with care for the employer by himself. The employee must work as he has explicitly or implicitly promised. Moreover, the employee also has duties to obey legitimate orders of employer, such as to be honest to the employer, to maintain confidentiality, and not to compete with the employers' business. The employee also has duty to deposit money to the Social Security Fund following the *Act on Social Security B. E.* 2533(1990). [1]

(2)Rights of employee

The principal right of employee is the right to receive remuneration for services, including overtime pay, holiday pay and holiday overtime pay. Moreover, the employee also has other rights as follows: the right to be taken care for his security during the service; the right to receive welfare provided by law and by provisions of contract concluded with the employer; the right to be treated equally by the employer; the right to receive certificate of work; the right to receive travel expense for returning to hometown in the case that the employee is legally hired from other region; as well as other rights protected under labor law and other relevant legislations, such as the right to receive benefits or subsidy provided by *Social Security Act*.

1.2.1. Employer

The employer who is a party to the employment contract has rights and duties as follows:

---

[1]　Hereinafter referred to as "*Social Security Act.*"

(1)Duties of employer

The main duty of employer is to pay remuneration for services done by the employee. The employer is obliged to pay remuneration not lower than the minimum wage following the *Labor Protection Act B. E.* 2541(1998)[①], Section 90 Subsection 1. Therefore, if the employer pays less than the minimum wage, the rest becomes money debt that the employer must pay interest upon default to the employee through out the default period at a rate of fifteen per cent per annum, which is a special rate provided by the labor protection law. (*Labor Protection Act*, Section 9, Subsection 1) If the employer fails to pay wage without reasonable cause, the employer shall pay surcharge to the employee every seven days at the rate of fifteen per cent of the unpaid money, from the expiration of seven days after the due date of such payment. (*Labor Protection Act*, Section 9 Subsection 2)

Moreover, the employer also have duties to take care of security, health and working environments of the employee, to arrange welfare for the employee, to treat every employee equally, to issue certification of work for the employee, and to pay the travel expense to the employee who is from other region for returning to hmoetown, as well as other duties provided by labor law and other relevant legislations.

Nevertheless, in the case that the employee commits wrongful to a third person in the course of his employment, the employer is jointly liable with the employee. (*Civil and Commercial Code*, Section 454) But the employer who has made compensation is entitled to get reimbursement from such employee. (*Civil and Commercial Code*, Section 456)

(2)Rights of employer

The primary right of employer is to receive services or benefits from work. If the employee does not work with care or does not act to protect the benefits of the employer and causes damage, the employer has right to claim any damage caused thereby for his non-performance of labour contract(*Civil and Commercial Code*, Section 215) and might also include the

---

① Hereinafter referred to as "Labour Protection Act".

compensation for damage caused by the act of employee (*Civil and Commercial Code*, Section 420).

1.3   The transfer of relations in employment contract

1.3.1   The transfer of rights

The employee may transfer the right to receive remuneration to a third person under the transferability of the right of claim. The employer may also transfer his right to a third person by the consent of the employee. (*Civil and Commercial Code*, Section 577 Subsection 1)

1.3.2 The transfer of duties

The employee may have a third person render the services in his place with the consent of the employer. (*Civil and Commercial Code*, Section 577 Subsection 1) The employer may also transfer the duty of paying remuneration and other duties to a third person by novation.

1.3.3   The transfer of the employee to work with the new employer

The employer may legally transfer the employee to work with the new employer under these following conditions:

(1) Getting consent of the employee; (*Civil and Commercial Code*, Section 577 Subsection 1)

(2) Non-degrading conditions of employment; (*Labour Relation Act B. E. 2518*, Section 20)

3) Transfering all rights and duties from old employer to new employer; (*Labour Protection Act B.E. 2541*, Section 13)

4) Counting work experience continually.

1.4   The termination of employment contract

There are two ways that take effect as termination of contract.

1.4.1   General termination

In general, employment contract is terminated in the following cases.

(1) Contract with fixed duration of hire may terminate in the following cases:

1) It comes to the end of fixed duration of hire;

2) The condition of hire or time clause is fulfilled; or

3) Both parties are agreed to cancel the contract.

(2) Contract without fixed duration of hire may terminate in the

following cases:

1) The services are completed, in the case of piecemeal work;

2) Bother parties are agreed to cancel the contract; or

3) There is an advance notice of termination before the next succeeding payment of wages.

1.4.2　Special termination

There are special cases that the contract of hire may terminate.

1.4.2.1　In the case that there is no fault of any parties

The employment contract may terminate despite no fault of any parties in the following cases:

1) Death of parties, especially the death of the employee. However, the death of the employer may take effect as termination of contract only in the case that the personality of the employer forms essential part of the contract;

2) It is impossible for the employee to render the service (*Civil and Commercial Code*, Section 219); or

3) It is impossible for the employer to deliver the condition of services. (*Civil and Commercial Code*, Section 219)

1.4.2.2　The case that there is fault of either party

The employment may terminate in the case that there is fault of either party.

(1) Fault of employee

The fault of the employee that takes effect to terminate the contract is as follows:

1) It is impossible for the employee to render services in consequence of the circumstance that he is responsible for; (*Civil and Commercial Code*, Section 218)

2) The employee either expressly or impliedly warrants special skills on his part, but he does not have such skills; (*Civil and Commercial Code*, Section 578)

3) The employee has a third person render the services in his place without consent of the employer; (*Civil and Commercial Code*, Section 577 Subsection 2) or

4) The employee willfully disobeys or habitually neglects the lawful command of his employer despite of warnings, absents from service, or acts in a manner incompatible with the due and faithful discharge of his duty. (*Civil and Commercial Code*, Section 583)

(2)Fault of employer

The fault of the employer that takes effect to terminate the contract is as follows:

1)It is impossible for the employer to deliver the conditions of service which is in consequence of the circumstance that the employee is responsible for; (*Civil and Commercial Code*, Section 218)

2) The employer transfers his right as an employer to a third party without consent of the employee. (*Civil and Commercial Code*, Section 577, Subsection 1)

3)The employer threatens the employee to resign;

4) There is severe wrongdoing of employer, such as non-payment of services and physical abuse that amount to criminal offence.

1.5　Difference of "hire of services" and "hire of work"

Some of business operators avoid being "employer" under employment contract concerning "hire of service" by alternatively concluding "hire of work" contract which has similar elements of work and payment for that work. However, these two types of contract are distinguished by the following four theories.

1.5.1　Classical theory

This theory focuses on the calculation of return for services or work. The remuneration under employment contract is calculated by the duration of services, while the payment under hire of work contract is calculated by the quantity and quality of work.

1.5.2　Object of contract theory

The hire of services contract has purpose for the labor, the remuneration is therefore paid for the services or labor itself. Even the work has not been completed, the remuneration must be paid. On the other hand, the hire of work contract has purpose for the completed work, the payment is the return for the achievement of work.

1.5.3 Commanding power theory

The employment contract(hire of services contract)has element of the employer's commanding power, which the hire of work contract does not have.

1.5.4 Integration test theory

If the work is the principal part of a business, such work must be subject to employment contract(hire of services contract). Therefore, even though the business operator pay for work in lump sum or on piecemeal basis, such person is considered to be the employer under hire of services contract. The hire of work contract can be concluded in the case of subsidiary work.

2. Labor protection law

The law of labor protection has been established because the protection of the employee under the *Civil and Commercial Code* was insufficient. Since the employee generally is at a disadvantage position comparing to the employer both in economic theory and practical situation, the employer can exploit the freedom of contract to his advantage. Therefore, the *Labor Protection Act* is necessary for setting the minimum standard of treatment with strict enforcement. The employer cannot agree with employee in the way that does not comply with the *Labor Protection Act*. This law concerns public order, therefore it must be strictly applied with criminal punishment.

The important contents of the *Labor Protection Act* are described below.

2.1 General provisions

The employer shall, in employment, treat male and female employees equally, except where it is not possible to do so due to the nature or conditions of work. (*Labor Protection Act*, Section 15)

2.2 General labor protection

The general labor protection provided by law is described below.

2.2.1 Ordinary working period

The employer must set ordinary working period no longer than eight hours and the total working period shall not be more than 48 hours a week. In the case of work which may be harmful to health and safety of the employee, the ordinary working period shall not be longer than seven hours a day and the total working period shall not be more than 42 hours a week. (*Labor Protection Act*, Section23)

2.2.2　Rest period

The employer shall, on the working day and during the working period, provide the rest period for the employee no less than one hour. The rest period shall not be counted as the working period, except where the total of the rest period per day is more than two hours; the excess of such two hours shall be counted as ordinary working period. In the case where there is the overtime work after the ordinary working period and such overtime work shall take not less than two hours, the employer shall provide the rest period for the employee for not less than 20 minutes before commencing the overtime work. (*Labor Protectio Act*, Section 27)

2.2.3　Holiday and leave

2.2.3.1　Holiday

The law stipulates about holiday as follows:

1)The employer shall provide weekly holiday for the employee for not less than one day per week; (*Labor Protection Act*, Section 28)

2)The employee has right to ask for traditional holiday not more than 13 days per year, including the labor day; (*Labor Protection Act*, Section 29)

3) The employee who has worked consecutively for one year has the right of annual holiday for not less than six working days a year. (*Labor Protection Act*, Section 30)

2.2.3.2　Leave

The *Labor Protection Act* stipulates six types of leave as follows:

1)Sickness leave—The employee has the right to leave for his sickness during the actual sickness period; (*Labor Protection Act*, Section 32)

2) Sterilization leave—The employee has the right to leave for sterilization and for rehabilitation from sterilization in accordance with the period determined and certified by the physician; (*Labor Protection Act*, Section 33)

3)Business leave—The employee has the right to leave for his necessary business in accordance with the working regulations;(*Labor Protection Act*, Section 34)

4) Military leave—The employee has the right to leave for military service in the case where the military has to mobilize troop for inspection, to provide military training or to test of alert under the law on military service; (*Labor Protection Act*, Section 35)

5)Training leave—The employee has the right to leave for training or knowledge and skill development under the rules and procedure as prescribed by the ministerial regulations;(*Labor Protection Act*, Section 36)

6)Parturition leave—A female employee who is pregnant has the right to leave for parturition not exceeding 90 days each time, including holiday during the leave. (*Labor Protection Act*, Section 41)

2.2.4   Remuneration

There are four types of remuneration—wage, overtime pay, holiday overtime pay and holiday pay.

2.2.4.1   Wage

The employer must pay wage to the employee not lower than the minimum wage(*Labor Protection Act*, Section 90 Subsection 1). There are two rates of minimum wage: nationwide Minimum Wage Rate at 300 baht per day; and the wage rates by skill standards which shall not be less than the nationwide minimum wage rate (*Labor Protection Act*, Section 87 Subsection3).

2.2.4.2   Overtime pay

In the case where the employer demands the employee to do work overtime, the employer shall pay the overtime pay to the employee at the rate of not less than one and a half times of the hourly wage rate paid on the working day(*Labor Protection Act*, Section 90 Subsection 61).

2.2.4.3   Holiday overtime pay

In the case where the employer demands the employee to do overtime work on holiday, the employer shall pay the holiday overtime pay to the employee at the rate of not less than three times of the hourly wage rate to be paid on the working day(*Labor Protection Act*, Section 90 Subsection 63).

2. 2. 4. 4   Holiday pay

In the case where the employer demands the employee to do work on holiday, the employer shall pay the holiday pay to the employee at the rate of not less than two times of the hourly wage rate to be paid on the working day(*Labor Protection Act*, Section 90 Subsection 62).

2. 2. 5   Welfare

The employer must provide necessary welfare as prescribed by law (*Labor Protection Act*, Section 95) which is welfare concerning health such as drinking water, toilet, first aid and healthcare, and also welfare necessary for safety at work such as emergency exit within the workplace and personal safety equipment which are required for preventing harmful consequence due to the nature of work. Moreover, the employer must provide welfare according to the duty under employment contract or agreement about conditions of hire.

2. 2. 6   Safety at work

The employer must manage and operate the occupational safety, health and environment in conformity with the standard prescribed by law [*Occupational Safety Health and Environment Act B. E.* 2554 (2011)[1], Section 8 and Section 32]. This special act establishes Safety Inspector who ensures that the employee will be under protection of law (*Occupational Safety Act*, Section 35 ~ 43). Moreover, this act also establishes the Occupational Safety Health and Environment Promotion Institute which has purpose to promote occupational safety, to develop and support the preparation of standards to promote such safety, to arrange research and study which helps improve human resources and relevant academic knowledge(*Occupational Safety Act*, Section 52).

2. 2. 7   Compensation

Even if there is safety measure in workplace, when the employee is in danger or suffers from sickness related to work, the employee must be protected and must have right of compensation prescribed by special law

---

[1]   Hereinafter referred to as "*Occupational Safety Act.*"

[*Workmen's Compensation Act B. E.* 2537(1994)[①], Section 13, 15, 16 and 18]. Compensation can be money paid for medical expense, rehabilitation expense, funeral expense or expense depended on cases.

2.2.8 Severance pay and special severance pay

The law provides rules for severance pay and special severance pay.

2.2.8.1 Severance pay

The employer shall pay the severance pay to the employee upon the termination of employment if the employee has worked consecutively for 120 days(*Labor Protection Act*, Section 118 Subsection 1) and does not fall within the exception prescribed by law(*Labor Protection Act*, Section 118 Subsection 3 and 4, Section 119). The employee has right to receive severance pay which is divided into five types as follows(*Labor Protection Act*, Section 118 Subsection 1~5).

	Rate	Consecutive Work Time
1	amount of the final wage for the period of 30 days	120 days but less than 1 year
2	amount of the final wage for the period of 90 days	2 years but less than 3 years
3	amount of the final wage for the period of 180 days	3 years but less than 6 years
4	amount of the final wage for the period of 240 days	6 years but less than 10 years
5	amount of the final wage for the period of 300 days	more than 10 years

2.2.8.2 Special severance pay

The employer shall pay the special severance pay when terminating contract by special causes as follows:

1) Relocation—The employer relocates the workplace and such relocation has adverse effect to the ordinary way of life of the employee or his families. The employer shall notify such relocation to the employee at least 30 days in advance before the relocation date. In the case where the em-

---

① Hereinafter referred as "*Workmen's Compensation Act.*"

ployee does not desire to continue working, the employees shall have the right to terminate the employment contract and the employer must pay the special severance pay to the employee not less than the severance pay rate in the case of ordinary termination of contract; (*Labor Protection Act*, Section 120 Subsection 1)

2) Redundancy—The employer has to terminate the employment to reorganize the undertakings or production, distribution or service line on account of the use of machine or the changing of competitors or technology. The employer shall notify the termination date of employment, reasons thereof and list of employees whose employment shall be terminated to all relevant employees in advance, which shall not be less than 60 days before the termination date. (*Labor Protection Act*, Section 121) If the employee has worked for six consecutive years, the employer shall pay the special severance pay in addition to the ordinary severance pay in an amount of not less than the final wage rate of the employee for the period of 15 days per year of work. The total special severance pay shall not exceed the final wage rate of the employee for the period of 360 days. (*Labor Protection Act*, Section 122)

2.2.9　The control of labor

The law stipulates that the employer who has 10 employees or more must arrange the following four types of documents for the inspection by the labor inspector:

2.2.9.1　Work regulations

2.2.9.2　List/registration of employees

2.2.9.3　Documents concerning remuneration

2.2.9.4　Documents concerning conditions of hire

2.2.10　The right of claiming for money

In the case where the employer violates, or fails to comply with the pro-visions related to payment under the *Labor Protection Act*, the employee has right to bring lawsuit as labor dispute. But if the employee does not desire to start the lawsuit, the employee may require any execution of the competent official under the *Labor Protection Act*, the employee shall have the right to request the labor inspector to investigate the fact and deliver the order.

(*Labor Protection Act*, Section 123 and 124) If one of the parties is not satisfy with the order of the labor inspector, he shall file the case to the Labor Court within 30 days from the date when he has acknowledged to such order.

2.2.11　Employee Welfare Fund

The employee in any undertaking having 10 employees or more shall be a member of the Employee Welfare Fund(*Labor Protection Act*, Section 130)and shall remit the cumulative money together with the employer who shall pay at the same rate but not exceeding five percent of the wage. This amount will be paid to the employee in the case of termination of employment or death. However, there is not yet an arrangement to collect such money because it is overlapped with the rights and duties of the employee under the *Social Security Act* which covers injury or out-of-duty sickness benefits, invalidity benefits, maternity benefits, death benefits, child benefits, old-age benefits, and unemployment benefits.

2.3　The protection of female employee

The female employee is specially protected.

2.3.1　Restricted work

Some types of work are restricted due to the nature of the work.

2.3.1.1　Work with overweight objects

The employer is prohibited to demand the female employee to lift, carry by shoulder, carry by head, drag or push a thing over 25 kilograms. [*Labor Protection Act*, Section 37 and *Ministerial Regulations on Allowed Loading Weight*, B.E. 2547(2004), Section 1 Subsection 3]

2.3.1.2　Work that may be harmful to health

The employer is prohibited to demand the female employee to do harmful works as follows(*Labor Protection Act*, Section 38):

1)Mining or construction to be made underground or underwater or in a cave, tunnel or crater, except where the nature of work is not harmful to health or safety of such employees;

2)Work to be done on the scaffold with 10 meters high or over from the ground;

3) Production or transportation of explosive or inflammable material

106

except where the nature of work is not harmful to health or safety of such employees.

2.3.2　Work during night-time

In the case where the employer demands the female employee to work during 24:00 to 6:00 and the labor inspector is of the opinion that such work may be harmful to health and safety of such female employees, the labor inspector shall report to the Director-General of the Department of Labor Welfare and Protection or a person entrusted by the Director General to consider and order the employer to change period of work or reduce the working hours of the female employee as he thinks fit. In this case, the employer shall act in compliance with such order.

2.3.3　Pregnant female employee

The law provides special protection for the female employee who is pregnant in addition to the protection for the female employee as described above. (*Labor Protection Act*, Section 39)

2.3.3.1　The employer is prohibited to do works as follows:

1) Work related to machine or engine which is vibrated;

2) Work related to driving of, or boarding on, any vehicle;

3) Work related to lifting, carrying by shoulder, carrying by head, dragging or pushing a thing over 15 kilograms;

4) Work to be done on a boat;

2.3.3.2　Prohibited working time

The employer is prohibited to demand the female employee who is pregnant to do work during 22:00 to 6:00, overtime work, or holiday work. (*Labour Protection Act*, Section 39/1 Subsection 1) However, in the event a pregnant employee works in a position of management, or performs in an academic work, administrative work, or any work relating to finance and accounting, the employer may allow such pregnant employees to work overtime in the working day if it does not affect health of the pregnant employee with prior consent of such employees each time. (*Labor Protection Act*, Section 39/2 Subsection 2)

2.3.3.3　The right to change duties temporarily

In the case where the female employee who is pregnant has a medical certificate of the first class physician certifying that she can no longer do her present duties, such female employee shall have the right to request the employer to change her duties temporarily either before or after parturition. (*Labor Protection Act*, Section 41)

2.3.3.4　Leave for parturition

A female employee who is pregnant shall have the right to leave for parturition for a period of not exceeding 90 days each time(*Labor Protection Act*, Section 41)and shall have the right to obtain wage in an amount equal to the wage to be paid for the working day throughout such leave but shall not exceed 45 days per year(*Labor Protection Act*, Section 59).

2.3.3.5　Prohibition of termination of contract

No employer shall terminate the employment of the female employee on account of pregnancy. (*Labor Protection Act*, Section 43)

2.4　Protection of child labor

The law provides special protection for child labor.

2.4.1　Age limitation

No employer shall employ a child less than 15 years of age as employee. (*Labor Protection Act*, Section 44)

2.4.2　The duty of the employer concerning child labor

In the case where there is an employment of a child less than 18 years of age, the employer shall have the following duties. (*Labor Protection Act*, Section 45)

2.4.2.1　Notification of employment

The employer shall notify such child employment to the labor inspector within 15 days from the date when such child starts the work.

2.4.2.2　Record on working conditions

The employer shall make a record on working conditions if there is a change thereof, and shall keep such record at the work place or office of the employer in ready condition for inspection of the labor inspector during working hours.

2.4.2.3　Notification of termination

The employer shall notify the termination of child employment to the labor inspector within 7 days from the date when such child is dismissed.

2.4.3 The duty to care during non-ordinary working time.

The law provides protection for child labor on non-ordinary working time.

2.4.3.1 Rest period

The employer shall provide the rest period for the employee who is a child for not less than one consecutive hour per day after working for not more than four hours. (*Labor Protection Act*, Section 46)

2.4.3.2 Work during night-time

The employer is prohibited to demand the employee who is a child to work during 22:00 to 6:00, except that a written permission is given by the Director-General of the Department of Labor Welfare and Protection or a person entrusted by the Director-General. The employer may demand the employee who is a child less than 18 years of age to do the work of film or drama actor or similar performances during such period. In this case, the employer shall enable the employee who is a child to have a suitable rest. (*Labor Protection Act*, Section 47)

2.4.3.3 Overtime work and holiday work

The employer is prohibited to demand the employee who is a child to do overtime work or to work on holiday. (*Labor Protection Act*, Section 48)

2.4.4 Work with overweight objects

The employer is prohibited to demand the employee who is a child to lift, carry by shoulder, carry by head, drag or push a thing over the weight rate prescribed by law as follows(*Labor Protection Act*, Section 37)

2.4.4.1 Object with over 20 kilograms in the case of female child employee;[*Ministerial Regulations on Allowed Loading Weight*, B.E. 2547 (2004), Section 1 Subsection 1]

2.4.4.2 Object with over 25 kilograms in the case of male child employee. [*Ministerial Regulations on Allowed Loading Weight*, B.E. 2547(2004), Section 1 Subsection 2]

2.4.5 Harmful work

The employer is prohibited to demand the employee who is a child to do the following works which may be harmful to health and safety of child:

(*Labor Protection Act*, Section 49)

2.4.5.1 Metal smelting, blowing, casting or rolling;

2.4.5.2 Metal pressing;

2.4.5.3 Work relating to heat, cold, vibration, noise and light at the difference level from normal level which may be harmful as prescribed by the ministerial regulations;

2.4.5.4 Work relating to chemical substances which may be harmful as prescribed by the ministerial regulations;

2.4.5.5 Work relating to poisonous microorganisms which may be a virus, bacteria, fungus or other germs as prescribed by the ministerial regulations;

2.4.5.6 Work relating to poisonous substances or explosive or inflammable materials, except working in fuel service station as prescribed by the ministerial regulations;

2.4.5.7 Driving or controlling a fork lift truck or crane as prescribed by the ministerial regulations;

2.4.5.8 Work with an electric or motor saw;

2.4.5.9 Working underground or underwater or in a cave, tunnel, or crater;

2.4.5.10 Work relating to radioactivity as prescribed by the ministerial regulations.

2.4.5.11 Cleaning machines or engines while they are in operation.

2.4.6 Prohibited workplace

The employer is prohibited to demand the employee who is a child to work in the place as follows:

2.4.6.1 A slaughter house;

2.4.6.2 A gambling place;

2.4.6.3 A place that is clarified to be entertainment place under the law.

2.4.7 Wage and insurance

2.4.7.1 Wage

The employer shall pay wage of the employee who is a child to other persons. (*Labor Protection Act*, Section 51 Subsection 1) In the case where the employer, employee who is a child, parent or guardian of the employee who is a child, pays or accepts money or other interests before employment, at the time of employment or before each payment of wage to the employee who is a child, such money or other interests shall not be deemed as the payment or acceptance of payment of wage for such employee who is a child, and the employer shall not deduct such money or interests from the wage to be paid to the employee who is a child upon due time. (*Labor Protection Act*, Section 51 Subsection 3)

2.4.7.2 Security money

The employer is prohibited to execute or accept security money for any reason from the employee who is a child. (*Labor Protection Act*, Section 51 Subsection 1)

2.4.8 The right to leave for training

In order to develop and promote quality of life and work of a child, the employee who is a child shall have the right to leave for attending any meeting, seminar, training, practice or other courses organized by the educational institution or State or private agency which is approved by the Director-General of the Department of Labor Welfare and Protection. In this case, such employee shall clearly notify the reason for such leave together with relevant evidence, if any, to the employer in advance, and the employer shall pay wage to such employee equal to the wage to be paid on the working day throughout the period of such leave, but shall not more than 30 days per year. (*Labor Protection Act*, Section 52)

3. Labor relations law

The *Labor Relations Act* B. E. 2518(1975)[1] is based on recognition and protection of the freedom of association to form labor organization to gain more negotiation powers between the employer and employee, by focusing on good relations between both parties. Moreover, the law also protects the

---

[1] Hereinafter referred as "Labor Relations Act."

employee from being abused by the employer because of invoking rights the employee has under the law. Such law covers the following issues.

3.1　Labor organization

The law recognizes and protects the freedom of association to form labor organization in three levels which are Labor Union，Labor Federation and National Congress of Thai Labor. The organizations of the employer are Employers Association，Employer Federation and Employers' Confederation of Thailand.

3.2　Agreement relating to conditions of employment and labor dispute settlement

"Agreement relating to conditions of employment" means an agreement between an employer and employee or between an employer or Employers' Association and a Labor Union relating to conditions of employment.

"Conditions of employment" means employment or working conditions，working days and hours，wages，welfare，termination of employment，or other gains received by an employer or employee relating to employment or work.

The agreement relating to conditions of employment must contain at least the following particulars(*Labor Relations Act*，Section 11)：

1) Employment or working conditions；

2) Working days and hours；

3) Wages；

4) Welfare；

5) Termination of employment；

6) Submission of complaints by employees；and

7) Amendment or renewal of an agreement relating to conditions of employment.

3.2.1　Types of agreement relating to conditions of employment

There are four types of agreement relating to conditions of employment.

3.2.1.1　The agreement relating to conditions of employment must be concluded by law

The employer is obliged to arrange such agreements when he has 20 employees or more in a place of business. (*Labor Relations Act*, Section 10 Subsection 1). Such agreements must be made in writing. (*Labor Relations Act*, Section 10 Subsection 2)

3. 2. 1. 2   The agreement relating to conditions of employment recognized by law

Where there is a doubt as to whether a place of business has an agreement relating to conditions of employment, the working regulations which the employer obeys under *Labor Protection Act* shall be regarded as the agreement relating to conditions of employment under the *Labor Relations Act*. (*Labor Relations Act*, Section 10 Subsection 3)

3. 2. 1. 3   The agreement relating to conditions of employment is concluded by implied act or by custom

Such agreements can be concluded by unilateral act of the employer without explicit acceptance of the employee but has always been observed. (The decision of supreme court no. 523, 531/2524 and the decision of supreme court 1448—1774/2541)

3. 2. 1. 4   The agreement relating to conditions of employment must be concluded by demand

Such agreements can be concluded by submitting demand in writen form. (*Labor Relations Act*, Section 13 or Section 15) Both parties enter into the amendment procedure of agreement relating to conditions of employment and agree upon the new agreement relating to conditions of employment in written form. (*Labor Relations Act*, Section 18)

3. 2. 2   Procedure of agreement relating to conditions of employment and labor disputes settlement

In the case that the employer or employee desires to conclude or amend the agreement relating to conditions of employment, without violating the duty to maintain peaceful employment, both parties have right to submit demand concerning the conditions of employment by following four steps of procedure prescribed by law:

3. 2. 2. 1   Submission of the demand

3. 2. 2. 2   Negotiation

3. 2. 2. 3   Mediation

3.2.2.4 Labor dispute settlement

3.3 The protection of employee in the case of invoking legal rights

3.3.1 The protection during the procedure of concluding or amending agreement relating to conditions of employment

Where a demand has been notified, if this demand is in the course of negotiation, settlement or arbitration, the employer shall not dismiss any employees, representatives of employees, committee members or sub-committee members or members of the Labor Union, or committee members or sub-committee members of the Labor Federation involved in the demand unless such persons have done the following faults(*Labor Relations Act*, Section 31 Subsection 1):

1)Such persons perform their duties dishonestly or intentionally commit a criminal offence against the employer;

2)Such persons intentionally cause damage to the employer;

3)Such persons violate the rules regulations or lawful orders of the employer after a written warning or caution has been given by the employer, except in a serious case where the employer is not required to give a warning or caution; provided such rules, regulations or orders have not been issued for the purpose of preventing the said persons from carrying out the demand.

3.3.2 Unfair practice

Unfair practice is an inappropriate treatment that the employer did to the employee including abusing, taking advantage of, or preventing the employee from invoking legal rights.

3.3.2.1 Protective measures concerning unfair practices

The employer is prohibited from doing the followings which amount to unfair practices.

(1)The employer is prohibited to(*Labor Relations Act*, Section 121):

1)Terminate the employment or act in any manner which may cause an employee, a representative of the employee, a director of the Labor Union or a director of the Labor Federation being unbearable to continue working due to the fact that the employee or the Labor Union calls for a rally, files a complaint, submits a demand, participates a negotiation or institutes a lawsuit or being a witness or submits evidence to the competent officials under the law of labor protection or to the registrar, conciliation officer, labor dispute arbitrator or Labor Relations Committee under the *Labor Relations Act* or to the Labor Court, or due to the fact that the employee or the Labor union is preparing to do so;

2) Terminate the employment or act in any manner which may cause an employee being unbearable to continue working due to the fact that the employee is a member of the Labor Union;

3) Obstruct the employee from being member of the Labor Union or cause the employee to resign from the Labor Union, or give or agree to give money or property to the employee or officer of the Labor Union to refuse the apply of the employee for membership, or to admit the applicant to be membership, of the Labor Union or in lieu of the resignation from the Labor Union;

4) Obstruct the operation of the Labor Union or the Labor Federation or obstruct the exercise of the employee in applying for membership of the Labor Union; or

5) Illegally interfere the operation of the Labor Union or the Labor Federation.

(2) No person shall do the following acts(Section 122):

1) Compel or threat the employee, directly or indirectly, to be a member of the Labor Union or to resign from there; or

2) Do any act which may cause the employer to act in violation of the *Labor Relations Act*, Section 121.

(3) The prohibition of dismiss concerning the demand for working conditions during the enforcement of the working condition agreement or award. (Labor Relations Act, Section 123)

During the enforcement of the working condition agreement or award, the employer is prohibited to dismiss the employee, representative of the employee or director, member of the subcommittee or member of the Labor Union or the director or member of the subcommittee of the Labor Federation who relating to the demand, unless they do the followings:

(1) Being dishonest in the discharge of duties or intentionally commit a

criminal offence against the employer;

(2)Willfully cause damage to the employer;

(3)Violate the regulation, rule or lawful order of the employer after a written warning or caution has been given by the employer. If there is a serious circumstance, such warning or caution may not be made. In this regard, the aforesaid regulation, rule or order shall not be made with a view to obstruct such persons from doing any act relating to the demand;

(4)Unreasonably neglect their duties for three consecutive days;

(5)Perform any acts which encourage, assist or induce any person to violate the working condition agreement or award.

3.3.2.2　The procedure of invoking rights

(1)First instance

The victim of unfair practices has right to submit a complaint against the violator to the Labor Relations Committee within 60 days from the date of violation. (*Labor Relations Act*, Section 134) The Labor Relations Committee shall, upon receiving a complaint, make an award and order thereon within 90 days from the date of receiving the complaint. The Committee has power to order the employer to employ the employee again, pay compensation thereto or compel the violator to do or refrain from doing any act inappropriate. (*Labor Relations Act*, Section 41 Subsection 4) If one of the parties is not satisfied with the order, he has the right to appeal.

(2)Appeal

If the employee desires to appeal to the Labor Court against a decision of the Labor Relations Committee [*Act on the Establishment of and Procedure for Labor Court*, B. E. 2522(1979)[①] Section 8 Subsection 4], the appeal may be proceeded in the Labor Court only after complaint is to be made to the competent official or must be complied with steps and procedure prescribed. (*Labor Procedure Act*, Section 8 Subsection 2)

---

① Hereinafter referred to as "Labor Procedure Act."

4. The procedure for labor cases

The *Labor Procedure Act* is concerned about the establishment of the Labor Court as specialized court, which comprises three types of court—Central Labor Court, Regional Labor Court and Provincial Labor Court. In the Labor Court, there shall be three people—one civil servant, one associate judge for employers and one associate judge for employees. (*Labor Procedure Act*, Section 11) These three types of Labor Court are to admit labor cases as the court of first instance and the cases can be appealed regarding legal issues within 15 days since the first decision, by filing the appeal to the Labor Department of the Supreme Court.

4.1 Types of labor disputes

Labor disputes mean the disputes between the employer and employee or person who has rights and duties under labor law.

There are seven types of labor disputes. (*Labor Procedure Act*, Section 8 Subsection 1)

4.1.1 Disputes concerning the rights or duties under an employment agreement or under the terms concerning the state of employment;

4.1.2 Disputes concerning the rights or duties under the law relating to the *Labor Protection Act*, the *Labor Relations Act*, the *State Enterprises Labor Relations Act*, the *Employment Arrangement and Job-Seeker Protection Act*, the *Social Security Act* or the *Workmen's Compensation Act*;

4.1.3 Disputes where the rights must be exercised through the court according to the law relating to the *Labor Protection Act*, the *Labor Relations Act* or the *State Enterprises Labor Relations Act*;

4.1.4 Cases of appeal against a decision of the competent official under the law relating to the *Labor Protection Act* or of the Labor Relations Committee or the Minister under the *Labor Relations Act*, or of the State Enterprises Labor Relations Committee or the Minister under the *State Enterprises Labor Relations Act*, or the *Appeal Committee under the Social Security Act*, or the Compensation Fund Committee under the *Workmen's Compensation Act*;

4.1.5　Disputes arising from the ground of wrongful acts between employers and employees in connection with a labor dispute or in connection with the performance of work under an employment agreement;

4.1.6　Labor disputes which the Minister of Labor requests the Labor Court to decide in accordance with the *Labor Relations Act* or the *State Enterprises Labor Relations Act* or the *Employment Arrangement and Job-Seeker Protection Act*;

4.1.7　Cases prescribed by law under the jurisdiction of the Labor Court.

Cases where the law prescribes preliminary procedure with the purpose of providing chance for the disputes to be settled before being brought to the court and for both parties to maintain good relationship, the cases may be proceeded in the Labor Court only after actions have already been complied with steps and procedure provided by the said laws. (*Labor Procedure Act*, Section 8 Subsection 2)

4.2　Principles for the settlement of labor disputes

There are four principles applied by the Labor Court in deciding the labor disputes.

4.2.1　Principle of cost-efficiency, convenience, expediency and fairness.

4.2.2　Principle of providing fairness to both parties.

4.2.3　Principle of giving judgment in excess of the relief sought in the case of interest of justice to both parties.

4.2.4　Principle of reinstating the employee at the same level of wage in the unfair dismissal cases.

4.3　Unfair dismissal

The idea concerning unfair dismissal comes from the desire to prevent the employee from being dismissed without reasonable causes, forced into the unemployment state and to help the employee derives salary to pay for the cost of living.

4.3.1　The characteristics of unfair dismissal

The unfair dismissal has the following characteristics:

1)Dismissal without reasons or not following the procedure prescribed *in the Civil and Commercial Code;*

  2) Dismissal that is contrary to the *Labor Protection Act*;

  3) Dismissal that is contrary to the *Labor Relations Act*;

  4) Dismissal that violates the principle of good faith;

  5) Dismissal that violates the principle of pacta sunt servanda.

  4. 3. 2 The consequence of unfair dismissal

If the Labor Court considers the dismissal is unfair, the Court has power to order the employer to reinstate the employee at the same level of wage at the time of dismissal. However, if the Labor Court considers that such employee and employer can no longer work together, the Court may instead fix the amount of compensation to be paid by the employer. Nevertheless, the Labor Court shall take into consideration the age of the employee, the working period of the employee, the employee's hardship when being dismissed, the cause of dismissal and the compensation that the employee is entitled to receive. (*Labor Procedure Act*, Section 49)

If the employer has basic knowledge concerning labor law described above and strictly observes the law without taking advantage of the employee, good relationship between the employer and the employee can be built and maintained. Such good relationship gives the employee positive incentive to work helping the employer make better production and benefits, and the employee gains more chances of being promoted. If the employer's business is operated well with interests, it will also gives good effect for the whole economic situation of the country.

公共部门与私人企业的合作模式

Anak Surasarang　　Jaruwan Onchan

张　璞　译

摘要　PPP模式指通过政府与私人部门的共同合作以实现某项公共服务项目的提供，在过去几十年中PPP模式在全球范围内受到广泛关注。本文主要介绍了泰国PPP模式的立法发展，并着重对新颁布的PPP法的主要内容作出说明以及对新旧两部PPP法进行简要比较。

　　PPP模式（Public-Private-Partnerships，即公共部门与私人企业合作模式）对于增强政府部门提供基本公共服务的能力有着重要作用，并已发展成为一种全球趋势。PPP模式指通过政府与私人部门的共同合作以实现某项公共服务项目的提供，通常依赖于私人企业的资金和技术并在公共部门的监管下完成。

泰国PPP模式的产生

　　由于受政府预算与公共债务的限制，大多数政府不能为公民提供完善的公共基础设施与公共服务，因此鼓励私人投资者与政府合作通过私人企业提供资金的方式以完成公共项目建设。

　　泰国的PPP项目主要受1992年颁布的《私人参与公用事业法》（*Private Participation in State Undertaking Act B. E. 2535*，以下简称"PPA"）以及在这之后所出台的一系列规章制度的调整。但是，由于PPA条款规定的模糊所带来的不确定性，PPP项目的实施在很大程度上依赖于个人对条款的解释。

　　特别是对哪些项目纳入PPA的规制范围不明确，同时政府的支持力度不足也严重制约了PPA发生效力。例如，PPA没有明确规定政府机构对PPP项目的监管方法，因而在什么时候需要政府干预以及何种情况下政府可以单方修改协定条款方面具有不确定性。此外，PPA 中也没有对关于合同的续订、终止以及违约的惩罚措施等问题作出相应规定。因此，PPA 的模糊性导致的法律缺乏执行力以及由此所产生的腐败问题制约了泰国 PPP 模式的发展。

PPP 项目主要集中在能源、通信、供水和环境卫生领域，比较典型的是曼谷大众运输系统（BTS）和曼谷城市地铁（MRT）。从过去的实践来看，PPA 主要涵盖私人投资以特许的形式进入公共基础设施建设中。

项目融资主要通过 BOO（建设—拥有—经营）模式，BTO（建设—转移—经营）模式，以及 BOT（建设—经营—转移）模式。土建工程主要依赖政府的财政预算或向多边机构贷款来支持建设。但是政府只为政府机构或国有企业提供资金担保，不针对私人部门企业。

泰国新 PPP 法

泰国的新 PPP 法即《私人参与公用事业法》（*Private Investment in State Undertaking Act B.E.* 2556 以下简称"PIA"）自 2013 年 4 月 4 日生效。虽然 PIA 的内容与结构跟 PPA 相似，但是在定义、程序、期限上有了更为具体的规定，此外还成立了 PPP 委员会来负责泰国 PPP 项目的发展。

PIA 的适用对象

根据新 PPP 法，当 PPP 项目价值超过十亿泰铢，若无其他行政法规规定，将自动适用 PIA 规定。而具体的规则和程序仍由行政法规等规定。根据 PIA 第 4 部分对"公用事业"的定义，"公用事业"应满足以下某一条件：

（1）政府机构、国有企业、其他国家机构或地方行政机构单独或共同具有义务建设的事业；

（2）需要自然资源投入或政府机构、国有企业、其他国家机构或地方行政机构单独或共同投入财产的事业。

PPP 委员会的成员涵盖公共与私人部门。政府方面的成员包括财政部长、总理、财政部常务秘书、国家经济与社会发展委员会秘书、国务院秘书长、预算局局长等。国有企业计划办公室（以下简称"SEPO"）作为 PPP 委员会的秘书处是委员会的核心机构，其主要任务是负责战略规划、为项目的可行性提供建议以及对 PPP 项目提供数据与信息支持。

PPP 项目考虑标准

根据 PIA 第 6 部分,以下因素是 PPP 项目中需要考虑的标准:

(1)项目的完成与费用以及对国家资源的使用;

(2)遵守财政政策;

(3)从项目中可能获得的社会与经济利益;

(4)政府决策的透明性

(5)公共部门与私营部门合理分担风险;

(6)使用者与服务提供者的利益;

(7)有意愿参与项目的私人投资者的公平竞争。

战略规划

根据 PIA 规定,PPP 委员会与国有企业计划办公室承担着 PPP 项目 5 年发展计划的规划任务。战略规划主要是明确能使国家受益的 PPP 项目以及项目实施的优先性和期限问题。并且 PIA 还规定战略规划发展中所产生的费用将由 PPP 发展基金负责。

关键程序

在 PPP 项目中,有五个关键步骤对于 PPP 项目的顺利实施具有重要作用,并且泰国 PPP 法中有相应规定:

第一步:PPP 项目的识别与选择;

第二步:审慎评估与项目可行性调查;

第三步:政府采购程序(包括资格预审与评标程序);

第四步:定标和授予合同;

第五步:合同管理。

审批原则

根据旧 PPP 法,PPP 项目的整合涉及复杂的部门体系,责任被划分到不同机构而缺乏统一的法律指导框架,因此费时费力不利于对 PPP 项目提供良好的发展环境。

而新的 PPP 法显然解决了这个问题,为了获得项目批准,主办机构首先需要获得外部顾问对项目可行性调查的报告,外部顾问是新的 PPP 法所特别规定的,其资格由 SEPO 事先规定。

有关项目规划与可行性研究的问题通常由外部顾问负责。项目的组成部分以及各自能力由可行性研究决定,项目的可行性报告一般包括以下几个方面:

(1)项目的合理性、必要性以及所带来的利益是否与战略规划相一致;

(2)项目费用;

(3)对使用政府预算与私人投资预算两者间的费用与价值进行比较,这种比较方法是新 PPP 法的规定;

(4)每种私人投资模式的替代方式,考虑包括利益大小以及私营部门的准备情况,其目的在于展示出所有的投资模式以便于决策者能选择最优的投资方案;

(5)项目影响;

(6)相关风险以及风险管理方法,这也是新 PPP 法的规定,而旧的 PPP 法并没有对 PPP 项目风险识别、分担和缓解作出相关规定;

(7)在需要使用政府预算的情况下,项目主办部门还要说明财政状况、资金来源、总体预算责任、获得政府财政支持但有能力不影响政府机构整体财政状况。

项目可行性研究将在 60 日内由各部门部长进行整合,如果各部长批准该项目,SEPO 对项目的进一步考虑与分析将在下一个 60 日之内完成,并且 SEPO 对项目问题的提出和提交补充文件的要求只能在前 30 日内作出。

如果项目获得 SEPO 批准,将被提交到 PPP 委员会做进一步审核。若 SEPO 未批准该项目,应将其决定告知各部门部长,并且部长有权利向 PPP 委员会提起申诉要求委员会作出最终决定。

相比旧 PPP 法来说,新颁布的 PPP 法将项目审批程序缩短到自收到项目可行性报告及相关信息之日起 60 日以内,若 PPP 委员会未在该指定期限内作出决定,该项目被视为批准。

遴选过程

PPP 项目采购程序要求公开、透明,并遵守相关的规章制度,并且各部门将组成遴选委员会负责遴选程序。

遴选委员会将负责规定有关授权范围、招标条件、招标邀请以及合同起草等问题。此外，遴选委员会还将负责采购程序，如规定投标者的资格预审，设定投标保证金和履约保证金，同投标者交换意见与信息反馈，确定并发布招投标文件，评估与筛选优势投标者等。

外部顾问将负责协助遴选委员会进行遴选程序、风险分析以及减少和控制潜在风险，外部顾问的资格与标准问题由 SEPO 事先规定。

确定合同条款与准备起草合同

PPP 合同条款通常包括以下几方面：

(1)合同期限；

(2)项目服务与经营条款；

(3)费用、付款方式以及其他涉及收款与拨款的财务问题；

(4)项目实施变更、合同当事人变更、分包和转让；

(5)项目资产、资产所有权以及资产估价；

(6)不可抗力和因不可抗力所产生的费用；

(7)合同终止、违约和合同解除产生的费用；

(8)合同担保、合同责任以及赔偿；

(9)争议解决。

若主办机构与遴选委员会认为不适宜采用招投标方式选择私人投资者并倾向于采用其他遴选方式，需经 SEPO 与 PPP 委员会批准。

若采用招投标方式只有一位投标者参与且遴选委员会认为该投标者能使国家获益，委员会可直接将项目授予此投标者。

项目监管

合同履行与合同管理是项目监管的关键环节。合同管理主要包括：

(1)设立监管程序与合同监管委员会；

(2)明确管理责任；

(3)财务监管；

(4)确保经营与服务交付的顺利进行。

合同管理涉及一系列程序的设立与合同文件的管理，主要包括变更管理、遵守合同条款以及财务管理。PPP法设立了项目监管委员会,其负责对每个PPP项目进行合同管理。项目监管委员的职权和职责包括:

(1)确保项目运营应遵守PPP合同、根据合同设立的项目实施计划以及遵守项目实施风险管理计划的规定;

(2)对项目实施中出现的问题提出解决意见以及建议项目主办者向外部顾问寻求帮助;

(3)有权要求项目主办者或合同当事人作出解释或提交相关文件;

(4)就项目执行的过程、结果、产生的问题以及解决问题的方法向负责该项目的部长报告;

(5)负责考虑PPP合同的修改。

违反合同规定

项目实施机构以及合同当事人要确保项目实施符合合同规定。一旦违反合同规定,项目监管委员会应向负责的部长报告。若出现严重后果,项目监管委员应立即向内阁报告。

合同变更管理

由于PPP合同周期长,一般在10～30年,因而在履行过程中会出现合同签订时无法预测的情况。并且合同当事人对合同解释与合同履行也会产生分歧,为了解决这些问题,需要对合同做相应变更。

新的PPP法对合同实施过程中的变更问题有明确的程序规定与指导。然而更为具体的标准应由SEPO发布。若合同变更确有必要,主办机构应向项目监管委员会提交修改建议,委员会应立即向负责的部长报告。

若合同修改涉及实质性条款,主办机构还应向项目监管委员会提交合同修改评估报告以及其他具体文件,以供总检察长进一步审核。内阁对合同的修改具有最终决定权。

合同续订

有关合同续订的事项由主办机构负责,内阁享有最终决定权,对续订的合同进行修改也需内阁批准。

项目发展基金(PDF)

新的 PPP 法规定由财政部设立项目发展基金为战略规划、项目建议以及分析评估报告提供资金支持。项目发展基金的资金来源于政府支持、招投标收入和合同签署费用。

违反 PPP 法规定

根据 PPP 法规定,若项目的实施未遵守 PPP 法,SEPO 可以要求主办机构作出澄清并说明是否继续该项目。相应的,SEPO 认为确有必要对违反 PPP 法程序规定的合同进行修改或终止,应获得内阁批准。

若 SEPO 认为该项目可以继续进行,可要求该项目在监管下进行并遵守 PPP 法的规定。

结　　论

尽管新 PPP 法相比旧法有所进步,但 PPP 法能否作为促进经济发展和吸引投资者的有效机制还依赖于相关行政法规的具体规定。新 PPP 法的规定更为明确、具体,这将对增强投资者信心和促进 PPP 模式的发展产生重要作用。为了给潜在的 PPP 合作方积极的信号,我们应该毫不迟疑地在新的 PPP 法下完成第一个 PPP 项目。

PPP

Anak Surasarang & Jaruwan Onchan

Introduction

The increasing need of state governments to provide fundamental public services for their people plays an important role in the development of Public-Private Partnerships ("PPPs") all around the world. It is a global trend that has over the years grown enormously. Thailand is not an exemption. The arrangement that offers the right combination of know-how, skills and management of the private sector, together with the public sector's regulatory actions provides appropriate safeguard for public interest.

In other words, PPPs setting is a form of cooperation between government and one or more private sector companies for the purpose of completing a project that will serve the public. The funding and operation of the project will be achieved through such partnership. PPPs often use private-sector investments to finance a public project when public funding is insufficient.

Origin of PPP in Thailand

Due to limited budget and restrictions on the level of public debt, most governments, in general, could not provide basic infrastructures and public services for its citizens. Private investors therefore are encouraged through a process to form an alliance with governments to provide, finance and maintain these public services and infrastructures.

In Thailand, since 1992, PPPs have, for the most part, been governed by the *Private Participation in State Undertaking Act B. E.* 2535(1992) (the "PPA"). Subsequent to the enactment of the PPA, rules and regulations were issued to address the selection process. Regrettably though, broad terms employed in the PPA create uncertainty, the implementation of which therefore depends very much on one's own reading of law.

In particular, it was unclear which projects were covered within the scope of the PPA. Due to the unclear definitions, there are over 100 requests sent to the Council of State for interpretation and clarification. Also, insufficient state support severely limits the effectiveness of the PPA. To be more precise, the PPA omits clear monitoring methods by state agencies of PPP projects, raising questions therefore as to when the State should intervene or under what circumstances can the State unilaterally amend the terms of agreements. Besides, several important issues, such as contract renewal, termination and penalties for breach of contract, are all largely left unaddressed.

From investors' perspective, therefore, there are difficulties involved in the realization of the law, and, as a result, such uncertainty prevents the development of PPPs in Thailand. In short, legal ambiguity leads to a lack of enforcement and rampant corruption.

Major PPP projects are energy, telecommunications, water and sanitation. Prominent examples of previous PPP projects in Thailand also include the Bangkok Mass Transit System("BTS") and the Metropolitan Rapid Transit("MRT"). Past experience shows that the PPA has been used in a broad sense to cover concession-based private investment in public infra-structure, made on the basis of traditional project finance structures.

The most common structures for project financing include Build-Own-Operate ("BOO"), Build-Transfer-Operate ("BTO") and Build-Operate-Transfer ("BOT"). Civil works are usually funded by the government through either the fiscal budget or through borrowing from multilateral in-stitutions. As an alternative, government contribution, such as equity, is also allowed under each project agency's establishment act. Note, however, that the Thai government cannot provide funding guarantee for private sectors. Its funding guarantee is merely provided for government agencies and State Owned Enterprises.

The Thailand's new PPPs law

Taking effect since 4 April 2013, resulting in a simultaneous repealing of the PPA, the *Private Investment in State Undertaking Act B. E.* 2556 (2013)(the "PIA"), offers a ray of hope for the new era of Thailand's PPPs development. Although the content and structure of the PIA, in general, are rather similar to the old PPA, the PIA makes available better specificity in definitions, procedures, and time frames. Besides, a new committee, the PPP Committee, has been established and will be responsible for PPPs in Thailand.

Projects governed by PIA

New PPP projects with a value of more than one billion baht, unless otherwise prescribed in ministerial regulations, will be subject to the PIA. Detailed rules and procedures have yet to be subsequently contemplated through ministerial regulations.

The "state undertaking" is defined, as per Section 4 of PIA, to mean an undertaking having one of the following descriptions:

(1) An undertaking which a government agencies, state enterprise, other state agencies or local administrative organizations, either singly or collectively, have a legal obligation to perform;

(2) An undertaking which requires the utilization of natural resources or properties of one or several government agencies, state enterprises, other state agencies or local administrative organizations, either singly or collectively.

The PPP Committee comprises members from the public and private sectors. On the government side, members include the Minister of Finance, the Prime Minister (Chair), the Permanent Secretary of the Ministry of

Finance, the Secretary of the National Economic and Social Development Board, the Secretary General of the Council of State, the Director of the Bureau of the Budget, the Comptroller, General, and the Director of the Public Debt Management Office of the Attorney General. The State Enterprise Planning Office("SEPO")functions as the secretariat of the PPP Committee as a central PPP unit. The key roles of the unit are to prepare strategic plans, provide recommendations on project feasibility and to provide database and information concerning PPP scheme.

At the time of writing, the total project value for PPP during the next six years(2014-2019)under the Ministry of Transportation is expected to be more than 1. 7 trillion baht(approximately USD 57 billion).

Criteria when considering PPPs

The following aspects, as contemplated in Section 6 of PIA, among other things, shall be taken into consideration when contemplating PPP projects:

(1) Accomplishment and costs of operation and the use of state resources;

(2)Adherence to fiscal discipline;

(3)Social and economic benefits from each project;

(4)Transparency of the decision-making process;

(5)Proper risk allocation between public and private sector projects;

(6)Rights and interests of the user and the service provider; and

(7) Encouragement of fair competition among private investors that desire to participate.

Strategic planning

Not only that the new PIA provides clarity and precise timelines, but also PIA contributes to the development of PPPs in Thailand. The PPP Committee, together with the State Enterprise Planning Office, are obliged to put in order a 5-year strategic plan for PPPs for the Cabinet's consideration. The strategic planning is supposed to identify sectors and specific projects in which PPPs would be of benefit to the country, the priority of each and timeframe for implementation. Expenses incurred in relation to the development of such strategic plan, such as hiring consultants, will be absorbed by the PPP development Fund, as stipulated in the PIA. This helps ensuring that the PPPs employed by such respective agencies will align with the PPP development plan.

An example of the method by which the project funding has been achieved is the BTS Rail Mass Transit Growth Infrastructure Fund, which are the first infrastructure fund created in Thailand and was approved by Thailand's Securities and Exchange Commission to offer fund units to the public.

For pre-existing projects or potential new projects, which are already undergoing consideration, a question may be raised as to which law shall apply, the old law or the new law. The PIA clearly addresses this issue.

Key procedure

In normal PPP project, the five key stages allow each PPP project to be individually tailored to its particular characteristic and environment, essential for successful implementation. These five steps are also mentioned under Thai PPP law.

Stage 1: Identification and selection of PPP project.

Stage 2: Due diligence and conducting feasibility studies.

Stage 3: Procurement process. This includes outlining prequalification of the bidders, bidding and bid evaluation process.

Stage 4: Award of contract.

Stage 5: Contract management and monitoring.

Principles in approval

Under the old PPP laws, coordinate PPP projects according to the legal framework are very time consuming as there are so many different bodies across several sectors assumed various responsibilities of the regulations. The responsible implementation agencies are left to various parties while there are no uniform legal framework as the guidance and the projects face lesser quality support. This previously lends itself to inefficiency and does not create positive investment climate. The new laws do fix these problems. In obtaining the project approval, the host agency having intention to initiate any PPP project, shall, first and foremost, require to engage the external consultant to conduct the project feasibility report. The engagement of the external consultant is the new development under the new PPP laws whereby only the external consultant must be limited to the external consultant approved by SEPO. The qualification of the approved external consultant shall be prescribed by SEPO. So far, this has yet to be announced by PPP.

The work involved in the project planning and feasibility study is generally undertaken by the external consultant. The physical components of the project and their capabilities are determined on the basis of the outcomes of the feasibility study. The host agency, upon engaging the external consultant shall conduct feasibility report in which the main elements of the report must contain at least the following subjects:

(1) Rationale, necessity and benefit of the project, consistency to the strategy plan.

(2) Project cost.

(3) Cooperation for cost and value for money between the use of government budget and the private investment budget.

This comparison method is the new improvement of Thai PPP laws that creates significant changes to Thai PPP laws.

(4) Alternative form of each private investment model including interest and readiness of the private sector.

This aims to lay out all possible forms of investment so that the decision maker shall opt to proceed with the best investment arrangement.

(5) Project impact.

(6) Related risks and approaches in managing the project risks.

This is also one of major improvements of the new laws. The old PPP laws do not provide the methodology in identifying, allocating and mitigating risks in PPP. This is considered one of the most important principles to the PPP projects especially the infrastructure project. allocation for the PPP projects.

(7) In the case where the project host intends to use the government budget, the project host shall demonstrate the financial status, source of funding, overall budgetary obligation committed to other projects, ability to obtain project funding without affecting overall financial status of the government agency.

Such feasibility study will then be consolidated, within the 60-day time frame, by respective ministers of the agency. In the event that the respective ministers approve the project, SEPO will then subject such project to further consideration and analysis, a process of which is to be completed within another 60 day period. Questions and additional documents could only be posed and requested within the first 30 days.

If SEPO agrees with the project, the PPP Committee will further review the project. In the event that the SEPO disagrees with project, SEPO shall notify the outcome to the ministers of the agency and the ministers of the agency are entitled to file the appeal to the PPP Committee to make the final judgment accordingly.

The project approval process is shorten comparing to the previous laws, i. e. 60 days upon receiving the complete set of the feasibility study and relevant information. Failure to issue the outcome upon the lapse of 60 days, the project shall be deemed as approved.

In this respect, If the project incurs government expenditure, cabinet approval would be required.

Selection process

The PPP procurement process needs to be transparent, neutral based on the common principles of good governance. Therefore, the selection of the private partner will be conducted in accordance with the rules and regulations which have yet to be issued. A selection committee is to be formed by the respective project agencies, in order to select a private sector operator to join the PPP project. The main objective of the process is to acquire the best proposal which serves the best interest of the government and provides value for money.

A selection committee shall prepare a draft of the terms of reference, tender conditions, and invitation to bids as well as a draft of PPP contract. Besides, a selection committee is empowered to undertake the following procurement processes, i. e. outlining the prequalification of the bidders, setting out the bid bond and performance bond, requesting for proposals from the prequalified bidders, exchanging information and getting feedback from the bidders, finalizing and issuing final tender, evaluating and selecting preferred bidder and negotiating contract, awarding and financial closing.

A selection committee may consider engaging the external consultant to provide assistance with respect to the selection process, risk analysis and method in minimizing and managing potential risks. The qualification and criteria in engaging the external consultant shall be prescribed by the SEPO.

The specific requirements for invitation letters and contract are subject to be further detailed by the forthcoming regulations, with which agencies pursuing PPP projects need to comply.

Setting the terms of contract and preparing a draft contract

The draft of PPP contract shall set out the terms and conditions which shall be developed and to be announced by the PPP. The main items that are generally covered in a PPP contract must include the following issues:

(1) Tenure of contract;

(2) Provision of service and operation of the project;

(3) Fee, payment method and other financial matters including collection and appropriation;

(4) Change of the project implementation, change of the contract party, subcontractor and assignment;

(5) Project assets, ownership over project assets and assets price evaluation;

(6) Force Majeure and payment in case of force majeure;

(7) Termination of contract, event of default and payment upon termination;

(8) Guarantee insurance, liability and indemnity;

(9) Dispute resolution.

In selection the private partner, if the host agency and a selection committee agree together that the bidding process is not appropriate and prefer to select the partner by other means, the approval from the SEPO and PPP committee must be obtained.

In the case where there is the sole bidder in the bidding process and the selection committee deems that the government shall benefit from the government interest, the selection committee shall allow to award the project to such bidder.

Once the decision on the selection is made, the selected bidder and the draft PPP contract shall be sent to the SEPO and the SEPO shall accordingly report the selection to the relevant minister within 45 days upon receiving the report and send the draft PPP contract to the Attorney General for final review within 45 days. The minister shall forthwith send the matter to the Cabinet to make final decision.

Accordingly, the successful bidder shall be notified the award after the approval of the Cabinet and after agreeing on the contract document, both the selected bidder and the implementing agency shall proceed to sign the contract. The contract signing is the last task of the procurement process.

Project supervising and monitoring

Upon execution of the contract, contract management is an essential activity in project administration. This is to ensure timely completion and satisfactorily of the project operation. Basically, the key elements of contract management include:

(1) Establishment of an administration process and contract supervising and monitoring committee;

(2) Formation of management responsibilities;

(3)Monitoring financial parts;

(4)Ensuring the smooth operation and service delivery.

Contract administration involves the establishment of processes to ensure that all the procedures and documents concerning the project are effectively managed. The major contract administration includes variation management, compliance with the contract provisions and financial monitoring.

As a part of the supervising and monitoring mechanism, PPP laws establish a committee appointed for each PPP project, which is supposed to perform its on-going task during the project execution to propose solutions to problems that may arise.

Project Supervising and Monitoring Committee shall have the following powers and duties:

(1)To monitor and supervise the project operation which shall be in compliance with the PPP contract, implementation plan provided under the PPP contract, plan for managing the potential problems arising during the project implementation;

(2)To recommend solutions to problems arising during the project implementation and may suggest the project host to engage the consultant in order to analyze and provide solutions to tackle problems occurring during the process of implementing the project;

(3)To demand the project host or the contractual party to give an explanation or to submit the relevant documents;

(4)To report the operational progress, result, problems and approaches in order to solve problems to the responsible minister;

(5)To consider the PPP contract amendment.

Non-compliance with the contract

The implementing agency needs to ensure that itself and the contracting party are in compliance with the contractual obligations. In the event that the host agency fails to comply with the contractual obligations under the PPP contract, the Supervising and Monitoring Committee shall be required to report such incident to the responsible minister. The responsible minister is forthwith empowered to enforce service performance and contract compliance. In case of severe consequence, the Supervising and Monitoring Committee must report the matter to the Cabinet for further consideration.

Dealing with contract change

During the life of typical PPP contract(e. g. up to 10~30 years), things will inevitably happen that could not have been predicted when the contract was signed. It is also likely that the parties will get into a dispute over how the contract should be interpreted, or whether both parties have been performing as agreed. In order to avoid such risks, contract amendment could be a way out.

The new PPP laws provide clear procedures and guidelines in amending the contract while implementation. However, the detailed criteria shall be announced by the SEPO.

In the case where it is necessary to amend the contract, the host agency shall submit the amendment proposal to the Supervising and Monitoring Committee. Should the Committee consider that the amendment is not substantial, the Committee shall forthwith notify the responsible minister.

In the event that there is proposed amendment to any material terms and conditions under the contract, the host agency shall submit along with the amendment proposal the evaluation report on the affect of the contract amendment and other details to the Supervising and Monitoring Committee for the Attorney General's further review. The Cabinet shall make final decision on the Contract's amendment.

The criteria in considering as to whether there is "substantial change" to the contract shall be announced by the SEPO.

Renewal of contract

With regard to the renewal process, a mechanism is put in place and the host agency will decide whether to renew the agreement with the private operator or not, and such is ultimately subject to the Cabinet's approval. Any amendment upon renewal would also require the Cabinet's approval.

Project Development Fund(PDF)

The new PPP laws require that the Project Development Fund shall be established under the Ministry of Finance in order to support the preparation of strategic plan, to support the project proposal by the host agency and to prepare the analytical report. The funding of the PDF derives from government contribution, income generated from bidding, contract signing fee.

Procedures and implications of the project failing to comply with the provisions under the PPP laws

The PPP laws do provide a specific section to handle the project failing to comply with the provisions under the PPP laws in such a way that the SEPO may instruct the host agency to clarify the fact and the possibility if they decide to continue the project. Accordingly, the SEPO, if it considers appropriate, shall seek approval from the Cabinet to amend or to terminate the PPP contract for the project that breaches the procedure stipulated under the PPP laws.

In any case, should the SEPO, having taken into the consideration of the availability of the service or the impact to the public interest, find it is beneficial to continue the project, the SEPO may instruct to continue the project provided that the project shall be monitored and followed up in compliance with the provisions under the PPP laws.

Due to the uncertainty relating the exposure to contract amendment or termination under these provisions, the private sector, investor and lender might take this as the key risk factor considering whether to participate in the project.

Conclusion

Though, the new PPP laws contain several improvements from the old laws, whether the PPP laws will be used successfully as the mechanism to boost economic and attract more investor will depend on the details under the ministerial regulations which have yet to be announced. Somehow, with clearer procedures under the new laws, it is expected that the new PPP will build more confidence to the investor and the acceleration of the PPP process will bring about numbers of profitable PPP projects. In order to send positive signal to potential PPP partners, it is important to get the first PPP project done under the new PPP laws without delay.

老年人社会福利保障法

Associate Professor
Dr. Wichitra(Foongladda)Vichienchom

仲 夏 译

　　摘要　这篇文章是基于对泰国老年人社会福利政策实施情况的调查而完成的,本文试图通过研究与老年人社会福利有关的法律强制机制、老年人权利保护团体以及老年人社会福利救济来找出问题的所在,并探索出合适的应对之策。

　　研究表明,通过法律建立起来的社会福利机制主要有以下几方面的不足:首先,国家老年人委员会主席工作的不公开性以及对老年人问题解决的力度太低;其次,从上述机构人员的构成上来看,并没有来自老年人团体的代表;再次,老年人国家基金会没有足够的资金来维持老年人的社会福利。

　　因此,为了从实质上解决这些问题,首先应当从法律上对国家老年人委员会主席及其人员的组成作出一些新的调整和规定,使其能够尽其所职,为保障和改善老年人生活质量做出应有的贡献;其次,与老年人社会福利有关的法律规则和程序必须被明确地制定和执行,以保证老年人能够真正享受到法律赋予其的权利;再次,国家应加大对老年人国家基金的投资,使其能够有足够的资金来为老年人提供更好的社会福利;最后,为了提高老年人的生活质量,加大对老年人的关心和照顾是必不可少的,而这种义务则更多地应当落在当地政府组织之上。

一、简介

　　为贫困人士特别是老年人提供社会福利是国家应尽的责任,尤其是在当今这个人口老龄化严重的时代,政府更应当肩负起这样一种使命。泰国虽然在 2003 年颁布了《老年人保护法》,但这一法案仅仅只有一章涉及了老年人享有社会福利的权利,并且这一章节并没有对这些权利加以明确,赋予其更加清晰、直观的意思。虽然,其他方面的立法也为老年人提供了社会保障措施,有的甚至规定建立了老年人国家储蓄基金,但是在提高老年人生活质量上,仍然存在着不足与缺陷。主要包括如下三个方面:

(1)社会福利措施实施上的问题

首先,老年人社会福利是由法律规定的委员会来执行的,然而这一委员会的组成人员却并不具备良好的职业素质和专业技能;其次,这一委员会并不能很好地与当地政府组织协同工作,而当地政府组织则是与当地老年人群体进行直接沟通的主体,这就使得这一委员会不能根据当地的实际情况实施社会福利政策;最后,当前的立法工作并没有老年人群体代表的实际参加,宪法赋予老年人的参与权因此没能得到保障。

(2)缺乏明确的与老年人权利有关的法律规定

泰国虽然颁布了一些有关老年人权利的法律法规,但是这些规定并不详细明确,不足以使得公众能够直观、清晰地理解有关社会福利方面的规定。尽管有关国家机关已经提供了一些社会福利,但是这些社会福利却与老年人的实际需要有很大的差异。

(3)老年人社会福利基金的不足与缺陷

泰国虽然通过法律建立起了一些老年人社会福利基金会,但是由于基金会自身组织的不合理以及财政资金的不足,使其不能发挥预期的功效,不同程度地影响了老年人四个方面的幸福感:

1)身体健康方面,即老年人对身体健康的需要;

2)物质方面,即与日常生活息息相关的基础设施的便捷程度;

3)精神方面,即有利于老年人娱乐消遣的社会服务;

4)环境方面,即自然资源的节约以及环境的保护。

上述问题使得对现行法律进行修改和补充,以使其能够与现阶段社会条件和社会需要相适应成为必要。为了使老年人能够老有所养、能够获得与其年龄相适应的机会以及延长其寿命,政府应当采取一些必要的措施。如政府应该加大对老年人的抚养和照顾,这种抚养应当持续到老年人死亡之后的阶段,同时,抚养费也应当及于老年人的家属。从这一角度来看,社会福利是社会服务组织或社会机构帮助老年人的一种方法,确保他们对生活的满意度。从这方面来讲,社会公共机构是社会在平等原则基础之上进行平稳社会化进程的一个重要手段,只有在这一原则的基础之上,才可能真正形成稳定和谐的社会。

社会福利的建立需要以下几个原则为基础:

1)独立原则;

2)平等原则;

3)经济福利和安全保障原则;

4)生存机会安全原则;

5)公众幸福感提高原则。

根据以上几个原则,在实施社会福利措施的时候,也应当考虑以下四个方面的情况:

1)经济方面,即确保老年人能够有足够的收入维持生活;

2)教育方面,即国家应提供生存和发展所必需的知识和技能培训;

3)社会方面,即一个社会普遍可以接受的生活标准和社会互助机制;

4)收入和资源分配方面,即收入和资源的分配方式应至少能够保证贫困人员可以幸福地生活。

就泰国而言,社会福利法规是在政府政体改革之后出现的。关于社会保障计划或者社会福利计划的概念是在 1934 年人民党的经济计划中首次出现的。在这一计划中,人民党提出了制定社会保障法的议案,然而,这个议案在当时并没有得到泰国人民的认可。之后,在 1971 年,泰国颁布了一部关于职工在受雇期间受伤的赔偿法。这部赔偿性质的法案实质上是包含了一部分社会保障和一部分规范社会保障机制的法律。上述法律构成了一部完整的职工劳动保护法。自成一格的社会保障立法在 1990 年得以成功颁布,名为《社会保障法》。这部法律为工人建立起了一个强制的社会保障基金,职工作为基金会的成员,必须为该基金筹集资金。职工有权在以下情况下得到该基金会的补偿:①不属于雇用期间的受伤和疾病;②疾病;③死亡;④分娩;⑤儿童救济;⑥年老;⑦失业。

2003 年,泰国颁布了《社会福利法》,旨在与《泰国宪法》的要求保持一致,为公民提供社会福利。这部法律定义了社会福利的概念和范围,制定了社会福利机构的活动原则,以及对这些福利机构负责的其他强制性机构的活动原则。事实上,在《社会福利法》之外,泰国还制定了两部不同的法律,一是《儿童保护法》,二是《老年人保护法》,这两部不同的法律主要处理有关儿童和老人的社会福利方面的问题。此外,这些法定的为老年人提供社会福利的法律规定是在宪法实施后对其他法律的要求,即国家有义务去保障老年人生存、发展的权利。基于这样一种宪法考虑,老年人也自发地成立了泰国老年人协会这样的旨在提高老年人参与性和积极性的组织。尽管如此,这种力度的措施和行动仍然不能满足老年人的需要,社会福利事业任重而道远。

二、社会福利法的基本原则

为保证人们生活在一个稳定和谐的社会中,以下五项基本原则是建立社会保障制度所必需的:

(1)稳定收入原则

基于这一原则,国家有义务保证公民有充足且合理的收入,即使是做家务以及照料小孩的妇女也应受到如此保护。

(2)就业原则

这一原则关系到社会集合,也是公民的基本权利之一。该原则规定公民有权利得到平等的就业机会,并且享受平等的工资待遇,以满足公民的基本生活需要。

(3)救助原则

这一原则规定国家有义务对公民提供援助,无论他们是否有子女、老人、残疾人及其他贫困情况。国家应提供给公民力所能及的长期关心、救助以及其他社会福利。

(4)机会和权利平等原则

这一原则要求国家消除来自社会各个方面的性别歧视,给予公民同等机会和权利。

(5)服务机构原则

为了能让老年人享受平等的机会和权利,国家应当建立有老年人参加的社会福利组织。

以上五项基本原则总的来讲可以归纳为两个主要的原则:社会正义以及公民权。

社会正义需要政府在经济竞争与社会公平之中作出选择,政府需要认识到公民才是整个国家最重要的资源,并且应当得到平等的社会福利待遇。公民权作为建立全球化社会福利制度的一个重要原则,要求国家采取直接有效的社会福利政策来保证宪法赋予公民的基本权利。

三、国际法和外国法律中的社会福利制度

1. 国际法中的社会福利制度

在国际法中,制定有关社会福利政策的国际性组织有两个,联合国以及国

际工人组织。

(1)联合国

联合国关于保护老年人权益的规定主要体现在其在 1991 年 12 月 16 日联合国大会决议中做出的五个基本原则之中:

1)独立原则。就该原则而言,老年人应当得到国家在收入、家庭以及社区等方面的帮助,并且得到其他增加收入的机会。他们应当有权参加与决定工作的时间,并且应当得到专业知识和技术的培训与指导。同时,老年人应当居住在安全的环境中,并尽可能地得到适当的其他个人优惠。

2)参与原则。该原则指老年人应当积极参加国家事务,积极参加讨论与自身福利有关的政策,多与年轻人交流沟通。同时,老年人应当多参加与自己能力和兴趣有关的社会服务和志愿者服务,多组织老年人之间的活动,加强老年人之间的交流。

3)自我实现原则。基于这一原则,老年人应当得到机会去充分发掘自身潜能,能够享受到社会提供的教育、文化、精神以及娱乐消遣的资源。

4)救助原则。基于这一原则,老年人应当得到来自家庭和社区的关心和照顾,能够获得维持或帮助其恢复身体以及心理状况的医疗条件。

5)尊严原则。这一原则要求社会应当尊重老年人,不应当因年龄、背景等因素而歧视或虐待老人。

此外,国际社会保障协会已经在瑞士的日内瓦建立起来了。这个组织致力于为世界各国的老人提供经济援助。

(2)国际工人组织

这一国际组织致力于提供一些特殊情况下的社会福利和社会保障,这些情况包括社会成员因疾病、怀孕、年老以及失业引起的入不敷出,经济陷入困境的情况。当然,这些社会福利中也包括为社会成员身体健康而提供的医疗救助。国际工人组织设计的这些社会保障制度以以下几个条件为基础:

第一,这些社会保障措施必须得到国家财政的支持;

第二,应当有详细、明确的立法保证人们的这些基本权利;

第三,社会保障措施应当由政府组织或者代表公民利益的其他独立组织来实施。实际上,国际工人组织已经提出了一些必须遵守的必要原则来保证公民享受到社会福利。

1)补偿金的最低限度标准应当是能够满足人的基本生活。

2)为了能够使社会经济福利最大化,标准金发放应当以一种能够促进经济和社会发展的方式进行。

国际工人组织第 10 次社会保障大会确立了社会保障的最低标准,同时也建立了 5 个不同类别的社会保障的基本框架。

1)家庭救济金。家庭救济金主要包括生活补助、税收减免、教育补贴和医疗补贴。

2)医疗救济金。包括医疗服务补贴、身体康复补贴以及健康保养服务补贴。收入损失的补助也是该救助金的一种。

3)无劳动能力者、老年人以及幸存者救助金。

4)工作意外救助金。这一救助金是为了保障职工因在工作期间受伤、生病甚至死亡所受的损失。包括赔偿金、救助金、医疗服务、护理服务以及其他恢复健康和工作能力所必需的服务。

5)失业救助金。这一救助金包括为失业工人及其家庭提供经济救助以及就业岗位培训,使其能够重新回到工作岗位。此外,为鼓励失业人员寻找新的工作,这项救助金还包括一个独立的补助项目。

2. 外国法律中的社会福利制度

(1)英国

英国著名学者贝弗里奇对社会福利的定义对英国社会福利事业有着深远的影响。贝弗里奇被称为英国社会保障制度之父,他提出为公民提供充分的社会保障措施,这些提议包括对最低工资、疾病、工伤、退休、因主要家庭成员死亡导致的经济困难、抚养小孩增加的经济负担、死亡、结婚、年老、残疾以及失业等方面的社会保障。

(2)丹麦

丹麦的社会福利立法主要致力于为老年人提供社会救助。丹麦法律在禁止歧视老人的前提下,以四项基本原则为基础建立了社会保障制度。

第一,所有社会救助都必须有法可依。

第二,社会福利资金必须来源于国家税收基金,并且必须用于保障贫困公民的基本生活,提高其幸福感。

第三,社会福利的形式必须合法。

第四,社会救助应当满足不同公民的需要。

(3)瑞典

瑞典的社会福利制度十分发达,1980 年的《瑞典法典》就正式地确定了公民享有获得维持生活的国家救助的权利。时至今日,瑞典已经建立了老年人基金,并通过该基金会的各种措施为老年人提供充分的社会福利。这些措施包括预防性和补助性措施。为了老年人的身心健康,瑞典还建立了健康护理

和长期护理制度,这大大地减少了公民因疾病而花费的金钱。以下两方面的考虑在瑞典的社会福利制度中尤为重要:

1)健康方面的考虑。

2)居住方面的考虑。

(4)日本

日本 1946 年宪法确立了公民有享受来自国家的社会福利的权利。这些社会福利包括护理、健康补助以及基本生活条件补助等方面。为了保障这些权利的实现,宪法第 25 章中明确规定了政府应当尽其所能来推动社会福利和社会保障以及公民的身体健康。

为了与日本当前人口老龄化的现状相适应,日本颁布了《老龄社会基本法》,这部特殊的法律规定了社会保障包括工作和收入保障(第 9 条)、健康和幸福保障(第 10 条)、教育和社会事务参与机会的保障(第 11 条)以及生活环境保障(第 12 条)。同时,该法还推动了针对老年人疾病预防和治疗的研究工作,要求政府积极听取公民对老年人政策的建议和意见(第 14 条),为此,日本实施了两个基本的社会福利制度。

1)退休金制度。

2)长期关心救助制度。这一制度又包括以下两个方面:

①该制度的实施机构。长期关心救助制度由当地政府组织进行实施,即市、县行政机构。

②该制度的覆盖面积。这一制度的覆盖面积是由 2005 年通过的《长期救助法》规定的,这一法案要求政府必须为老年人提供帮助和服务,特别是提供健康的食物和护理服务。

(5)新加坡

在新加坡,由于传统习惯的影响,子女是照顾父母、维护家庭温暖的主体。

(6)澳大利亚

澳大利亚建立了为老人因受遗弃和虐待的法律援助。其中年龄稍大的律师应当更多地被派去为老年人提供法律援助。

四、泰国法律制度下的老年人社会福利制度

1."老年群体"的概念

法律规定的老年人指具有泰国国籍的 60 岁以上的公民。(《老年人保护法》,第 3 章)

2. 国家责任机构

在泰国,老年人社会福利保障责任由不同的部门承担,包括社会发展和人权保障部门、公共健康部门、旅游体育部门、信息交流部门、文化部、教育部以及司法部。

3. 社会团体

法律规定的促进老年人社会福利事业发展的组织主要有:①国家社会福利促进委员会;②地方社会福利促进委员会;③曼谷社会福利促进委员会。

在泰国,老年人社会福利责任主要由以下准司法团体承担:

(1)国家老年人委员会

这一委员会由泰国总理担任主席、社会发展和人权保障部门担任第一副主席、泰国王妃赞助的泰国老年人协会的负责人担任第二副主席,其他的一些与老年人社会福利有关的社会福利组织和机构也参与其中。这些职位都是由《老年人保护法》第4章规定的。这一委员会有权制定维护老年人权利、地位的政策和决定,也可以为政府和私人机构提供保护老年人权益方面的援助。这些权利在《老年人保护法》第9章中有规定。

(2)社会保障委员会

这一委员会由职工终身大臣担任主席,由财政部代表、公共健康部门代表以及一个国家预算局的代表组成。此外,该委员会另有总理提名的5位职工代表和雇主代表。这些职位在《社会保障法》第8章中有规定,这一委员会旨在提供与社会保障有关的政策措施以及法律事务方面的建议,包括《社会保障法》第9章中规定的退休补偿金。

4. 老年人社会福利基金会

泰国有许多为老年人提供社会福利的基金组织,包括:

(1)社会福利促进基金会。

这一基金会是由社会发展和人权保障部门建立的,旨在为社会福利事业提供财政支持。(《社会福利促进法》,第24章)该基金会的资金来自国家的设立资金以及年度拨款、社会捐款、国外组织的捐助、提供法律服务和司法活动的收入以及由基金会自身经营所得的其他收入。

(2)老年人基金会

这一基金会是由弱势群体关爱部门创立的,旨在为老年人权益保护提供财政支持。(《老年人保护法》,第14章)其资金来源与社会福利促进基金会相似。

（3）国家储蓄基金会

这一基金会是一个国家机构,同时,它也是一个不同于政府机构或国有企业法人的组织。该基金会鼓励社会成员进行个人储蓄,并在成员退休后为成员提供退休补助和其他补助。(《国家储蓄基金法》,第 5 章)这一基金会的资金主要来源于其成员的储蓄,即 15 岁以上、60 岁以下的泰国公民和其他社会保障法规定的成员。

（4）社会保障基金会

这一基金会由社会保障部门和劳动部创立。这一基金会旨在为其成员、社会保障法规定的委员会以及该部门的行政机构提供资金支持。其资金来源于政府、雇主以及其成员的投资。其中,作为该基金成员之一的 15 岁以上、60 岁以下的职工需要缴纳与雇主同样水平的基金。超过 60 岁仍参加工作的,也应当缴纳上述费用。此外,该基金会也接受来自外界的捐助和投资。

5. 老年人社会福利法

根据泰国的社会福利制度,社会福利将会以特定的标准发放给特定的公民。以下是一些关于社会福利的基本情况:

1）社会福利的范围。社会福利包括:社会服务、教育、健康、房屋、职业培训、就业、娱乐以及司法援助。

2）社会福利的性质、形式和程序。社会福利的形式包括促进发展、提供援助、保护、预防以及帮助恢复。个人、家庭、社区当地政府组织、专业机构、宗教组织以及其他机构都可以积极参加推动社会福利事业的发展。

为了使宪法规定的主体能够得到适当的社会福利,泰国现行宪法规定了不同领域的平等保护原则:

1）教育。宪法赋予了老年人接受平等教育的权利。基于这一目的,国家应当保障和促进专业机构教育、私人机构教育、私人教育以及长期教育事业的发展。(《泰国宪法》,第 80 章)

2）医疗卫生事业。宪法规定,老年人有权享受高质量的公共医疗服务,并且贫困老人有权接受国家公共卫生中心的免费医疗服务。同时,对于致命性的传染性疾病,国家还应当免费地为老年人提供及时的治疗,直至痊愈。《泰国宪法》、2007 年颁布的《国家卫生法》对此进行了规定。

3）房屋。泰国宪法规定了老年人有定居自由,并且有享受安静的居住环境的权利。(《泰国宪法》,第 33 章)

4）就业与报酬。宪法规定,老年人有自由参加劳动、自由选择职业以及自由平等地竞争的权利。(《泰国宪法》,第 43 章)并且,国家应无歧视地保证老年人在工作期间以及下班后的安全。(《泰国宪法》,第 84 章)同时,60 岁以上老年人以及收入不足以维系正常生活的人有权得到国家提供的社会福利和公共设施。

5)娱乐休养。宪法虽没有直接的条款对这一领域进行规范,但却对社区权利有着明确的规定。宪法规定,社区有权保留自己的风俗、习惯、文化和艺术,有权参与管理,有权保护自然资源、生态环境以及生物多样性,并有权以合理的方式对其加以利用。(《泰国宪法》,第 66 章)宪法还要求国家应为公共健康事业提供福利支持。(《泰国宪法》,第 80 章)

6)司法援助。在这一领域,老年人有权获得方便、快捷、广泛的司法援助,享有案件审理过程中的基本权利(即公开审判、法官人数符合法定要求以及合乎逻辑的判决)。国家权力的行使也必须与这些宪法权利保持一致。(《泰国宪法》,第 81 章)

7)社会服务。宪法第 53 章对社会服务进行了规定。宪法规定,60 岁以上的老年人以及收入不足以维持正常生活的人有权以一种不伤及尊严的方式获得国家提供的福利和公共设施。

(1)《老年人保护法》之下的社会福利制度

《老年人保护法》第 11 章规定了国家应当在下列领域对老年人的权益进行保护。

1)便捷的医疗卫生服务。

2)教育、宗教信仰以及生活所需的信息。

3)合适的职业或职业培训。

4)自我发展、社会活动参与以及互动组织或社区的建立。

5)房屋、经营场所、交通工具以及其他公共设施的便利与安全。

6)交通费用的补助。

7)国有旅游景点的免费参观。

8)对被遗弃、虐待以及其他受不合理对待老人的援助。

9)便捷的老年人法律援助。

10)广泛的老年人所需的住房、食物以及衣物补助。

11)必要的零用钱。

12)丧葬补助。

尽管《老年人保护法》在以上多个领域对老年人的社会福利做了规定,但是这些法律规定并没有得到严格的执行。究其原因,还是在于该法案的规定不够明确和清晰。

(2)涉及养老储蓄福利的法律

国家经济政策中的一些决定性原则规定,国家应当为公民以及政府官员提供养老储蓄金,以保障其老年的生活。(《泰国宪法》,第 84 章)这些宪法要求在 2011 年颁布的《国家养老储蓄法》中得到了贯彻实施。

(3)涉及退休补助社会福利的法律

根据《社会保障法》,老年人满足以下条件的可以享受退休金或退职金补助:

1)参加了社会保障计划。

2)连续 180 个月缴纳了社会保障基金。

3)退休年龄不低于 55 岁。

五、中老年人社会福利制度存在的问题

1. 社会福利实施方面的问题

在这一方面,主要是这些实施机构规定的不合理。比如,为了保持一致,国家老年人委员会继《老年人保护法》更名为了《老年人生活质量改善法》后,改名为老年人生活质量改善委员会。根据这一法律,该委员会主席由总理担任。但是,这一规定似乎并不合理,总理可能因为繁忙的国家大事而无暇顾及委员会主席的事务。此外,这一法定委员会的各个组成部门不能与公私部门以及当地的政府组织进行有效的配合。然而这些地方政府组织与当地居民联系紧密,因此更加可能以一种有效的方式分配社会福利,满足老年人的需要。该委员会的另一缺点在于该委员会的委员代表中并没有来自老年人群体的代表。为了解决上述不足,以下几点建议值得考虑:

首先,为了提高这一委员会的工作效率,应当将其置于社会发展和人权保障部门的直接领导之下。

其次,为了提高该委员会运作的便捷性和灵活性,应当剔除委员会中没有老年人社会福利方面经验的成员,增加来自老年人群体的代表,从而保护宪法赋予老年人的参与权。

再次,根据该法,国家老年人委员会并没有老年人社会福利战略计划方面的权利和义务。因此,法律有必要赋予该委员会这方面的权利和义务。

最后,立法机关应对该法进行修改,使委员会能够迅速地得到有关老年人问题和需要的信息,并提供援助满足他们的需要。

2. 老年人权利方面的问题

(1)教育权

《泰国宪法》第 49 章和第 80 章规定了老年人有权接受谋生所需的教育培训和信息。对此,教育部应当制定推进教育福利的措施。首先,教育部应当组织与老年人年龄相适应的教育培训项目。其次,为了提高老年人的自我独立能力和幸福感,教育部也应提供一些对老年人生活有帮助的信息。再次,为了促进家庭幸福和谐,国家应当提供一些活动来加强老年人与其子女和其他年轻群体的交流。

(2)健康权

为使老年人能够正常独立地生活,国家应对老年人的身体状况加强关心和照顾。

(3)居住权

根据《老年人保护法》第 11 章的规定,国家有义务保护和改善老年人衣食住行方面的条件。但该法关于这些方面社会福利的规定却并不详尽。为此,为了满足无家可归老人的需要,国家应提供可供老年人居住的房屋,改善老年人的居住环境。同时,对那些并不是无家可归,但居住条件不适宜于他们所处年龄阶段需要的老人来说,国家应当提供援助,改善其居住条件。当然,基于这些事务所花费的资金都应当由老年人基金会提供。

(4)就业及薪酬权

《老年人保护法》第 11 章规定,国家有义务为老年人提供工作和职业培训。同样,由于缺乏明确的法律条文,这一规定也未取得实质性的效果。因此为满足那些达到退休年龄但仍需要工作维持生活的老人的需要,国家就业办应当为他们提供报酬合适、与他们年龄和健康相适应的工作。另外,对于身体健康的老人,将退休年龄从 60 岁提高到 65 岁也是一个不错的选择。

(5)娱乐休养权

法律虽然没有明确的规定,但《老年人保护法》第 11 章却规定了老年人有免费参观国有景点的权利。但同样由于规定不够详细,这一权利并没有得到很好的保障。为此,在老年人基金会的支持下,国家应当联合私人组织、团体或当地的政府组织开展一些有利于老年人娱乐休养的活动。另外,为了提高社会整体责任感,国家应当呼吁私人社团和组织在享受社会福利的同时,也为社会福利事业提供一些捐款,或者鼓励他们多多参与社会福利事业,作为回报,国家可以适当减免他们的税收。

(6)司法援助权

一些老人可能因为种种情况而遭受不幸与痛苦,这些情况包括:用于养老的储蓄被盗、被诈骗或者成为家庭暴力或者第三人侵害的主体。在这些情况下,老人不容易得到便捷的司法援助,因此,国家应为这些老人提供便捷的法律援助。首先,他们至少应享受公平公正的司法程序对待。其次,《老年人保护法》第11章规定,国家应当为受虐待的老人提供帮助和建议,并且应当采取有关的措施解决家庭矛盾。但由于法律在这方面的规定不明确,所以权利并没有得到很好的保障。

(7)社会服务权

社会服务是泰国老年人保护事业中一个不可忽视的薄弱环节。为此国家应从以下几个基本方面为老年人提供社会福利:

首先,老年人有权享受老年生活补助。法律规定收入低于法定水平的老年人有权享受与其年龄阶段相适应的4个等级的生活补助。但不幸的是,这4个等级还是低于老年人的贫困水平。为此,可以参考《劳动保护法》中关于职工每日最低工资等级的最高限度的规定来发放老年人的生活补助。这4个等级包括:

1)60岁以上,不满70岁的老人,可以按月获得10倍于职工每日最低工资等级中最高等级工资的补助。

2)70岁以上,不满80岁的老人,可以按月获得15倍于上述工资的补助。

3)80岁以上,不满90岁的老人,可以按月获得20倍于上述工资的补助。

4)90岁以上的老人,可以按月获得25倍于上述工资的补助。

其次,老年人有获得公共交通和公共设施社会保障的权利。目前,老年人在搭乘各种交通工具时,仍需支付票价,也不能在其他服务中获得合理的方便。

再次,老年人葬礼费用补助。由于现行法律没有规定任何标准的葬礼费用补助,有关国家机构就以2000泰铢作为标准为老年人提供葬礼费用补助。但这一标准显然不够。为此,应当以职工每日最低工资等级中最高等级工资的100倍为标准确定葬礼费用补助。

最后,国家应当鼓励家庭成员多关心、照顾老人。《税法典》规定,纳税人可以在应缴纳税款中扣除扶养老人所需的费用。尽管如此,这些费用依旧太少。为此,为了鼓励子女扶养老人,维护家庭温暖、和谐,应当提高从应缴纳税款中扣除的这部分用于扶养老人的费用的比例。

3.基金会方面的问题

根据《老年人保护法》第 13 章建立起来的老年人基金会,由于组织结构的不合理以及资金的不足,不能发挥应有的作用。为解决这一问题,需要与老年人社会福利事业联系紧密的当地政府组织为该基金投资、捐款。另外,为该基金还款的捐赠者,应当享受与捐款总额相适应的税收减免。

六、总结和建议

1. 社会福利实施方面

首先,这一机构应当被重新命名为"老年人生活质量促进和发展委员会",相应的法律应更名为《老年人生活质量促进和发展法》。

其次,为弥补该委员会组织结构上的不足,应当将这一委员会置于社会发展和人权保障部门的直接领导下。同时,在人员组成上,也应当增加来自老年人群体的代表。

再次,该委员会的职能仍不完善,为此,可以通过修改法律来赋予该委员会以战略决策权。

2. 老年人权利方面

尽管《老年人保护法》第 11 章规定了一些与老年人社会福利相关的权利,但遗憾的是,这些规定并不明确、清晰,不具备可操作的程序。这些立法上的不足主要存在于以下几个方面:

第一,职业培训和信息畅通方面,国家并没有真正地以法律形式保障这些权利。因此,为了提高老年人的生活质量,国家应开展一系列的与老年人年龄相适应的技能培训项目,提供更多的信息,以满足老年人的需要。

第二,医疗卫生方面,法律并没有提供综合的医疗卫生社会福利。因此,国家应为老年人提供更多彻底的医疗卫生服务,特别是加大在增强老年人健康、增加便捷的医疗卫生服务、增加医疗卫生中心以及增加医护人员方面的投入。

第三,房屋居住方面,有关房屋居住的社会福利仍不充分,不能满足无家可归的老人的需要。同时,具备资格的护理人员也十分缺乏。为此,国家有必要为老年人提供良好的居住条件以及专业的护理人员。

第四,就业和报酬方面。在这一方面,法律并未规定适当的社会福利。因此,有必要为那些仍有工作能力的老人提供与他们年龄和健康状况相适应的工作,使其获得适当且公平的劳动报酬。

第五，娱乐休养方面。法律在这一方面的规定并不健全，因此，国家有必要为老年人提供一些娱乐项目，使他们能够与子女和年轻人在活动中进行交流、沟通，以维持老年人的身心健康，节约社会资源。

第六，司法援助方面。在这一方面，法律并没有明确清晰的条文保障老年人的权益。因此，国家应免费为老年人提供法律服务，特别是为老年人提供年纪稍大的律师。

第七，社会服务方面。在这一方面，法律并没有一个固定的老年人生活补助标准。法定标准的缺乏，导致了一些责任机构自行制定的标准不能满足老年人的基本生活需要。这一生活补助的缺乏，也存在于葬礼补助方面。为此，为满足老年人的需要，有必要以一种适当且充足的方式来确定社会福利标准，即这一标准应当高于贫困等级。另外，立法也应当鼓励老年人的家属、亲人、公共和私人机构积极地参加到关爱老年人这一行动中来。

3. 老年人社会福利基金会方面

在这一方面，由于基金会自身组织结构的问题，这一基金会没有足够的资金为老年人提供社会福利。为此，法律应当要求当地政府组织为该基金会捐款，以解决资金上的不足。

总之，只有秉承着"改善和提高老年人的生活质量"这一理念去修改法律，以最广泛、最便捷的方式为老年人提供社会福利，以最充足的资金去保证这些社会福利的实施，老年人的权利才可能真正得到尊重和保障，老年人的需要才可能真正得以满足。

The Provision of Social Welfare for Old-Aged Persons

Associate Professor Dr.
Wichitra(Foongladda)Vichienchom[*]

Abstract: This article is based on research on the administration of social welfare for old-aged persons in Thailand and is indeed intended to grasp problems, and find solutions to them, in connection with the statutory mechanisms or body in charge of the administration of rights of old-aged persons as well as the fund for social welfare for the elderly. The study reveals that inaptness of the body established by the law lies in that the Chairman of the National Commission on Old-Aged Persons is not in the position to know, or puts full dedication to solving problems surrounding old-aged persons. In addition, the composition of the above—mentioned body has no representative from old-aged persons. As far as the rights of old-aged persons are concerned, this research reveals deficiencies of provisions of law which determine clear rules and procedures for the delivery of services practically accessible by old-aged persons. Further, the national fund for old-aged persons has had an insufficient amount of money to be expended on the provision of social welfare for the elderly.

Thus, as practical solutions to the problems hitherto spelled out, it is advisable that the revision be made of the provisions of law concerning the

---

    * Professor of Law at Thammasat University. (LLB Thammasat University, LLM Chulalongkorn University, Docteur en droit Université de Paris II). This article is translated from Thai to English by Thitirat Thipsamritkul, Lecturer of Law at Thammasat University.

Chairman of the National Commission on Old-Aged Persons and the composition of this body to the effect that the Commission, in its performance of official duties, shall dedicate particular attention to the protection, promotion and development of the quality of life of old-aged persons. Also, rules and procedures in connection with the provision of social welfare for old-aged persons should clearly be formulated to ensure that old-aged persons may have real access to their statutory rights. In addition, the national fund statutorily established should be allocated such a sufficient amount of money for financing costs incurred in the operation of work in favor of social welfare for old-aged persons. The prime objective apparently lies in improving health, both physically and mentally, of old-aged persons and enabling them to live their independent lives. In the case where old-aged persons may not live their normal lives, they should be assisted by volunteers well equipped with the service mind towards the elderly in the interest of the achievement of good quality of life as well as happiness in the late period of their remaining days. In this connection, regard should also be had to participation by old-aged persons and bodies or agencies concerned in both private and public sectors, in particular, local government organizations. In effect, given that local government organizations assume direct responsibilities in the delivery of services for old-aged persons and have close ties with old-aged persons in their local areas, local government organizations are therefore in the position to perceive problems encountered by old-aged persons and, as such, may administer social welfare in promotion and development of the quality of life of old-aged persons in a manner actually suited to their needs and demands.

It is submitted that the measures recommended above will, when effectively put in place, be conducive to efficient protection, promotion and development of the quality of life of old-aged persons, with a view to the attainment of their better lives and greater happiness.

Introduction

It is the State's duty to take care of its underprivileged people, especially old-aged persons, and ensure their access to basic welfare. Indeed, one has witnessed the growing number of old-aged persons in consequence of technological advancements conducive to high development in food and pharmaceutical science as well as in environmental conservation. The demographic imbalance as a result of such rising number of old-aged persons amidst the downward trend of birth rate has now formed the present elderly society in several countries such as Japan, Singapore and Thailand. As such, in providing social welfare, the States have dedicated particular attention to old-aged persons. As far as Thailand is concerned, despite the promulgation of the *Old-Aged Persons Act*, *B. E.* 2546(2003)which is currently in force, the rights of social welfare for old-aged persons are embodied in only one section of this act and this only section indeed fails to specify clear criteria or standards. Also, although other legislation provides social security schemes for the elderly or even establishes the National Savings Fund for the Old-Aged Persons, there remain problems and obstacles affecting good quality of life of old-aged persons. In this regard, three principal problems are summarized below.

(1) Problems Surrounding the Administration of the Provision of Social Welfare

In this connection, the provision of social welfare for old-aged persons is administered by the statutorily established Commission the composition of which is made of persons not in the position to have real devotion of their knowledge and expertise to this area of work. Also, the Commission is not in the position to coordinate with local government organizations, which are the public bodies having closest ties with elderly people in their respective localities. Further, current legislation does not rest upon actual participation by old-aged persons and is therefore not in line with the fundamental principle enshrined in the constitution.

(2) Lack of Clear Statutory Criteria Pertaining to Rights of Old-Aged Persons

The law on old-aged persons establishes rights of old-aged persons without specifying clear criteria or rules in connection with the provision of social welfare to meet really acceptable standards. Although state agencies concerned have provided social welfare, in certain areas, for elderly people, the services thus far provided remain at variance with necessities and needs of the elderly in the light of appropriate cultural and social backgrounds of Thailand.

(3)Problems Encircling the Statutory Fund for Social Welfare for Old-Aged Persons

The act establishes a specific fund dedicated to financing the provision of social welfare for the elderly but, due to the inappropriate composition of the fund itself, the amount of money constituting the fund becomes insufficient for the effective provision of social welfare in the interest of old-aged persons. This deficiency is incapable of remedy by the National Savings Fund established under the law on national savings, simply because of certain problems restraining elderly people's access to certain types of savings-related services made available to them and also problems encircling the management of the Fund. All these problems prevent activities supposed to be actually carried out by the State for the happiness of the people in four dimensions, namely, ① physical happiness, which refers to good health of the people, ② material happiness, denoting the availability of daily-life facilities, ③ spiritual happiness, which centers on recreational services in the interest of the people's happy sentiments and ④ environmental happiness, signifying the conservation of natural resources and the environment to ensure good conditions conducive to happy feelings.

The problems spelled out above make it necessary for revising legislation in force to ensure appropriate application in line with social needs and conditions of the present time, in the interest of the efficient provision of social welfare and the development of social welfare projects or plans for old-aged persons, in order that the elderly will be well nurtured, afforded opportunities increasingly suitable to their old age and able to live their normal lives to the extent possible. In effect, such nurture should be carried out up to the post-mortem stage, whereby payment is to be made to old-aged persons' dependents upon their dealth as well. [1] In this light, it can be said that "social welfare" denotes the organization of social services and social institutions to assist people in society in a manner ensuring their satisfaction with standards of living and health. In this connection, social institutions are an essential instrument for social integration so as to ensure smooth socialization on the basis of the principle of equality, which is indeed the most important factor bringing society to fairness, efficiency and genuine harmony. Social welfare is founded upon the following fundamental principles, namely, ①the independence principle, ②the equality principle, ③ the economic welfare and security principle, ④the life-opportunity security principle and⑤the public well-being promotion principle. Actions are to be undertaken as are necessary and appropriate by reference to four considerations：①the economic consideration—ensuring sufficient income for the living, ②the educational consideration—contemplating the acquisition of knowledge and capacity through education to be reasonably provided by the State for future living, ③the social consideration—signifying livelihood in a manner of securing a socially acceptable status and mutual assistance and, ④ the consideration as to income and resources distribution—attempting to bring into existence the distribution of income and resources in the way that underprivileged persons may live their lives happily in society. Notwithstanding, the notion as to the assistance to be rendered by the State to underprivileged persons has gained global momentum when countries around the globe established the United Nations(UN)which subsequently issued the Declaration of Human Rights 1948 to protect welfare of all men.

This instrument, which is an important international law, holds that every human-being, as a member of the international community, has the right to social security so as to achieve such economic, social and cultural rights as essential for dignity and for the development of personality along the line of liberties and through attempts by the State and international co-

---

① International Labor Office, *Social Security Principles*, Geneva： International Labour Office, 1998, p. 7.

operation. Another important instrument in this sphere lies in the *Social Security (Minimum Standards) Convention* 1952 as adopted by the United Nations, under which every human-being is entitled to such standard of living as sufficient for living a life and having family well-being, including food, clothing, housing, medical care (sanitary services), education and necessary social services on the basis of three social preferences, namely, ① eradication of physical poverty plaguing the living, ② social protection of all human-beings born with rights and, ③ recognition of such economic and social disparity of persons as arising for intended purposes and in compliance with rules and regulations of society.

As far as Thailand is concerned, the provision of social welfare began its life after the reform of government regime. A notion as to social security schemes or social welfare schemes entered its appearance for the first time in 1934 as reflected in the economic plan of the People's Party wherein a proposal was made for preparation of a law bill on social security. However, this proposal failed to secure a public welcome, the reason being that such scheme and its value were unknown in Thailand and not conceived by the Thai people at that time. Later, in 1972, the law on employees' compensation was brought into being to protect employees from suffering injuries in the course of their employment. Such compensatory scheme was, in essence, part of social security and part of the principles governing social security mechanisms. The said law constituted an integral part of the labor protection law which was, at that particular time, legislation made by the executive, as it took the form of the Notification of the Ministry of Interior Re: Labor Protection, dated 16th April 1972.

The *sui generis* legislation on social security *per se* was successfully enacted in 1990 and was entitled the "Social Security Act, B. E. 2533(1990)" under which mandatory social security schemes have been established in favor of employees, who are indeed required by the act to be members of the Social Security Fund and make contribution payment to this Fund. Member employees are entitled to obtain compensation in seven circumstances: ① injury or sickness suffered not in the course of employment, ② infirmity, ③ death, ④ child delivery, ⑤ child aid, ⑥ old age and ⑦ unemployment.

In 2003, the *Act on Promotion of Social Welfare Provision*, B. E. 2546 (2003) has been promulgated with a view to affording people social welfare along the line of requirements set forth in the *Constitution of the Kingdom of Thailand*, B. E. 2540 (1997). As a result of this act, people have become increasingly familiar with social welfare mechanisms. The act defines "social welfare", makes provisions for the organization of social welfare and sets forth statutory bodies responsible for the organization of social welfare. In effect, two more pieces of legislation have been enacted in this area, namely, the *Children Protection Act*, B. E. 2546 (2003) and the *Old-Aged Persons Act*, B. E. 2546 (2003) which deal with the provision of social welfare for children and old-aged persons. Indeed, the statutory provision of social welfare for the elderly under the law on old-aged persons is the implementation of the requirement, laid down by the constitution, that the State be under the duty to protect, promote and foster rights of the elderly. Alongside such constitutional concerns, elderly people themselves have formed Old-Aged Persons' Councils of Thailand in the interest of promoting participation by elderly people and carrying out activities for them. Apart from such attempt at the initiative of the elderly, the State has carried out activities in certain areas for elderly people but actions on the part of the State remain insufficiently capable of meeting appropriate necessities and needs of the elderly by reference to the standard pertaining to the social welfare organization for old-aged persons.

Principles underlying social welfare law

The provision of social welfare must be based upon the preventive principles intended to curb risks to the extent possible in order that people can live peaceful lives in society under the protective umbrella of law handling all disturbances against peaceful livelihood of human-beings, *whether in domestic or professional affairs.* ① In effect, the social welfare mission, which is actually the duty of the State, is founded on family security, as it will be apparently conducive to national security. Social welfare to be provided embraces the efficient provision of food, clothing, housing, health, safety and emotion as well as brain growth②, whilst social needs must be responded in an economical and state-centered manner and also on the basis of public participation. In this connection, five underlying principles are to be pursued to put forth desirable security: (1) income maintenance, (2) work, (3) care, (4) equal opportunities and rights and (5) service organization.

1. Income maintenance principle

Under this principle, it is the duty of the State to ensure that people in the State have sufficient and appropriate incomes. This duty extends to women doing housework and looking after children at home as well.

2. Work principle

This principle holds that work is essentially associated with social integration and constitutes a fundamental right of citizens of the nation. As such, people must be afforded equal opportunities in the labor market and entitled to fair remuneration by reference to minimum standards of payment, which must be sufficient for the living. In this regard, the State is obligated to give its citizens equal treatment to ensure that they are equally looked after.

3. Care principle

According to this principle, the State is under the duty to take care of people in society, whether they are children, elderly people, disabled people or underprivileged people. For this care to be materialized, the State must provide them with choices, support, facilities and benefits as much as it can.

---

① International Labour Office, *Into the Twenty-First Century: The Development of Social Security*, Geneva: International Labour Office, 1984, pp. 20~21.

② Louise C. Johnson & Charles L. Schwartz, *Social Welfare: A Response to Human Need*, 4th Ed., Massachusetts: Allyn & Bacon, A Viacom Company, 1997, p. 77.

In particular, as an essential mission borne by the State, care must be provided on a long-term basis.

4. Equal opportunities and rights principle

This principle requires the State to eradicate sexual discrimination in all respects in order that its people or citizens, as users of social welfare services provided by the State, shall have equal opportunities and rights in society through elimination of unfair discrimination.

5. Service organization principle

Access by the elderly to equal opportunities and rights explained above entails appropriate and efficient mechanisms for managing the provision of social welfare to the elderly in each society. In effect, this must be carried out in the way that allows participation by old-aged persons as well.

From the above principles, it can be concluded that, with respect to the provision of social welfare by the State, those principles boil down to two main principles, [1] namely, (1) social justice and (2) citizenship. The first principle serves as a crucial flavor in the social welfare notion and, based upon it, the government needs to choose between social justice and economic competition, given that human beings are the most valuable resource of the State and are thus eligible for social welfare on an equal basis. The second principle—citizenship—is a crucial condition to be taken into account in formulating social welfare policies in the context of globalization society. The State must put in place directive policies in connection with the provision of social welfare to its citizens so as to materialize their fundamental citizen rights to which they are entitled in accordance with the constitutional requirement.

---

[1] Nongluk Aimpradit, Decha Sangkhawan, Kitiphat Nonthapatamadul, Malee THammalikhitkul and Chokchai Suthaves, *Comparative Study on Labour and Social Welfare Policies in Developed and Undeveloped Countries*, Bangkok: Faculty of Social Administration, Thammasat University, p. 7, 9.

Social welfare schemes in international laws and foreign laws

Schemes for providing social welfare for the benefit of the elderly in international laws as well as laws of other jurisdictions will now be explored in comparison with the schemes embodied in Thai law. Our explanations will be given in turn, as follows.

1. Social welfare schemes in international laws

At an international law level, rules and regulations which deal with social welfare schemes for old-aged persons have thus far been put forward by two international organizations, viz, the United Nations(UN)and the International Labor Organization(ILO).

(1)United Nations

Elderly people are afforded protection in accordance with the principles introduced by the United Nations. In this instance, [①] principles have been declared by the *United Nations Principles for Older Persons Adopted by General Assembly Resolution* 46/91 of 16 December 1991, will be explained as belows.

1)Independence. As far as this component is concerned, elderly people (referred to, in the UN instrument above, as "older persons")should have access to adequate necessities through the provision of income, family and community support and self-help and should have the opportunity to work or have access to other income-generating opportunities. They should be able to participate in determining when and at what pace withdrawal from the labor force takes place and should have access to appropriate educational and training programs. Also, they should be able to live in environments that are safe and adaptable to personal preferences as long as possible.

2)Participation. This principle requires that the elderly should remain integrated in society, participate actively in the formulation and

---

① www. 2. ohchr. org/english/Law/oldpersons. htm.

implementation of policies that directly affect their well-being and share their knowledge and skills with younger generations. It is also required that the elderly should be able to seek and develop opportunities for serving the community and serving as volunteers in positions appropriate to their interests and capabilities and should be able to form movements or associations of older persons.

3)Care. According to this principle, older persons should benefit from family and community care and protection in accordance with each society's cultural values and should have access to health care to help them maintain or regain the optimum level of physical, mental and emotional well-being. Also, they should be able to utilize appropriate levels of institutional care providing protection, rehabilitation and social and mental stimulation in a humane and secure environment and should be able to enjoy human rights and fundamental freedoms.

4)Self-fulfilment. Based upon this principle, the elderly should be able to pursue opportunities for the full development of their potential and should have access to the educational, cultural, spiritual and recreational resources of society.

5)Dignity. This principle ensures that the elderly should be able to live in dignity and security and be free of exploitation and physical or mental abuse and should be treated fairly regardless of age, gender, racial, ethnic or religious background, disability, economic status or other status.

In addition, the International Social Security Association has been established in Geneva, Switzerland. This Association lends economic support to elderly people in all countries. [1]

(2)International Labor Organization

The International Labor Organization has dedicated particular attention to matters concerning social welfare or social security, which is regarded as

---

[1]　International Social Security Association, *The Implications for Social Security of Structural Adjustment Policies*, Geneva: International Social Security Association, 1993, pp. 17~82.

preventive measures to be made available to members of society for combating economic and social hardship resulting from a decrease or pause of income on account of illness, maternity, ageing, death or unemployment. In effect, measures contemplated by the International Labor Organization also include the provision of medical care for relieving or alleviating suffering or pain occasioned by illness. Social security schemes envisaged by the International Labor Organization must conform to the following descriptions. First, the provision of social security must lie in the distribution of financial assistance for the purposes of providing medical treatment, preventing harm to health, maintaining income in the event of involuntary loss or loss of material earnings or supplementing income of persons bearing family responsibilities with a view to ensuring good quality of life within the family and enabling family members to live together happily. Second, there must be legislation recognizing rights of persons, with clear conditions and details. Third, social security must be administered by governmental or independent organizations in the interest of individuals. In effect, the International Labor Organization has also come up with the imperative principles to be adhered to in the protection of people in the sphere of social security or social welfare, as follows.

1) Payment of compensation is to be made by reference to such minimum standards as to enable people to live a reasonable life.

2) Distribution of benefits must be managed in a manner strengthening national economic and social development, with a view to achieving economic well-being.

The Social Security(Minimum Standards)Convention No. 102(1952)of the International Labor Organization sets minimum standards of social security schemes and, in this connection, sets a framework of common important basic social security principles in five categories as follows.

1) Family benefits. Family benefits are granted in the form of living ma- intenance compensation, tax reduction, the provision of educational or medical welfare or the provision of living necessities for the family.

2) Medical sickness and maternity benefits. These benefits are to be made available through the provision of medical services, maternity services

and health promotion services. Compensation for loss of earnings is also one form of these benefits.

3) Invalidity, old-aged persons and survivors' benefits. These benefits are compensations awarded to persons with inability to engage in any gainful activity, old-aged persons and persons suffering loss of support in order to enable their rest in their late stage of life.

4) Accidental work benefits. These benefits are granted as compensation for the injury or disease resulting from employment so that employees are protected against risks in the course of employment and thereby enjoy work efficiency as well as security in the case of sickness, disability or death in consequence of their work. The benefits are granted in the form of compensation, maintenance, medical services, nursing supplies and services as well as supplies necessary for health and vocational rehabilitation.

5) Unemployment benefits. These benefits are in the form of paying compensation for loss of earnings for personal and family living and providing jobs as well as training for unemployed persons in order to put them back into employment. In addition, separate payment is also granted as an incentive for finding a new job.

2. Social welfare schemes under foreign laws

Several countries, including the United Kingdom, Denmark, Sweden, Japan, Singapore and Australia, give serious concerns for social security schemes. The legislation in this area is therefore discussed below.

(1) Law of the United Kingdom

Concepts addressed by Beveridge, a leading scholar in the area of social welfare, have had significant influences on the provision of social welfare in the United Kingdom. Beveridge is acclaimed as the "Father of Social Security Schemes" in recognition of his attempts to put forward such efficient social security schemes as necessary for human beings. These attempts have led to a guarantee of minimum wages of persons and the provision of social welfare in relation to sickness, employment injury, retirement, loss of support as a result of death of a family member, increasing costs resulting from birth, death or marriage, ageing, disability and unemployment.

167

(2)Law of Denmark

In Denmark, legislation on social welfare places emphasis on allocating social aids to the elderly. The law considers that treatment of the elderly without dignity is absolutely improper and, in this instance, the provision of social aids is founded upon four fundamental principles as follows. Firstly, social aids are to be provided as of right under the law and are recognized and protected by the State, with a view to the well-being of citizens. Secondly, the provision of social welfare must be financed out of the State fund derived from taxation and must be carried out for the happiness of underprivileged people. Thirdly, forms in which social welfare is to be granted must be determined on the conception that the need of welfare is not prompted by any fault of eligible persons but rests upon legitimate rights to be conferred by the State itself. Fourthly, aids must be granted in accordance with varying needs of individuals. In this connection, social security under Danish law is objectively provided, in a uniform standard, in three forms: 1) cash allowances as envisioned in the allowances awarded under the pension schemes for old-aged persons retired from work in certain low-income generating careers e. g. factory workers, 2) goods or kinds, which are reflected in the provision of necessities for the living and 3) services to be provided to enable people to live with reasonable ease and comfort in society, including medical services and other free public services to facilitate livelihood or daily life.

(3)Law of Sweden

Sweden is one of the countries well known for providing social welfare for old-aged persons. The Swedish law, enacted in 1980, recognizes the elderly rights to be granted by the State, such aids are necessary for their lives. This legislation, which has undergone gradual development to achieve efficient operation, has established the Old-Aged Persons Fund and sets out its administration to ensure a sufficient sum for managing and providing social welfare for the elderly. Both preventive and remedial measures are employed. Also, health care and long-term care are provided with a view to a good condition of both physical and mental health of old-aged persons, thereby bringing about significant reduction of costs incurred in their medical care in case of serious illness. In providing social welfare for old-aged persons in Sweden, the following considerations receive particular attention: 1) health consideration and 2) housing consideration. As far as the health consideration is concerned, the State directly assumes the duty to take care of health of its population. This duty is indeed assumed by local government organizations as well and, as such, county councils also administer, as part of their functions, local nursing establishments, out-patient treatment centers and medical clinics. Similarly, municipalities provide health services as well. As far as the housing consideration is concerned, Swedish old-aged citizens are provided such housing care as to live their normal lives in their own residences. Municipalities, in fulfilling their responsibilities in relation to the provision of welfare, assist old-aged persons in the acquisition of necessities in life and provide them with catering services. Also, municipalities, with respect to housing, provide cleaning services, give warnings of hazards and make available housing-repair services to ensure livelihood suitable to the elderly. Transportation services are also put in operation for comfortable use by the public.

(4) Law of Japan

The constitution of 1946 of Japan takes recognition of fundamental rights of the people and guarantees people's rights of social welfare provided by the State in order that all citizens are entitled to such care, health support and basic livelihood as shall be provided by the State. To fulfill these duties, the State shall exercise its best endeavor to promote and extend social welfare, social security and public health, as specified in Section 25 of the national charter. In this regard, to be in line with the old-age society structure in the wake of the greater growing number of old-aged persons than other generations of its population, Japan has enacted the *Basic Law on Measures for Ageing Society* (Law No. 129, 1995). This specific legislation affords protection in relation to working and incomes (Section 9), health and welfare (Section 10), opportunities for learning and social involvement (Section 11) and living environments (Section 12). Also, this basic law promotes research concerning the prevention and treatment of diseases characteristic of old-aged persons (Section 13) and requires the government to adopt measures necessary to establish a system for reflecting views of people in government policies for the aging society(Section 14). In this connection, two principal schemes are put in operation in Japan with regard to the provision of social welfare for ageing people, namely, 1) the public pension scheme and 2) the long-term care insurance scheme. The public pension scheme is concerned with the national pension and employees' pension insurance plans, as to which the said basic law requires the State to make a larger amount of contribution to the Social Security Fund and also amends criteria regarding the age of employees eligible for the retirement payment under the employees' pension insurance plans(indeed, the age of 60 has been changed into 65 in an attempt to reduce burdens of employees joining the pension plan at a subsequent time, with the result that those employees will not assume too heavy burdens for the benefit of retired old-aged persons eligible for the retirement payment). As far as the second scheme—the long-term care insurance scheme—is concerned, its operation may be considered in two respects as follows.

①Administrative structure of the scheme. In this respect, the long-term care insurance scheme is administered by local government organizations, namely, municipalities and prefectural offices in the case of metropolitan administrative units. The administration by such local organizations is, in effect, under support and assistance by the government as well as prefectures and also by members of other schemes related to old-aged persons, that is to say, members of the health insurance scheme and members of the pension scheme, who make contribution payment to the respective funds in proportion to their incomes, as to which a lesser portion may be required of members with lesser earnings accordingly.

②Coverage of the scheme. The long-term care insurance scheme for old-aged persons covers such preventive services as specified in the *Long-Term Care Insurance Act* 2005. The act makes it compulsory for the State to provide services at residences of old-aged persons, with particular emphasis on the provision of healthy food and nursing care. Also, the act ensures that old-aged persons are offered convenient access to services available at nursing care centers.

(5) Law of Singapore

The position of social welfare in Singapore is different, as Singaporean society takes a cultural conception that it is the duty of children to take care of their parents to ensure family warmth as well as family security. [1]

(6) Law of Australia

In Australia, public bodies have been established to take care of elderly people who are in need of legal aids as a result, for instance, of abandonment or torture. In effect, old-aged lawyers are specifically made available to help old-aged persons for protecting their rights. [2]

Our exploration of the provision of social welfare for the elderly under international laws and the laws of other jurisdictions reveals that several countries dedicate particular attention to old-aged persons' rights to social welfare and, in doing so, ensure that both physical and mental health should be nurtured and that long-term care should be provided as well.

Social welfare schemes for old-aged persons under the Thai law

The provision of social welfare for old-aged persons in Thailand is explained in this part, as follows.

1. Meaning of the "old-aged person"

The law on old-aged persons defines an "old-aged person" as a person of over 60 years of age and of Thai nationality. [Section 3 of the *Old-Aged Persons Act*, *B.E.* 2546(2003)]

---

[1]　Associate Professor Narong Jaiharn, Lecturer of Law at the Faculty of Law, Thammasat University, discussing at a seminar on "Directions for Revision of Law on Social Welfare for Old-Aged Persons", held on 24th September 2012 at TK Palace Hotel, Bangkok. See discussion paper on "Approaches to Cooperation on the Development of Welfare for Old-Aged Persons", by the Committee in charge of considering the revision and development of social security law, dated.

[2]　"Approaches to Cooperation on the Development of Welfare for Old-Aged Persons", p. 17.

2. State agencies responsible for social welfare for old-aged persons

Responsibilities in connection with the provision of social welfare for elderly people are assumed by different ministries, namely, Ministry of Social Development and Human Security, Ministry of Public Health, Ministry of Tourism and Sports, Ministry of Information and Communication Technology, Ministry of Culture, Ministry of Interior, Ministry of Education and Ministry of Justice.

3. Public bodies administering social welfare for old-aged persons

The administration of social welfare for old-aged persons is placed under the responsibility of the following statutorily established bodies.

(1)Bodies in charge of social welfare promotion

The law on promotion of social welfare provision establishes the following quasi-judicial bodies in charge of promoting the provision of social welfare, namely, 1) National Commission on the Promotion of Social Welfare,2)Provincial Committees on the Promotion of Social Welfare and 3) the Bangkok Metropolitan Administration Committee on the Promotion of Social Welfare. In this regard, the National Commission on the Promotion of Social Welfare makes recommendations of policies in connection with the social welfare provision, social welfare law and relevant plans and determines social welfare measures as well. [Section 13 of the *Act on Promotion of Social Welfare Provision*, B. E. 2546(2003)]

(2)Bodies in charge of social welfare for the elderly

As far as the social welfare for the elderly is concerned, statutory responsibilities are assumed by the following quasi-judicial bodies.

1) National Commission on Old-Aged Persons. This Commission is chaired by Prime Minister and its remaining composition is made up of Minister of Social Development and Human Security, as first vice chairman, President of the Association of Old-Aged Persons' Councils of Thailand under royal patronage of Princess Srinagarindra, as second vice chairman, Permanent Secretary for Finance, Permanent Secretary for Foreign Affairs, Permanent Secretary for Social Development and Human Security, Permanent Secretary for Interior Affairs, Permanent Secretary for Labor, Permanent Secretary for Education, Permanent Secretary for Public Health,

Permanent Secretary for the Bangkok Metropolitan Administration, Director of the Bureau of the Budget, Director-General of the National Economic and Social Development Commission, President of the National Council on Social Welfare of Thailand under royal patronage, Secretary-General of the Thai Red Cross Society, as *ex officio* members, and not more than five qualified persons appointed by the Council of Ministers from representatives of non-governmental organizations working in the areas concerning the protection, promotion and support of the status, roles and activities of old-aged persons, as members. In addition, this commission is also joined by Director of the Office of Promotion and Protection of Children, Youth, the Elderly and Vulnerable Groups(an agency within the Ministry of Social Development and Human Security), as a member and secretary, and by Director of the Bureau of Empowerment for Older Persons(OPPO), which is within the Office of Promotion and Protection of Children, Youth, the Elderly and Vulnerable Groups, as well as Director of Medical Sciences for the Elderly(attached to the Department of Medical Services, Ministry of Public Health) as an assistant secretary. Such composition is laid down by Section 4 of the *Old-Aged Persons Act*, B.E. 2546(2003). This commission has powers and duties in connection with the formulation of policies and plans for the protection, promotion and support of the status, roles and activities of old-aged persons, with participation of their families. The commission also provides support and assistance for State and private agencies in relation to their activities dedicated to helping and developing old-aged persons. Such powers and duties are specified in Section 9 of the act.

2) Social Security commission. This commission consists of Permanent Secretary for Labor, as chairman, a representative of the Ministry of Finance, a representative of the Ministry of Public Health and a representative of the Bureau of the Budget as members. In addition, the commission is also composed of five representatives of the employers' side and five representatives of the employees' side as appointed by the minister, with Secretary-General of the Social Security Office being a member and secretary and persons appointed by the commission as assistant secretaries. The Minister may appoint advisers to the commission not more than five

qualified persons experienced social security affairs, medical affairs and legal affairs. All this composition is the requirement under Section 8 of the *Social Security Act*, B. E. 2533(1990). The powers and duties of this commission center on the giving of opinions on social security policies and measures and legal matters in relation to social security, including retirement payment, as apparent from Section 9 of the act.

4. Funds established for providing social welfare for old-aged persons

Several funds are available for the provision of social welfare, as will be brought out below.

(1)Fund for the Promotion of Social Welfare Provision

This fund is established within the Office of Permanent Secretary for Social Development and Human Security and intends to finance expenses incurred in the promotion of social welfare provision. [Section 24 of the *Act on Promotion of Social Welfare Provision*, B. E. 2546(2003)] This fund is made up of inauguration money allocated by the State, money from the annual appropriation, donated money or property, subsidies from foreign sources or international organizations, money or property vesting in the fund or received by the fund by operating laws or by any other juristic acts, and fruits arising from the money or property of the fund. (Section 25 of the act)

(2)Old-Aged Persons Fund

This fund is set up within the Office of Promotion and Protection of Children, Youth, the Elderly and Vulnerable Groups with a view to financing expenses incurred in the protection, promotion and support of old-aged persons. [Section 13 of the *Old-Aged Persons Act*, B. E. 2546(2003)]. The fund consists of money similar to that forming the fund for the Promotion of Social Welfare Provision. (Section 14 of the act)

(3)National Savings Fund

This fund has a status as a state agency. Indeed, it is statutorily ascribed a status of a juristic person that is not a government agency or a state enterprise. The fund carries out, as its objects, the promotion of savings of members and serves as security for payment of pensions and benefits to members (i. e. old-aged persons) upon termination of membership. [Section 5 of the *National Savings Fund Act*, B. E. 2554

(2011)] Money forming this fund is essentially the accumulated contribution payment made by members, who are Thai nationals of not lower than 15 years of age and not more than 60 years of age and who are not members under the law on social security. Such contributions are made in return for entitlement to compensation at the retirement age. In this connection, members of the Government Pension Fund, Bangkok Metropolitan Administration Pension Fund, Local Government Pension Fund, Provident Fund under the law on provident fund and Aids Fund under the law on private schools and members of such funds or of such other pension schemes as prescribed in the ministerial regulation are, under Section 30 of the act, eligible for applying for membership of the National Savings Fund. Those members are required, by Section 31 of the act, to make contribution payment to the National Savings Fund in an amount not lower than 50 Baht and not more than the amount prescribed in the ministerial regulation. The contribution payment to be made by the government towards the fund, which varies with the age of members, is in proportion to the accumulated sum and is in accordance with the list of contribution payment attached to the *National Savings Fund Act*, *B. E.* 2554(2011)(Section 32 of the act). [1] In addition to the contribution payments, the National Savings Fund is also formed by money or property donated to the fund, money allocated by the government, other incomes and fruits of the money and property in the fund. (Section 7 of the act)

---

[1] The list of contribution payments is prescribed as follows.

(1)In the case of membership not exceeding 30 years, the ratio of the contribution payment to the accumulated amount is 50 percent, with the maximum contribution payment of 3,000 Baht *per annum*.

(2)In the case of membership exceeding 30 years but not exceeding 50 years, the ratio of the contribution payment to the accumulated amount is 80 percent, with the maximum contribution payment of 4,800 Baht *per annum*.

(3) In the case of membership exceeding 50 years, the ratio of the contribution payment to the accumulated amount is 100 percent, with the maximum contribution payment of 6,000 Baht *per annum*.

(4)Social Security Fund

This fund is established within the Social Security Office, Ministry of Labor, for funding payment of benefits to which its members are entitled and also for financing expenses of the commission and committees under the act as well as expenses incurred in general administration of the Social Security Office under the law on social security. [Section 21 and Section 24 of the *Social Security Act*, *B. E.* 2533（1990）] This fund consists of contribution payments made by the years of age up to 60 years of age is required to be a member of the social employee who works for an employer having at least 1 employee and who is of 15 Security Fund and make contribution payment to the Fund at the same rate as that required of the employer in accordance with the List annexed to the law on social security. Employees over 60 years of age who remain their status as employees of employers under the law on social security are also subject to these statutory requirements above. Apart from the compulsory contribution payments, this fund is also made up of donated money, subsidies, money vesting in it, subsidies or money advanced by the government, money from fines payable in settlement of offences and other revenues. Such composition of the fund is laid down by Section 22 of the said act.

5. Provision of social welfare to old-aged persons

Under the social welfare schemes of Thailand, social welfare is provided, in accordance with the prescribed standards, for persons suffering social problems(statutorily called "recipients of social welfare services")and such matters as will be explained below are to be taken into account. [Section 5 and Section 6 of the *Act on Promotion of Social Welfare Provision*, *B.E.* 2546(2003)]

1)Areas of social welfare. Social welfare services are to be provided as necessary and appropriate in the following areas: social services, education, health, housing, vocational training, occupation, recreation and justice administration.

2)Nature, forms and procedures of social welfare. Social welfare is to be provided in the form of development promotion, assistance, protection, prevention, resolution and rehabilitation. In effect, individuals, families, communities, local government organizations, professional organizations, religious institutions and other agencies are encouraged and promoted to participate in the provision of social welfare as well.

In this instance, public interest organizations (namely, foundations or associations having objects in connection with the provision of social welfare) or non-governmental organizations carrying out work concerning the provision of social welfare in accordance with such standards accredited by the Social Welfare Promotion Commission may receive financial support from the Fund for the Promotion of Social Welfare Provision.

That having been said, the State has thus far made available social welfare in the form of development promotion, assistance, protection, prevention, resolution and rehabilitation for the benefit of old-aged persons who are "recipients of social welfare services," pursuant to the definition provided by the *Act on Promotion of Social Welfare Provision*, B. E. 2546 (2003). In this regard, Section 3 of the act defines the "old-aged person" as a person who is over 60 years of age and is of Thai nationality.

Social welfare services are to be provided for old-aged persons in such areas as necessary and appropriate and in line with such rights of recipients of social welfare services as recognized and protected by the constitution. In this instance, the current constitution—the *Constitution of the Kingdom of Thailand*, B. E. 2550(2007) affords protection on the basis of the equality principle (Section 30) in a variety of areas as follows.

1) Education. As far as education is concerned, old-aged persons are afforded constitutional recognition and protection with respect to an equal right to education. To these ends, the provision of education by professional organizations or the private sector, alternative education by the people, self-tuition and life-long learning shall be protected and promoted by the State as appropriate. [Section 49 Paragraph one and Paragraph three of the *Constitution of the Kingdom of Thailand*, B. E. 2550 (2007)] Given the constitutional requirements above, the State is expected to provide social welfare in this area in a manner compatible with such constitutionally recognized rights. [Section 80(1) and Section 80(4) of the national charter]

2) Health. With respect to health, old-aged persons' rights are constitu-

tionally recognized and protected, as to which they enjoy an equal right to receive public health services which are appropriate and up to the quality, and indigent old-aged persons shall have the right to receive free medical treatment from public health centers of the State. Such public health services from the State are required to be provided thoroughly and efficiently.

Also, old-aged persons have the right to be appropriately protected by the State against harmful contagious diseases and to have such diseases eradicated, without charge and in a timely manner. These requirements are embodied in Section 51 of the national charter. In effect, health involves a human-being's state of perfection in physical, mental, intellectual and social dimensions in a well-balanced manner. In order to materialize this, there has been enacted the *National Health Act*, B. E. 2550(2007), which provides health-related rights and duties and ensures that persons enjoy the right to live in environments and surroundings facilitating good health. (Section 5 of the act)

3) Housing. Elderly persons' rights relating to housing are recognized and protected in that they shall enjoy the liberty of dwelling and be protected for peaceful habitation in and possession of their dwelling places. [Section 33 of the *Constitution of the Kingdom of Thailand*, B. E. 2550 (2007)] Further, in the case where old-aged persons are homeless and have insufficient income for the living, they shall have the right to receive appropriate aids from the State. [Section 55 and Section 80 (1) of the *Constitution of the Kingdom of Thailand*, B. E. 2550(2007)]

4) Employment and earnings. In this sphere, the constitution also recognizes and protects elderly persons' rights by affording them with the liberties to engage in an enterprise or an occupation and to undertake a fair and free competition [Section 43 paragraph one of the *Constitution of the Kingdom of Thailand*, B. E. 2550(2007)] and ensuring their safety at work and security after work without unfair discrimination [Section 84 (7) of the national charter]. Also, persons who are over 60 years of age (old-aged persons) and have insufficient income for the living are granted the right to such welfare and public facilities as suitable for their dignity to be provided by the State. [Section 53 of the *Constitution of the Kingdom of Thailand*,

B. E. 2550(2007)]

5)Recreation. In the recreational regard, despite no direct provision in the constitution, certain provisions in the national charter protect community rights. It is, in this respect, specified that persons so assembling as to be a community, a local community or a traditional community shall have the right to conserve or restore their customs, local knowledge, good arts and culture of their community and of the nation and to participate in the management, maintenance, preservation and exploitation of natural resources, the environment and the biodiversity in a balanced and sustainable fashion. (Section 66 of the constitution) The national charter requires the State to provide welfare in accordance with state policies in relation to public health. [Section 80(2)]

6) Justice administration. In this area, the elderly are afforded constitutional recognition and protection for the purpose of their having easy, expeditious, speedy and comprehensive access to justice, having fundamental rights in legal proceedings (in respect of which fundamental assurances must accord with the openness of trials as well as trials by judges of a duly constituted quorum and reasoned decisions, judgments or orders) and having the right to have their cases tried in a correct, speedy and fair manner. (Section 40 of the national charter) Actions by the State must be carried out along the line of these constitutionally rights. (Section 81)

7)Social services. With respect to social services, the constitutional recognition and protection find their established place in Section 53 of the national charter itself. Under this provision, persons who are over 60 years of age and have insufficient income for the living have the right to such welfare and public facilities as suitable for their dignity as well as appropriate aids to be provided by the State. The State must take action in fulfillment of these requirements of social services.

(1)Social welfare provision under the law on old-aged persons

The State ensures that old-aged persons are afforded rights of protection, promotion and support in the following areas as specified in Section 11 of the *Old-Aged Persons Act*, B. E. 2546(2003), namely,1) medical and health care services specially made available to old-aged persons for their easy and expeditious access,2)education, religion and information useful for the living,3)appropriate occupation or vocational training(in this connection, officials of the employment offices give old-aged persons advice on job availability meeting their varying needs, provide training on occupational skills and attempt to find suitable jobs for them and, in addition, focal points have been established for serving occupational information to old-aged persons),4)self-development, participation in social activities and formation of networking or communities,5)convenience and safety in buildings, premises, vehicles and other public utilities, 6) transportation assistance through appropriate reduction of fares for the benefit of old-aged persons, 7) exemption of fees for admission to state-owned places of attraction[although this statutory requirement is, in some ways, not complied with, as reflected in the fact, for instance, that the Ministry of Tourism and Sports encourages agencies in both public and private sectors to make available services to old-aged persons at reduced (rather than fully exempted)fees for admission or for participation in activities], 8) assistance against torture and unlawful exploitation or abandonment(in respect of which aggrieved old-aged persons are to be assisted in two dimensions, namely, the social dimension and legal proceedings dimension—the former involving getting tortured, exploited or abandoned old-aged persons out of the torture, exploitation or abandonment in question and providing advice on solutions to family problems and the latter dealing with the provision of advice on legal rights and interests and the pursuit of other related actions as solutions to family problems,9)legal aids or aids relating to the resolution of family affairs, to be specially provided for old-aged persons in a convenient and expeditious manner,10) comprehensive provision of housing, food and clothing meeting the needs of old-aged persons,11)necessary subsistence allowances, to be granted to old-aged persons in a comprehensive and fair manner, as to which monthly payment will be made on a step-up basis in accordance with the age of old-aged persons and subject to four rates(the lowest rate at 600 Baht and the highest rate at 1,000 Baht) and 12)funeral aids in the form of payment of 2,000 Baht for the purpose of organizing a customary funeral.

Despite the rights statutorily enjoyed by old-aged persons in various areas under the *Old-Aged Persons Act*, B. E. 2546 (2003) as explained above, the provision of social welfare for old-aged persons has not been effectively carried out and, as such, fails to give them good livelihood and quality of life. This failure is indeed generated by the fact that the act itself provides no clear criteria or standards.

(2) Provision of welfare relating to savings

The directive principles of state policies in relation to economy require the State to provide, inter alia, savings for the people and state officials for their living at the old age. [Section 84(4) of the *Constitution of the Kingdom of Thailand*, B. E. 2550(2007)] Such constitutional requirement has now been implemented through the enactment of the *National Savings Act*, B. E. 2554(2011), which has entered into force from 12th May 2011.

Notwithstanding, up till now no action has been taken to fulfill the savings scheme under the act. In effect, draft legislation is even under preparation for repealing the said act.

(3) Provision of welfare relating to retirement compensation

Under the law on social security, old-aged persons who are members of the social security scheme and have made contribution payments towards the Social Security Fund, in the case of children aids and in the case of retirement payment, for not less than 180 months and whose status as an employee has ended at least at the age of 55 are entitled to retirement compensation in the form of old-age pensions and old-age gratuities.

Apart from the protection afforded under the social security scheme, social welfare law is regarded as the law of particular importance, as it offers enhanced security to members of society, especially the elderly. This being so, serious attention should be dedicated by the State to the provision of social welfare for the elderly.

Problems encircling the provision of social welfare to the elderly

This research reveals three main problems surrounding the provision of social welfare to old-aged persons under the laws of Thailand, as will now be canvassed below.

1. Problems in relation to the Administration of Social Welfare Provision

In this respect, some hitches apparently plague the statutory body in charge of administering the provision of social welfare. The law on old-aged persons contains inappropriate provisions on the administering body. It is suggested that the "National Commission on Old-Aged Persons" be renamed in line with the title of the act. In this connection, given that the act should be given a new title as the "Act on Promotion and Development of Old-Aged Persons' Quality of Life," the statutory body administering the welfare schemes—the "National Commission on Old-Aged Persons"—should be renamed as the "Commission on Promotion and Development of Old-Aged Persons' Quality of Life." Under the act, the commission is chaired by the Prime Minister. [Section 4 Paragraph one of the *Old-Aged Persons Act*, B. E. 2546(2003)] This appears inapposite, given that the Prime Minister's too hectic schedules in the administration of the state affairs simply do not allow efficient chairmanship in this sphere of work. Further, the composition of the commission provided by the act fails to facilitate coordination with agencies in both public and private sectors as well as with local government organizations which should ideally assume responsibilities in connection with the efficient provision of social welfare in the locality, along the line of the principle of decentralization, with support from the government, as envisioned in social welfare schemes in Sweden. As such local government organizations have closest ties with local residents, social welfare may be provided by them in a manner genuinely meeting the needs of old-aged persons in the locality accordingly. Another deficiency plaguing the commission lies in that the commission's composition has no adequate representation from old-aged persons. The shortcomings spelled out above provide substantial room for the recommendations, firstly, that the composition of the commission in charge of the social welfare for old-aged persons be changed to the effect that the commission shall be placed under direct chairmanship of the Minister of Social Development and Human Security, given the Minister's direct expertise and responsibilities in these areas and, secondly, that persons whose experience and work bear no relevance to social welfare for old-aged persons are to be made redundant from the existing composition of the commission in the interest of expediency and flexibility and, in this connection, more persons representing old-aged persons should be made members of the commission along the line of the principle, as laid down in the present constitution, of participation by old-aged persons. In addition, under the act, the National Commission on Old-Aged Persons does not have any powers and duties in connection with the preparation of strategic plans for the provision of social welfare for the elderly. It is therefore recommended that this commission be given powers and duties to draw up strategic plans for promoting and developing the quality of life of old-aged persons in an appropriate, equal, comprehensive and fair manner encompassing both short-term and long-term care schemes for the benefit of old-aged persons, having regard to participation by old-aged persons themselves, agencies and organizations concerned and local government organizations as well. Also, the act should be amended in order that the commission may have prompt information on troubles and needs of old-aged persons and consider necessary assistance suiting their needs.

2. Rights of old-aged persons

The law on old-aged persons as currently in force provides rights for old-aged persons without laying down clear criteria, as may be explained below.

(1)Education

With respect to education, training or information useful for the living, old-aged persons are entitled to social welfare in connection with education, training or information useful for their lives, in accordance with Section 49 and Section 80(3)of the *Constitution of the Kingdom of Thailand*, B.E. 2550(2007). As old-aged persons will leave employment at their retirement age, they will face loneliness and some suffering effects, which will in turn affect their physical and mental health. Thus, educational and training activities should be provided for them. In this instance, state agencies in charge of educational affairs, namely, agencies within the Ministry of Education, should put in place measures dedicated to educational welfare.

To these ends, educational or training programs should be organized for old-aged persons in a way suitable for their age. Attempts should also be made for disseminating useful information to old-aged persons for their lives and their good quality of life in the interest of their self-dependence and happiness during their late days. Further, as a large number of old-aged persons are valuable assets of the country and are in the position to give contribution to the resolution of social problems, the State should make available activities so as to give old-aged persons opportunities to have suitable participation together with children and the youth. In such activities, old-aged persons may, for example, be employed as trainers passing on their rich knowledge and experience to those younger generations. Through these endeavors, problems in relation to violent or aggressive juveniles may, to some extent, be subtly curbed.

(2) Health

In this respect, old-aged persons' naturally deteriorating health needs special care to enable their normal self-dependent living. In case of sickness, old-aged persons need to be given such medical treatment as to be restored to their healthy condition. For these purposes, old-aged persons need to be offered integrated health-services, to be made available comprehensively and efficiently at state-owned health centers, which should cover both physical and mental health.

(3) Housing

Under Section 11(10) of the *Old-Aged Persons Act*, B.E. 2546(2003), old-aged persons are afforded comprehensive protection, promotion and support in the areas of housing, food and clothing in accordance with their needs. The act, however, fails to set out clear and important rules for the provision of social welfare in these areas, despite a large number of old-aged persons in need of it. In effect, homeless old-aged persons should be housed at old-age homes to ensure their happy living in good environments, although they should first be encouraged to live with their families in the interest of domestic solidarity and warmth, in line with the principles of the United Nations. At present, social welfare in this sphere is not sufficiently provided by the State. It is therefore necessary to increase availability of old-age homes and adjust living conditions in response to the needs of homeless old-aged persons. Also, with respect to those old-aged persons who are not homeless but live at residences not suitable for the normal life at their old age, the State should render assistance in repairing such residential unsuitability. Further, when old-aged persons are incapable of taking care of themselves, suitable persons should be provided by the State to take care of old-aged persons. In this regard, costs incurred under the provision of such welfare should be financed out of the Old-aged Persons Fund.

(4) Employment and earnings

Under Section 11(3) of the *Old-Aged Person Act*, B. E. 2546(2003), old-aged persons are afforded protection, promotion and support in respect of work and vocational training. However, lack of clearly important rules in the act itself results in old-aged persons not receiving social welfare in this regard in a practical sense. Thus, to help old-aged persons who have reached their retirement age but remain in need of employment for earnings, the State should ensure that agencies in employment offices provide jobs which are suitable for the age and health of old-aged persons and which trigger appropriate and fair pay. For instance, old-aged persons may serve as speakers, qualified persons or counselors providing advice in specific areas to working people. However, old-aged persons will enjoy labor protection in accordance with international standards, as to which work allowed to be carried out by old-aged persons must be one not posing risks of danger to them. Alternatively, the retirement age may be changed from 60 to 65 so as to allow healthy old-aged persons to continue their employment.

(5) Recreation

The law on old-aged persons makes no candid recognition of old-aged persons' rights of protection, promotion and support in respect of recreational activities. Rather, the law provides exemption of fees for admission to state-owned places of attraction, as laid down in Section 11(7) of the *Old-Aged Persons Act*, B.E. 2546(2003). Nonetheless, no essential rules and clear procedures have been found in the act. Given that a large number of old-aged persons face mental-health problems associated with loneliness caused by lack of employment and also by an environmental shift from living amongst colleagues to living in isolation, the State is thus obligated to put in place recreational activities beneficial to society as well as the elderly. Such activities may be held by the State or through coordination with agencies or bodies in the private sector as well as local government organizations, under financial support from the Old-Aged Person Fund. In addition, to promote corporate social responsibility(CSR), the State may launch campaigns whereby organizations in the private sector may make donations for the provision of social welfare or may be encouraged to have some participation in social welfare for the elderly in return for certain tax preferences.

(6)Law and justice administration

Some old-aged persons suffer misfortunes or grievances when their savings accumulated for use at their non-working age are taken away by deceitful culprits or thieves or when they become victims of torture by family members or third persons. In such a case, old-aged persons do not have easy, convenient and prompt access to justice administration. There arises therefore compelling need for easy access to justice for the benefit of the aggrieved elderly. At least, they should be provided fundamental assurances as to fair legal proceedings in order that their cases may be tried openly, correctly, expeditiously and fairly in courts. Indeed, such facilities are to be made available in fulfillment of the directive principles of fundamental state policies in relation to administration of justice set forth in the constitution. Furthermore, Section 11(8)of the *Old-Aged Persons Act*, *B. E.* 2546(2003) also requires the State to provide assistance and advice to old-aged persons who are victims of torture and take other relevant actions to solve family problems. However, such requirements are plagued with misfortune when the act provides no clear rules as to operations to be taken to materialize the provision of social welfare in this sphere. The dearth of such rules results in old-aged persons not enjoying guaranteed protection in a real sense. To curb these shortcomings, lawyers should be made available for legal assistance and counseling in the interest of old-aged persons and other actions should also be carried out in an endeavor to solve problems encountered by old-aged persons in relation to law and administration of justice.

(7) Social services

It has been a witnessed fact that a large number of old-aged persons en-counter problems in relation to social services. Their good quality of life is prevented by poverty, lack of ability to take care of themselves, abandonment, and neglect of warm care or health problems. Despite all these problems, the law on old-aged persons provides no clearly important rules and procedures governing the provision of social welfare in the sphere of social services. In this regard, old-aged persons should be entitled to state social welfare in the following principal respects. First, they should be entitled to old-age subsistence allowances. In this respect, payment under current legislation is to be made at step-up rates (of 600 Baht to 1,000 Baht) commensurate with the age of the old-aged persons. These rates unfortunately stand below the poverty level. To curb this deficiency, subsistence allowances should be made at four rates by reference to the maximum rate of an employee's minimum daily wage under the labor protection law. Such determination allows appropriate adjustment corresponding to costs of living and the standard of living without any need to make amendment to the law. These rates are as follows: 1) old-aged persons of 60 years but below 70 years of age are entitled to a monthly sub-sistence allowance in an amount 10 times the maximum rate of the minimum daily wage under labor protection law; 2) old-aged persons of 70 years but below 80 years of age are entitled to a monthly subsistence allowance in an a-mount 15 times the maximum rate of the minimum daily wage under labor protection law; 3) old-aged persons of 80 years but below 90 years of age are entitled to a monthly subsistence allowance in an amount 20 times the maximum rate of the minimum daily wage under labor protection law and 4) old-aged persons of 90 years of age upwards are entitled to a monthly subsistence allowance in an amount 25 times the maximum rate of the minimum daily wage under labor protection law. Second, old-aged persons should be entitled to social security in respect of public transport and public facilities. At present, old-aged persons using public transport are required to pay fares for certain types of transportation and do not receive reasonable convenience in the services available. To enable them to live their normal lives with a reasonable degree of comfort, old-aged persons should be eligible for free inland and water transportation and also for half-fare air transportation. They should also be provided with comfort in using other public services to be made available indoors and outdoors at appropriate places. State agencies concerned should therefore perform their duties in relation to the provision of social welfare in the sphere of public transport as well as other public facilities explicated above. Third, funeral expenses should be granted in the interest of old-aged persons' demise. In this regard, as legislation in force does not specify any fixed rate, the state agency concerned fixes the rate at 2,000 Baht which is obviously insufficient for funeral expenses. This deficiency should be rectified by allowing payment of funeral allowances in an amount of not less than 100 times the maximum rate of the minimum daily wage under labor protection law. Fourth, families should be encouraged to have due participation in the care of old-aged persons. In this regard, although the law on old-aged persons has no candid provisions encouraging families of old-aged persons to take care of them, such encouragement is reflected at least in the *Revenue Code*, under which taxpayers are allowed to deduct, from assessable incomes, expenses incurred in taking care of their parents. Nonetheless, such tax-deductible expenses as allowed by the code are subject to an unreasonably low ceiling. Such ceiling should be elevated for the purpose of effectively encouraging children of old-aged persons to take care of their ageing parents, which will bring about mental warmth and security within the family as well.

3. Fund financing expenses incurred in social welfare for old-aged persons

The Old-Aged Person Fund established under Section 13 of the *Old-Aged Persons Act*, *B. E.* 2546(2003) has an inappropriate composition and an insufficient sum to finance the provision of social welfare for the elderly in response to their real needs. It is, in this instance, desirable to require local government organizations to participate in social welfare for the elderly by paying contribution money towards the fund, given that local government organizations have close relationship with old-aged persons in their respective areas. Further, donations of money towards the fund should be promoted on the basis that donors are granted tax deduction on the ground of their donated amounts.

Conclusions and recommendations

The study under this research leads to the conclusions and recommendations, as may be below summarized:

1. Social welfare administration

With respect to the administration of social welfare provision, inaptness is found in the statutory body in charge of this matter in three respects as follows. First, this body should be renamed as the "Commission on Promotion and Development of Old-Aged Persons' Quality of Life." In effect, the title of the law should also be changed into the "Act on Promotion and Development of Old-Aged Persons' Quality of Life" accordingly. Second, the composition of the commission appears inappropriate. For rectification, this commission should be chaired by the Minister of Social Development and Human Security rather than by the Prime Minister. Also, the commission's current composition fails to accommodate real participation by old-aged persons. Thus, the commission should also consist of members who truly represent old-aged persons. Third, the commission's functions remain incomplete, thereby resulting in its inability to know and solve problems encountered by old-aged persons in relation to their social welfare. It is therefore recommended that the law be amended to the effect that the commission shall have powers and duties to formulate a strategic plan and consider old-aged persons' complaints as well.

2. Rights of old-aged persons

Although the law on old-aged persons sets out, as embodied in Section 11 of the *Old-Aged Persons Act*, *B. E.* 2546 (2003), main principles in connection with the provision of social welfare for the elderly, the act fails to prescribe detailed rules and procedures, including those on rates of financial aids to be granted to the elderly. Such lack of clear statutory criteria results in problems encircling rights of old-aged persons in a variety of aspects. First, in the sphere of training or information useful for the living, old-aged persons do not enjoy statutory rights in a real sense. This shortcoming may be put right through making available learning or training programs suitable to the age of the elderly and disseminating useful information contributing to elderly people's good quality of life and enabling them to live independently and happily. Second, as far as health is concerned, the law on old-aged persons fails to provide health-related social welfare measures in an integrated manner. Thus, thorough health services should be made available to old-aged persons, with particular emphasis on strengthening old-aged persons' health, increasing fast-track health services as well as the number of care centers specifically for old-aged persons and providing suitable care-takers for them. Third, with respect to housing, housing welfare remains insufficient and fails to meet the demand and need of homeless old-aged persons. In effect, a shortage of persons well qualified to take care of old-aged persons has also been witnessed. Thus, accommodation and suitable care-takers should adequately be provided for old-aged persons. In fact, even old-aged persons who live at residences not well suited to their normal livelihood should receive assistance in the improvement of their accommodation so as to enable their comfortable, happy and self-dependent lives. In this connection, old-aged persons should first be housed at the same place with their own family members in the interest of mental warmth and in promotion of security of the family institution. Fourth, with respect to employment and earnings, the law makes no provision on appropriate social welfare measures for old-aged persons. It is thus desirable to make available for old-aged persons, who possess promising potential, jobs suitable to their age and physical health and allow them to receive suitable and fair remuneration. Fifth, in the area of recreation, the law currently in force does not make provisions for social welfare relating to recreation in the interest of relaxation of the elderly from stress and in facilitation of their happy lives. Recreational programs should therefore be put in place in a manner that the elderly may join activities together with children and the youth and thereby derive entertainment as well as opportunities to conserve natural resources for the benefit of society as a whole. Such activities will contribute to good mental and physical health of the elderly. Sixth, as far as law and justice administration is concerned, no clear rules and procedures related are found in the law. To achieve the concrete provision of social welfare in this aspect, lawyers, who may be old-aged persons alike, should be made available to help alleviate or eliminate grievances of old-aged persons. Seventh, with respect to social services, standard rates of subsistence allowances for old-aged persons are not fixed in the law on old-aged persons. The absence of such statutory rates results in the responsible agency fixing the rates in a too small amount to meet the standard of living of old-aged persons. The fixing of insufficient amount is also witnessed with respect to funeral allowances (in the event of the elderly's demise) as well as other social services. Social welfare in these respects should be provided in a manner well suited to old-aged persons and capable of meeting their needs. Indeed, such social welfare should be provided not below the poverty level and with reasonable standards, which should be directly laid down in parent legislation—the act itself. Measures encouraging families of old-aged persons to participate in the care of old-aged persons should also be clearly set out by such legislation, with emphasis on participation of relatives, family members and agencies or bodies in both public and private sectors as well.

3. Fund financing the provision of social welfare for old-aged persons

In this instance, the composition of the fund becomes inept and thereby results in the insufficient amount of money to finance costs incurred in the provision of social welfare for the elderly. This deficiency should simply be mended by requiring local government organizations to make contribution payments to the fund as well.

It is submitted that when the law on social welfare for old-aged persons is reshaped towards the "Law on Promotion and Development of Old-Aged Persons' Quality of Life" in a manner that social welfare measures are to be made available in such directions as recommended in this article with participation of all sectors concerned and out of a sufficient sum from the fund, then social welfare for old-aged persons may be provided in an appropriate and efficient way well responding to necessities and needs of old-aged persons.

泰国适合成为《联合国全程或部分海上国际货物运输合同公约》缔约国

Professor Pathaichit Eagjariyakorn[①]

胡 旭 译

摘要 海上货物运输是泰国当今社会经济发展中重要一环,而海上货物运输方面的恰当立法工作能为泰国本行业保驾护航。因此,采用何种海上货物运输规则,如何适用法律原则,关系到泰国是否能在国际海上货物运输方面处于恰当位置,从而得到世界各国认可,促进本国经济发展。本文从泰国现有的海上货物运输立法方面的现状与不足出发,引申论述加入《联合国全程或部分海上国际货物运输合同公约》的各种优点,最后提出一些对本国现有法律修改的建议,最终证明,泰国适合成为《联合国全程或部分海上国际货物运输合同公约》缔约国。

关键词 泰国法律;"鹿特丹规则";海上货物运输

一、泰国国内关于海上货物运输立法现状

(一)泰国国内单独立法及优点

泰国《海上货物运输法》自 1991 年颁布,是建立在 1924 年《统一提单的若干法律规则的国际公约》("海牙规则"且包含"海牙—维斯比规则")和 1978 年《联合国海上货物运输公约》("汉堡规则")原则之上,而如法国和韩国法律等外国法也被作为该法律的有益指导。

[①] Professor of Law, Director of the Transport and Maritime Law Institute and Director of the Law Center of the Faculty of Law, Thammasat University.

值得注意的是,尽管世界许多国家已经是"海牙规则"或"海牙—维斯比规则"的成员,但泰国尚未成为这些国际公约的缔约国。

(二)泰国国内单独立法的不足

首先,单独立法的《海上货物运输法》将置泰国的收货人和托运人于不利地位并危害国家利益。究其原因,是上述海上货物运输法律的受益方大多是外国人,适用在发展中国家(包括泰国)的一些法律条款,原则上就明显倾向于外国船队(就"汉堡规则"较"海牙规则"和"海牙—维斯比规则"倾向于保护承运人而言)。

其次,即使采用"汉堡规则"为泰国法律,仍然会导致本国法律与其他司法管辖区法律的不同。未来起草关键条款应综合考虑"海牙规则"和"汉堡规则",来实现一个理想的承运人和托运人利益的平衡。

再次,更大的并发症是由于引入国外法律规则时,翻译的不完整,或者吸收运用之时与国内法不能一一对应。泰国虽没有成为"海牙规则"或者"海牙—维斯比规则"的缔约国,但由于《海上货物运输法》在运用中遇到具体困难,引发了各种有争议的案件,最终国会决定准备《海上货物运输法草案》。

(三)国内对加入"鹿特丹规则"的准备

目前,国际上正尝试制备新的海上货物运输国际公约。公约草案定稿为《联合国的全程或部分海上国际货物运输合同公约》("鹿特丹规则"),并开放供成员国签署。最主要的,此公约是"海牙规则"、"海牙威斯比规则"和"汉堡规则"主要原则的综合体现,致力实现海上运输各方更大利益的平衡。因此,本公约已经广受欢迎,目前已有 24 个缔约国。预计"鹿特丹规则"将很快生效,最终取代"海牙规则"、"海牙—维斯比规则"以及"汉堡规则"以实现海上货物运输的协调。

就泰国而言,其作为联合国国际贸易法委员会的一员,一直参与"鹿特丹规则"的起草和讨论,但是,当公约成为定稿之时,泰国未能签署。原因是签署当时,泰国方面怀疑"鹿特丹规则"能否适应泰国国内法律,如多式联运、海运单、国际贸易中港口运营者的提单民事责任等方面。而目前,围绕着上述货物运输的种种问题,新的立法草案将充分考虑。

泰国对加入"鹿特丹规则"的准备,颇有一段时间。早在 1995 年,联合国国际贸易法委员会对于海上具体货物运输问题进行研究时,便向国际海事委员会寻求帮助,想要深入解决这类问题。该草案是由国际海事委员会于 2002

年准备完毕,随后提交给联合国直至定稿。2008 年,联合国大会批准这项草案,并于 2009 年在荷兰鹿特丹正式批准成为公约。目前,已有 24 个国家成为公约的签署国,但公约需要 20 个缔约国批准才能生效。目前,只有 2 个国家,即西班牙和多哥已签署并批准该公约。值得注意的是,"海牙规则"、"海牙—维斯比规则"和"汉堡规则"的缔约国,对于"鹿特丹规则"的这种事先约定的行为猛烈抨击。

二、泰国成为"鹿特丹规则"缔约国的必要性

泰国准备签署《联合国全程或部分海上国际货物运输合同公约》。理由如下:

第一,全球范围内对海上货物运输公约的适用没有统一性。前文提到"海牙规则"(连同"海牙维斯比规则")和"汉堡规则",已经被依靠外国船只进出口货物的国家所指责,原因是上述两个规则倾向于保护船主和承运人,特别是对于承运人的责任承担。条约中有大量免责条款,同时,在承运人对货物损毁进行赔偿时,赔偿金固定在一个较低的数额。相比之下,"汉堡规则"的规定显然更现代化,也更有利于货方,更少的免责条款无疑加重了承运人对货物毁损的责任。同时,"汉堡规则"固定较高的赔偿,且对承运人诉讼时效期间制度更长。如今,在两个公约都有大量缔约国的情况下,加入"鹿特丹规则"无疑是正确之举。

第二,今天,海上货物贸易越来越涉及包括电子记录交易等新技术的使用。因此,传统纸质提单不适合且不便交易。和"海牙规则"和"汉堡规则"相比,"鹿特丹规则"的规定更现代化,更能适应时代的发展。

第三,目前,虽然海洋运输是最重要的模式,但国际货物运输通常涉及多种而非单一的运输方式。很多时候,在货物海运之前,需要通过公路或铁路运到预定港口,同样,在船舶到达目的地之时,货物将通过公路、铁路等方式到达收货方。与规定单一的"海牙规则"和"汉堡规则"相比,"鹿特丹规则"在这方面的规定更为详细。

三、"鹿特丹规则"的优点

事实上,泰国长期以来的贸易中,国际贸易占有重要的比例。在国际贸易中,首先是出售或交换商品,付款和交付紧随其后。相邻国家的货物运输通过

陆运,不相邻国家可以通过海运,运输贵重物品可能空运。然而,90%的泰国进出口货物依靠海洋运输,与其他运输方式相比,这种运输方式允许笨重货物或大质量的货物。现实问题是,泰国自己的船队有限,很多时候需要使用外国船队,在国际上,泰国被归类为"托运人"国家。因此,由托运人和收货人利用外国舰队所提供的服务关系到国家利益。我们决定对泰国海上货物运输进行立法或者成为"鹿特丹规则"的缔约国。如果泰国国内立法或者加入的规则更有利于承运人,则在泰国占较多数的托运人和收货人将处于弱势地位。泰国应采取各种行动捍卫托运人和收货人的利益,这也可以说是在捍卫国家利益。而成为"鹿特丹规则"的缔约国,将会有利地将外国船只置于不利地位,从而使泰国托运人获得无与伦比的好处。具体如下:

第一,与《海上货物运输法》《海上货物运输法草案》体现的原则相比,"鹿特丹规则"包含的原则更有利于托运人、收货人以及整个国家。与"海牙规则"、"海牙维斯比规则"和"汉堡规则"相比,"鹿特丹规则"能为泰国国内处于多数的托运人和收货方提供更高的赔偿金和较长的诉讼周期,而外国船队占大多数的承运人则需要承担更为严苛的责任和更多的赔偿金额。

第二,"鹿特丹规则"引进了一些新的、泰国海上货物运输方面没有涉及的条款,包括执行条款、海运履约方、批量合同、托运记录、控制权、控制方等,其中更包含了对世界新技术的贡献,如电子运输单据记录等运用。

第三,相对于《海上货物运输法案》,"鹿特丹规则"提供给泰国更多好处,并针对《海上货物运输法》在运用过程中遇到的难题,提供一些解决方案,具体体现在包括侵权的诉讼时效周期、承运人的诉讼代理或雇员、低数量的补偿、租船合同、承运人的识别等方面。

第四,一般国家在海洋运输方面采用的规则往往只是一个特定的海上货物运输公约,而泰国是两种原则的混合。成为"鹿特丹规则"的缔约国之一,将使泰国法律原则得到国际海上运输规则的认可,也与其他司法管辖区的法律不产生过大冲突。

第五,通过成为"鹿特丹规则"缔约国,泰国的法律规则将得到其他国家的认可,从而产生了良好的国家声誉和形象,使其在国际舞台上的负面形象成为过去。

四、加入"鹿特丹规则"对国内立法的影响

(一)对《海上货物运输法》的影响

如果泰国成为本公约缔约国,则需要废除或修改《海上货物运输法》。在深入分析了"鹿特丹规则"的基本原则和《海上货物运输法》所蕴含的原则的基础上,我们会发现它们之间的深刻不同。一批体现"鹿特丹规则"的规定可以解决《海上货物运输法》在实际运用中的困难,从而完善泰国的《海上货物运输法》,以实现更大的国际认可。事实上,加入"鹿特丹规则"将会使托运人和收货人具有更大的价值。如果泰国成为"鹿特丹规则"的缔约国,《海上货物运输法》(1991)不足以成为实用的解决方案,因此,适当的解决方案在于《海上货物运输法》的废除和起草新法律,并使这些基本原则体现在新法律之中。

(二)对《多式联运法》的影响

在这一点上,笔者认为,泰国成为"鹿特丹规则"缔约国,则不需要废除或修改《多式联运法》。理由如下:

第一,对当事人(托运人和承运人或多式联运经营人)的意图,必须确定当事人是否打算订立一个海上运输合同(不论任何涉及其他运输模式)或打算订立一个多式联运合同。如果他们打算做一个海上运输合同,将适用新法;如果当事人打算订立多式联运合同,这些合同将由多式联运的法律规定。因此,《多式联运法》与"鹿特丹规则"的当事人不会发生交叉。

第二,就距离而言,很可能的情况是,主要的有关运输距离只是短途却涉及不同的运输方式。设想在海上货物运输的情况下,如通过公路或铁路运输或在情况需要通过公路运输作为一个辅助,主要通过空运运输货物到收货人住所,这种情况下被认为是多式联运是不合理的。相比之下,一个给定的构成多式联运运输额外的运输,需要显著的长途。因此,我们需要做的是仔细区别多式联运是否真的存在。

第三,运输单据可以揭示有关运输的本质。如果使用提单在每个运输方式,运输不是多式联运。相比之下,多式联运的运输单据签发(如使用多式联运提单或联运提单),构成了多式联运的运输问题。

如果泰国成为缔约国的"鹿特丹规则"和需要特定的立法的实施规则,这样的追求不可能对《多式联运法》产生负面影响,前提是确定运输方式是海上

货物运输或联运性质。因此,不存在令人信服的需要废除或修改《多式联运法》。

(三)对《国际运输港口民事责任法草案》的影响

笔者认为,只要各个国家尚未制定专门立法规范港口运营商和在国际贸易运输港站经营人责任或者这类的法律尚未生效,而这些国家像泰国一样成为"鹿特丹规则"的缔约国,泰国就应该给予这些国家与"鹿特丹规则"相同的法律规则待遇,这样的规定会比颁布《国际运输港口民事责任草案》等特别法的方式更受欢迎。笔者认为,如果泰国成为"鹿特丹规则"缔约国之时,《国际运输港口民事责任法草案》尚未批准,立法过程应该被终止。但是,如果《国际运输港口民事责任法草案》已经生效却与"鹿特丹规则"相矛盾,那就应该制定新的法律。

综上所述,我们有理由相信,泰国适合成为《联合国全程或部分海上国际货物运输合同公约》缔约国。

Suitability for Thailand's Becoming a State Party to the *United Nations Convention on Contracts for the International Carriage of Goods Wholly or Partly by Sea* 2009

Professor Pathaichit Eagjariyakorn[①]

Since the promulgation of the *Carriage of Goods by Sea Act*, B. E. 2534 (1991), Thailand has had specific legislation applicable to maritime carriage without relying on the provisions of the *Civil and Commercial Code on Carriage* as, by way of analogy[②], the provisions closest to the matters concerned, as previously witnessed. The enactment of such sui generis

---

① Professor of Law, Director of the Transport and Maritime Law Institute and Director of the Law Center of the Faculty of Law, Thammasat University.

② Section 4 of *Civil and Commercial Code* "The law must be applied in all cases which come within the letter or the spirit of any of its provisions.

Where no provision is applicable, the case shall be decided according to the local custom.

If there is no such custom, the case shall be decided by analogy to the provision most nearly applicable, and, in default of such provision, by the general principles of law."

legislation has indeed been a response to the spirit of Section 609[1], Paragraph 2 of the *Civil and Commercial Code*, which anticipates specific law on carriage of goods by sea in lieu of the provisions on carriage encapsulated in the code.

The draftsmanship of the *Carriage of Goods by Sea Act*, B. E. 2534 (1991) was founded upon fundamental principles embodied in a couple of international conventions, namely, (1) the *International Convention for the Unification of Certain Rules of Law* relating to Bills of Lading, done on 25th August, 1924 (the Hague Rules 1924) as amended in 1968 and 1979 (the Hague-Visby Rules) and (2) the *United Nations Convention on the Carriage of Goods by Sea*, signed at Hamburg on 30th March, 1978 (the Hamburg Rules), while Thai law and certain foreign laws such as French and Korean laws have also been consulted as useful guidance for the preparation of this draft[2]. Notably, Thailand has not become a State Party to any of these international conventions despite the membership of the Hague Rules or the Hague-Visby Rules by a large number of countries. The decision by the draftsmen of the *Carriage of Goods by Sea Act*, B. E. 2534 (1991) to rely on both rules in framing this specific legislation was prompted by the view that approximately 90 percent of Thai imports and exports in Thailand remained dependent on foreign fleets of ships. [3] The importation of the provisions of the Hague Rules or the Hague-Visby Rules into Thai law would, on the one hand, bring Thai law in line with those of the countries

---

[1] Section 609 of the *Civil and Commercial Code* "The carriage of goods or passengers by Royal State Railways Department of Siam or of postal articles by the Post and Telegraph Department are governed by the Laws and Regulations concerning such Department.

The carriage of goods by sea id governed by the Law and Regulations relating thereto."

[2] Somporn Paisin, *The Carriage of Goods by Sea Act*, B. E. 2534 (1991) and the Hague/Hague-Visby Rules and the Hamburg Rules, *Maritime Affairs Journal*, Vol. 11, 1, January 1992, pp. 15~16.

[3] Pathaichit Eagjariyakorn, *Maritime Law*, Vol. 2, 2014, Vinyuchon Publisher, p. 219.

whose ships served imports and exports from or into Thailand, on the other hand, would place Thai shippers and consignees at a disadvantage and jeopardize national interests, given that the principles of these conventions have been formulated in a manner favorable to the sea carriers, most of whom are foreigners. As far as the Hamburg Rules are concerned, although essential principles embodied in these rules appear well-suited to the developing countries (including Thailand) apparently dependent on foreign fleets (in view of the fact that the provisions of the Hamburg Rules impose on sea carriers greater liability than in the Hague Rules or the Hague-Visby Rules), any adoption of the Hamburg Rules into Thai law whilst such rules had not yet come into force would nonetheless result in the enacted law being dissimilar to the laws of other jurisdictions. In an endeavor to overcome this difficulty, the drafters elected to blend key provisions of the Hague Rules and the Hamburg Rules to achieve a desirable balance of the interests of the shipper and of the carrier, whilst international characters were to be preserved amidst such mélange.

However, such blending track has triggered certain problems in consequence of dissimilarity of the principles of the international conventions on which Thai law is founded in light of interests of those involved in the carriage. Greater complication has also been engendered by incomplete translation, or even erroneous adaptation of the provisions of the rules into the domestic law intended to be enacted. The difficulties encountered in the application of the *Carriage of Goods by Sea Act*, *B. E.* 2534 (1991) to disputed cases have eventually led to the decision to prepare draft amendment to this legislation, which has later emerged as the *Carriage of Goods by Sea Bill* (No. ...), *B. E.* ... despite no intention on the part of Thailand to become a State Party to the Hague Rules 1924, the Hague-Visby Rules and the Hamburg Rules. Although its preparation had long been accomplished, this draft law simply remained as such with too little progress towards parliamentary approval.

Concurrently, elsewhere and in particular at an international level, attempts have been made in the preparation of a new international convention on carriage of goods by sea. The draft convention was finalized as *the United Nations Convention on Contracts for the International Carriage of Goods Wholly or Partly by Sea* 2009(the Rotterdam Rules) and open for signature by intending States. [1] In the main, these rules are the product of a combination of key principles enshrined in the Hague Rules 1924, Hague-Visby Rules and Hamburg Rules with a view to achieving a greater and more acceptable balance of interests amongst parties involved in the carriage of goods by sea. These rules have due regard to a carriage of goods by sea involving any other mode of carriage and also take recognition of the use of electronic transport records. This convention seems to have received wide welcome, indeed with 24 signatories at present[2], and it is expected that the Rotterdam Rules will soon come into force and, as intended, eventually replace the Hague Rules 1924 or the Hague-Visby Rules as well as the Hamburg Rules so as to achieve real harmonization of rules applicable to carriage of goods by sea. In effect, the preparation of the Rotterdam Rules was participated by, and welcomed opinions from, a large number of nations with a view to arriving at wide acceptance from all countries, whether in the position of shippers, consignees or other parties. As such, the Rotterdam Rules tends to gain extensive recognition from countries around the globe.

As far as Thailand is concerned, Thailand, as a member of the UNCITRAL, consistently followed and participated in meetings at which the Rotterdam Rules was drafted[3] and discussed but, when the convention became finalized, Thailand failed to sign it and has indeed remained indecisive as to whether to become a party to these rules. This indecisiveness has been prompted by the doubt as to whether the Rotterdam Rules would be well suited to Thailand and produce any undesirable impacts on relevant Thai laws and draft laws, including the *Multimodal Transport Act*, *B. E.*

---

[1]   United Nations, New UN Convention Rotterdam Rules Open for Signatures, http://www. rotterdamrules2009. com/cms/index. php.

[2]   Infra.

[3]   Transport and Maritime Law Institute Project, Proceedings of the seminar on "Should Thailand Sign the UNCITRAL Convention on Carriage of Goods?", held on 13th May, 2008 at Conference Room 222, Faculty of Law, Thammasat University, p. 90.

2548(2005), the *Carriage of Goods by Sea Bill* (No. ...), B. E. ... and the *Bill on Civil Liability of Port Operators in International Transport*, B. E. ... Much uncertainty surrounds the manner in which the above-mentioned legislation and draft legislation would be adapted in response to these new rules.

The idea towards the preparation of the Rotterdam Rules began in 1995 in the course of the study by the UNCITRAL of certain matters in connection with the carriage of goods by sea. A request was addressed by the UNCITRAL to the Comité Maritime International(CMI) for a thorough exploration of these matters so that the result of the study would further be submitted to the UNCITRAL. The preliminary draft convention as prepared by the CMI was, in 2002, subsequently referred to the UNCITRAL, which worked out such preliminary draft until its finalization. The General Assembly of the United Nations endorsed this draft convention on 11th December, 2008 at its 63rd meeting at New York. A ceremony for the opening for signature of this convention was held on 23rd September, 2009 in Rotterdam, the Netherlands. After such signing ceremony, all States may also sign the convention at the Headquarters of the United Nations in New York. At present, 24 States have become signatories but the convention has not yet come into force until ratified by 20 signatory States. At present, only 2 States, viz, Spain(on 19th January 2011) and Togo have signed and ratified the convention. Upon the Rotterdam Rules' entry into force, the countries which are State Parties to the Hague Rules 1924, Hague-Visby Rules or Hamburg Rules are obligated to denounce such prior conventions.

There appeared three main reasons for the preparation of this convention on *Contracts for the International Carriage of Goods Wholly or Partly by Sea* 2009, as explained below.

Firstly, the conventions applicable to international carriage of goods by sea as existing prior to the new convention have failed to achieve uniformity. As earlier mentioned, the two antecedent conventions are the Hague Rules 1924(together with the Hague-Visby Rules) and the Hamburg Rules. It has been claimed by the countries dependent on foreign fleets of vessels for imports and exports(most of which are developing countries) that the Hague

Rules 1924 (as well as the supplementing Hague-Visby Rules) lays down principles in favor of ship owners and carriers. In particular, the rules impose on carriers low liability. A large number of exceptions of liability are provided, under which the carrier will assume too little liability in the event of loss of or damage to the goods carried. Also, where the carrier is liable, compensation is fixed at a rather low amount. In contrast, the Hamburg Rules lays down principles more modern and apparently more favorable to owners of the goods carried, as fewer exceptions of liability there under lead to greater liability of the carrier for loss of or damage to the goods. Also, with a higher amount of compensation fixed under the Hamburg Rules, shippers or consignees tend to be entitled to greater compensation and are subjected to a longer limitation period for institution of an action against the carrier concerned. Both conventions have a large number of States Parties and are in force up to present.

Secondly, trade today involves the use of new technologies including the use of electronic records in transactions increasingly. As such, traditional transport documents in the form of paper-based bills of lading now become inappropriate and inconvenient for modern transactions nowadays.

Thirdly, it has long been envisaged that international carriage of goods usually involves multimodality rather than any single mode of transport, although the sea carriage is the most important mode. In effect, prior to the sea leg, goods are carried by road or by rail to the port where the intended ship is located and, similarly, upon the arrival of the ship at the destination, the goods will be unloaded from the vessel and subsequently carried by road, rail or otherwise to the domicile of the consignee.

The Rotterdam Rules contains 96 articles in 18 chapters as follows: General Provisions; Scope of Application; Electronic Transport Records; Obligations of the Carrier; Liability of the Carrier for Loss, Damage or Delay; Additional Provisions Relating to Particular Stages of Carriage; Obligations of the Shipper to the Carrier; Transport Documents and Electronic Transport Records; Delivery of the Goods; Rights of the Controlling Party; Transfer of Rights; Limits of Liability; Time for Suit; Jurisdiction, Arbitration; Validity of Contractual Terms; Matters Not Governed by This

Convention; and, finally, Final Clauses. Key details of the convention are now brought out below.

The Rotterdam Rules applies to contracts of carriage in which the place of receipt and the place of delivery are in different States, and the port of loading of a sea carriage and the port of discharge of the same sea carriage are in different States, if, according to the contract of carriage, any one of the following places is located in a Contracting State: the place of receipt, the place of delivery, the port of loading, or the port of discharge[①]. This application is without regard to the nationality of the vessel, the carrier, the performing parties, the shipper, the consignee, or any other interested parties[②], but this convention does not apply to liner transportation, charter parties or other contracts for the use of a ship or of any space thereon. Also, the convention does not apply to contracts of carriage in non-liner transportation except when there is no charter party or other contract between the parties for the use of a ship or of any space thereon and a transport document or an electronic transport record is issued.

The Rotterdam Rules provides general details, identification of the carrier, signatures, verification of particulars of a contract, evidentiary effects of the contract particulars and freight prepayment. In particular, with respect to validity of contractual terms, any term in a contract of carriage is void to the extent that it directly or indirectly excludes or limits the obligations of the carrier or a maritime performing party under this convention, or directly or indirectly excludes or limits the liability of the carrier or a maritime performing party for breach of an obligation under this convention or assigns a benefit of insurance of the goods in favor of the carrier or a person referred to in Article 18.

Similarly, for the sake of equality and in fairness to the carrier and having regard to other contractual terms usually contained in a bill of lading which have the effect of increasing obligations and liability of the shipper,

---

① Article 5(1).

② Article 5(2).

consignee and other parties on the part of the shipper in a manner disadvantageous to the shipper or consignee or even place the carrier at a disadvantage, the convention also provides that any term in a contract of carriage is void to the extent that it directly or indirectly excludes, limits or increases the obligations under this convention of the shipper, consignee, controlling party, holder or documentary shipper, or directly or indirectly excludes, limits or increases the liability of the shipper, consignee, controlling party, holder or documentary shipper for breach of any of his obligations under this convention. [1]

Another aspect of matters governed by the Rotterdam Rules lies in the obligations and liability of the shipper. In this regard, the convention provides essential requirements as follows.

a) Unless otherwise agreed in the contract of carriage, the shipper shall deliver the goods ready for carriage and in such a condition where they will withstand the intended carriage, including their loading, handling, stowing, lashing and securing, and unloading and that they will not cause harm to persons or property. [2]

b) The carrier and the shipper shall respond to requests from each other to provide information and instructions required for the proper handling and carriage of the goods if the information is in the requested party's possession or the instructions are within the requested party's reasonable ability to provide and they are not otherwise reasonably available the requesting party. [3]

c) The shipper shall provide the carrier in a timely manner such information, instructions and documents relating to the goods that are not otherwise reasonably available to the carrier and that are reasonably necessary for the proper handling and carriage of the goods, including precautions to be taken by the carrier or a performing party and for the

---

[1] Article 79.

[2] Article 27.

[3] Article 28.

carrier to comply with law, regulations or other requirements of public authorities in connection with the intended carriage, provided that the carrier notifies the shipper in a timely manner of the information, instructions and documents it requires. [1]

d) The shipper is liable for loss or damage sustained by the carrier if the carrier proves that such loss or damage was caused by a breach of the shipper's obligations under this convention. [2]

e) The shipper shall provide the carrier in a timely manner accurate information required for the compilation of the contract particulars and the issuance of the transport documents or electronic transport records, including the particulars referred to in article 36, Paragraph 1. [3]

f) When goods by their nature or character are, or reasonably appear likely to become, a danger to persons, property or the environment, the shipper shall inform the carrier of the dangerous nature or character of the goods in a timely manner before they are delivered to the carrier or a performing party. If the shipper fails to do so and the carrier or performing party does not otherwise have knowledge of their dangerous nature or character, the shipper is liable to the carrier for loss or damage resulting from such failure to inform. In addition, the shipper shall mark or label dangerous goods in accordance with any law, regulations or other requirements of public authorities that apply during any stage of the intended carriage of the goods. If the shipper fails to do so, the shipper is liable to the carrier for loss or damage resulting from such failure. [4]

g) The shipper is liable for the breach of his obligations under this convention caused by the acts or omissions of any person, including employees, agents and subcontractors, to which it has entrusted the performance of any of his obligations, but the shipper is not liable for acts or omissions of the carrier or a performing party acting on behalf of the carrier,

---

[1] Article 29.

[2] Article 30.

[3] Article 31.

[4] Article 32.

to which the shipper has entrusted the performance of his obligations. ①

In addition to the obligations and liability of the shipper, the Rotterdam Rules provide two important obligations of the consignee as follows(Article 43 and 44).

a) When the goods have arrived at their destination, the consignee that demands delivery of the goods under the contract of carriage shall accept delivery of the goods at the time or within the time period and at the location agreed in the contract of carriage or, failing such agreement, at the time and location at which, having regard to the terms of the contract, the customs, usages or practices of the trade and the circumstances of the carriage, delivery could reasonably be expected.

b) At request of the carrier or the performing party that delivers the goods, the consignee shall acknowledge receipt of the goods from the carrier or the performing party in the manner that is customary at the place of delivery. The carrier may refuse delivery if the consignee refuses to acknowledge such receipt.

Another party standing on the same side as the shipper and the consignee is the controlling party, which is entitled to give the carrier instructions relating to the goods. In this connection, the controlling party has the right to give or modify instructions in respect of the goods that do not constitute a variation of the contract of carriage, the right to obtain delivery of the goods at a scheduled port of call or, in respect of inland carriage, any place en route, and the right to replace the consignee by any other person including the controlling party. The carrier shall execute the instructions as received if the instructions can reasonably be executed according to their terms at the moment when they reach the carrier and the instructions will not interfere with the normal operations of the carrier, including his delivery practices.

As far as the obligations and liability of the carrier are concerned, the Rotterdam Rules sets out the following.

a) The carrier shall carry the goods to the place of destination and

---

① Article 34.

deliver them to the consignee. ①

b) During the period of his responsibility, the carrier shall properly and carefully receive, load, handle, stow, carry, keep, care for, unload and deliver the goods. Notwithstanding, the carrier and the shipper may agree that the loading, handling, stowing or unloading of the goods is to be performed by the shipper, the documentary shipper or the consignee. ②

c) The carrier is bound before, at the beginning of, and during the voyage by sea to exercise due diligence to make and keep the ship seaworthy, properly crew, equip and supply the ship and keep the ship so crewed, equipped and supplied throughout the voyage, and make and keep the holds and all other parts of the ship in which the goods are carried, and any containers supplied by the carrier in or upon which the goods are carried, fit and safe for their reception, carriage and preservation. ③

d) The carrier shall, at the shipper's request, issue transport documents or electronic transport records which may be negotiable or non-negotiable.

e) When neither a negotiable transport document nor a negotiable electronic transport record has been issued, the carrier shall deliver the goods to the consignee at the time and location referred to in Article 43, but the carrier may refuse delivery if the person claiming to be the consignee does not properly identify himself as the consignee at the request of the carrier.

f) The carrier shall not carry the goods on the deck of a ship as the carriage on deck triggers greater risks of loss of or damage to the goods than in case of carriage in the holds of the ship, including the risk of loss or damage caused by water or light.

g) The carrier has the right to retain the goods to secure payment of the sums due. ④

---

① Article 11.
② Article 13.
③ Article 14.
④ Article 49.

h) The carrier may decline to receive or to load, and may take such other measures as are reasonable, including unloading, destroying, or rendering goods harmless, if the goods are, or reasonably appear likely to become during the carrier's period of responsibility, an actual danger to persons, property or the environment. ①

i) The carrier may sacrifice goods at sea when the sacrifice is reasonably made for the common safety or for the purpose of preserving from peril human's life or other property involved in the common adventure.

With respect to liability of the carrier, it is specified by the Rotterdam Rules that the period of responsibility of the carrier for the goods begins when the carrier or a performing party receives the goods for carriage and ends when the goods are delivered. However, if the law or regulations of the place of receipt require the goods to be handed over to an authority or other third party from which the carrier may collect them, the period of responsibility of the carrier begins when the carrier collects the goods from the authority or other third party and, also, if the law or regulations of the place of delivery require the carrier to hand over the goods to an authority or other third party from which the consignee may collect them, the period of responsibility of the carrier ends when the carrier hands the goods over to the authority or other third party. As regards the basis of liability②, the carrier is liable for loss of or damage to the goods, as well as for delay in delivery if the claimant proves that the loss, damage, or delay, or the event or circumstance that caused or contributed to it took place during the period of the carrier's responsibility. In this connection, delay in delivery occurs when the goods are not delivered at the place of destination provided for in the contract of carriage within the time agreed.

---

① Article 15.

② Presumption of liability, Berlingieri Francesco, Philippe Delebecque, Tomotaka Fujita, Rafael Illescas, Michael Sturley, Gertjan van Derziel, Alexander von Ziegler, Stefano Zunarelli, The Rotterdam Rules: An Attempt to Clarify Certain Concerns That Have Emerged, http://www. mcgill. ca/maritimelaw/ sites/mcgill. ca. maritimelaw/files/ Rotterdam _Rules_An_Attempt _To_Clarify _Concerns. pdf, p. 21.

The carrier is relieved of all or part of his liability described above if he proves that the cause or one of the causes of the loss, damage, or delay is not attributable to his fault or to the fault of any performing party, the master or crew of the ship, employees of the carrier or a performing party or any other person that performs or undertakes to perform any of the carrier's obligations under the contract of carriage.

In addition, the carrier is also relieved of all or part of his liability if he proves that one or more of the following events or circumstances cause or contribute to the loss, damage, or delay: (Article 17(3))

—Act of God;

—Perils, dangers, and accidents of the sea or other navigable waters;

—War, hostilities, armed conflict, piracy, terrorism, riots, and civil commotions;

—Quarantine restrictions; interference by or impediments created by governments, public authorities, rulers, or people including detention, arrest, or seizure not attributable to the carrier or any performing party, the master or crew of the ship, employees of the carrier or a performing party or any other person that performs or undertakes to perform any of the carrier's obligations under the contract of carriage;

—Strikes, lockouts, stoppages, or restraints of labor;

—Fire on the ship;

—Latent defects not discoverable by due diligence;

—Act or omission of the shipper, the documentary shipper, the controlling party, or any other person for whose acts the shipper or the docu mentary shipper is liable pursuant to Article 33 or 34;

—Loading, handling, stowing, or unloading of the goods performed by the shipper, the documentary shipper or the consignee, unless the carrier or a performing party performs such activity on behalf of the shipper, the documentary shipper or the consignee;

—Wastage in bulk or weight or any other loss or damage arising from inherent defect, quality, or vice of the goods;

—Insufficiency or defective condition of packing or marking not performed by or on behalf of the carrier;

—Saving or attempting to save life at sea;

—Reasonable measures to save or attempt to save property at sea;

—Reasonable measures to avoid or attempt to avoid damage to the environment;

—Acts of the carrier in pursuance of the powers exercisable in connection with the goods which are, or reasonably appear likely to become during the carrier's period of responsibility, an actual danger to persons, property or the environment or in connection with the sacrifice of goods at sea when the sacrifice is reasonably made for the common safety or for the purpose of preserving from peril humans life or other property involved in the common adventure.

Further, the carrier is liable for the acts or omissions of any performing party, the master or crew of the ship, employees of the carrier or a performing party or any other person that performs or undertakes to perform any of the carrier's obligations under the contract of carriage to the extent that the person acts, either directly or indirectly, at the carrier's request or under the carrier's supervision or control.

When the carrier is liable without any defense or limitation, the carrier is allowed to limit his liability. In the case of loss of or damage to the goods, the carrier's liability is limited to 875 units of account (the Special Drawing Right as defined by the International Monetary Fund) per package or other shipping unit, or 3 units of account per kilogram of the gross weight of the goods that are the subject of the claim or dispute, whichever amount is the higher. [①]

The carrier's liability for delay and liability for economic loss due to delay are limited to an amount equivalent to two and one-half times the freight payable on the goods delayed; and in the event of both loss of or damage to the goods and loss due to delay, the total amount of compensation payable may not exceed the limit that would be established in respect of the

---

① Article 59(1).

total loss of the goods concerned. [1]

Although the carrier or persons described above may limit liability in accordance with the Rotterdam Rules, such limitation of liability does not apply when the value of the goods has been declared by the shipper and included in the contract particulars, or when a higher amount than that of limitation of liability set out in this article has been agreed upon between the carrier and the shipper, or when the loss was attributable to a personal act or omission of the carrier, any performing party, the master or crew of the ship, employees of the carrier or a performing party or any other person that performs or undertakes to perform any of the carrier's obligations under the contract of carriage to the extent that the person acts, either directly or indirectly, at the carrier's request or under the carrier's supervision or control, done with the intent to cause such loss recklessly and with knowledge that such loss would probably be caused.

The compensation payable by the carrier for loss of or damage to the goods or for the delay is calculated by refering to the value of such goods at the place and time of delivery. The value of the goods is fixed according to the commodity exchange price or, if there is no such price, according to their market price or, if there is no commodity exchange price or market price, by refering to the normal value of the goods of the same kind and quality at the place of delivery. The carrier is not liable for payment of any compensation beyond the value described above except when the carrier and the shipper have agreed to calculate compensation in a different manner.

In the event of apparent loss of or damage to the goods, the consignee is required to give notice of the loss or damage, indicating the general nature of such loss or damage, to the carrier or the performing party that delivered the goods before or at the time of delivery, and, when the loss or damage is not apparent, such notice must be given within seven working days at the place of delivery after the delivery of the goods. In the absence of such notice, the carrier is presumed to have delivered the goods according to their description in the contract particulars. However, such notice is not required in respect

---

[1]　Article 60.

of loss or damage that is ascertained in a joint inspection of the goods by the person to which they have been delivered and the carrier or the maritime performing party against which liability is being asserted.

Also, in respect of delay, the consignee is required to give notice of loss due to the delay to the carrier within 21 consecutive days of delivery of the goods. Without such notice, the carrier is relieved from liability for payment of compensation for such loss.

No judicial or arbitral proceedings in respect of claims or disputes arising from a breach of an obligation under the Rotterdam Rules may be instituted after the expiration of a period of two years[1]. Such limitation period commences on the day on which the carrier has delivered the goods or, in cases in which no goods have been delivered or only part of the goods have been delivered, on the last day on which the goods should have been delivered. The day on which the period commences is not included in the period. Notwithstanding the expiration of the limitation period, one party may rely on his claim as a defense or for the purpose of set-off against a claim asserted by the other party.

From a brief account of the substances of the Rotterdam Rules above, a question may arise as to whether, if Thailand becomes a State Party to this convention, any need occurs for a repeal or amendment of the *Carriage of Goods by Sea Act*, B. E. 2534(1991). A thorough analysis of the essential principles of the Rotterdam Rules and of the *Carriage of Goods by Sea Act*, B. E. 2534(1991) reveals sharp inconsistency between them. A number of principles embodied in the Rotterdam Rules may solve difficulties found in the *Carriage of Goods by Sea Act*, B. E. 2534(1991) and may be relied on in ameliorating the law on carriage of goods by sea of Thailand in order to achieve greater international recognition, in particular, in relation to the use of electronic transport records. Indeed, adoption of international practices brought into the Rotterdam Rules as well as their essential principles will result in Thai law on carriage of goods by sea being of greater value to both

---

[1] Article 62(1).

shippers and consignees as well as Thailand as a whole than the value derived from the existing provisions of the *Carriage of Goods by Sea Act*, B. E. 2534(1991). Compelling need is thus apparently vindicated for Thailand to become a State Party to the Rotterdam Rules. That having been said, amendment to the *Carriage of Goods by Sea Act*, B. E. 2534(1991) does not constitute a practical solution, given a very large extent of the required amendment. As such, an appropriate solution lies in a repeal of the *Carriage of Goods by Sea Act*, B. E. 2534(1991) and the drafting of a new law along the line of the essential principles enshrined in the new convention.

There emerges another ensuing question as to whether, if Thailand becomes a State Party to the convention, it is necessary to repeal or amend the *Multimodal Transport Act*, B. E. 2548 (2005), given that the Rotterdam Rules also apply to a sea carriage as well as a carriage of goods by sea which involves any other mode of carriage. Our preliminary perusal reveals that the convention, if adopted, will have impacts on the *Multimodal Transport Act*, B. E. 2548(2005) as well simply because the said Act applies to a transport involving at least two modes. If a contract is made for a multimodal transport incorporating a sea carriage as an essential mode, there will certainly be an overlap between the *Multimodal Transport Act*, B. E. 2548(2005) and the new legislation to be enacted in the imple-mentation of the new convention in case Thailand becomes a State Party to it. In this instance, if the *Multimodal Transport Act*, B. E. 2548(2005) is to be amended to the effect of its application only to a multimodal transport without a sea carriage(i. e. a multimodal transport involving a carriage by road and a carriage by air), the scope of application of the *Multimodal Transport Act*,B. E. 2548(2005) will simply be too narrow to retain its sig-nificance, with the result, in particular, that regulation of the operation of a multimodal transport will be limited to a multimodal transport involving a combination of a carriage by road and a carriage by air. Also, if regulation of a multimodal transport combining an essential sea carriage and any other mode of carriage is to be located in the new legislation to be enacted, such an approach seems to run counter to the nature of the operation of sea carriage, which has been, since its early life, founded upon autonomy without any requirement of business registration. At this point, it is submitted by the author that the decision, if made, by Thailand for becoming a State Party to the Rotterdam Rules entails no repeal of or amendment to the *Multimodal Transport Act*, *B. E.* 2548 (2005). Indeed, regard must be had to the intention of the parties, transport documents and the distance involved in the carriage. First, with respect to the intention of the parties (i. e. the shipper and the carrier or the multimodal transport operator), it must be determined whether the parties intend to make a contract of carriage by sea (irrespective of any other mode of carriage involved) or intend to enter into a contract for a multimodal transport. In case of their intention to make a contract for a carriage by sea (with or without any other mode of carriage), the new act to be enacted will apply to the ensuing contract. In contrast, if the parties intend to conclude a contract for a multimodal transport, such contract will be governed by the law on multimodal transport. Such an intention may be reflected in such transport documents as a bill of lading which usually contains a paramount clause specifying the law governing the bill of lading or rights, obligations or liability of the parties. For instance, if it specifies that the law on carriage of goods by sea or the Hague Rules 1924 or the Hague-Visby Rules or the Hamburg Rules shall govern the matters, an inference can be drawn that the parties intend their legal relations to be governed by the law on carriage of goods by sea, which is the new legislation to be enacted along the line of the Rotterdam Rules. By comparison, if it is specified by the paramount clause or any contract term that the law on multimodal transport or the rules on multimodal transport [1] shall apply, such indication constitutes an inference of the parties' intention to have their legal relations governed by the law on multimodal transport.

Secondly, as far as the consideration of the distance is concerned, it may well be that the main distance of the carriage concerned is merely supplemented by a rather short-distance involving a different mode of carriage, as envisioned in the case where a carriage of goods by sea is supplemented by

---

[1] e. g. The UNCTAD ICC Rules for Multimodal Transport Documents.

another auxiliary mode of carriage such as a carriage by road or by rail or in the case where a carriage by road is required as an auxiliary mode after the main carriage by air in order for the goods to be delivered to a domicile of the consignee. In such a case, such transport is, in no wise, perceived of as a multimodal transport. In contrast, a given carriage constitutes a multimodal transport if the additional transport takes a significantly long distance.

Thirdly, transport documents may reveal the true nature of the carriage concerned. If a bill of lading is used in each mode of transport, that transport is not a multimodal transport. By way of comparison, where a transport document is issued for a multimodal transport(as in the case of the use of a multimodal transport bill of lading or a combined transport bill of lading), the transport in question constitutes a multimodal transport.

Indeed, another matter which triggers a practical concern is a possible attempt by an operator of an auxiliary transport to circumvent the requirement as to registration of a multimodal transport operation under the *Multimodal Transport Act*, B. E. 2548(2005) through an interpretation that such supplementing transport is not a multimodal transport under the act.

In this regard, it is submitted by the author that, if Thailand becomes a State Party to the Rotterdam Rules and needs specific legislation in the implementation of the rules, such pursuit is unlikely to produce negative impacts on the *Multimodal Transport Act*, B. E. 2548(2005), provided that the above-mentioned criteria are employed to determine whether the carriage in question is a carriage of goods by sea or a carriage of a multimodal nature. However, in order to prevent circumvention of the registration requirement which, inter alia, seeks to protect users of the services, it is desirable for the law to treat the operator of such supplementary transport as a multimodal transport operator. As such, no compelling need exists for a repeal of or amendment to the *Multimodal Transport Act*, B. E. 2548 (2005). It suffices to require an operator of a supplementary transport to register, whilst its civil liability is to be governed by specific legislation to be enacted in the implementation of the Rotterdam Rules.

As regards adverse effects on the *Carriage of Goods by Sea Bill* (No. ...),

B. E. ... , although this draft law has been intended to provide solutions to difficulty encountered in the application of the *Carriage of Goods by Sea Act* , B. E. 2534(1991) , [1] the preparation of the draft became complete prior to the finalization of the Rotterdam Rules. Several issues under the *Carriage of Goods by Sea Act* , B. E. 2534(1991) have been intended to be revised. But, this act, when amended by the *Carriage of Goods by Sea Bill* (No. ...), *B. E. ...* (if such bill is approved through the legislative process) in the main retain legal principles founded upon the Hague Rules 1924, the Hague-Visby Rules and the Hamburg Rules, which differ from the principles enshrined in the Rotterdam Rules in various respects as earlier explained. Further, an analysis of compatibility with legal principles found in the laws of the countries which are Thailand's important trading parties reveals that the underlying principles in the *Carriage of Goods by Sea Act* , B. E. 2534(1991) as shall be amended by the *Carriage of Goods by Sea Bill* (No. ...), *B. E. ...* are not genuinely compatible with the laws elsewhere, simply because the *Carriage of Goods by Sea Act* , B. E. 2534(1991) as shall be amended by the *Carriage of Goods by Sea Bill* (No. ...), B. E. ... remains founded upon a combination of the principles in the two main international conventions relating to the carriage of goods by sea, viz, the Hague Rules 1924 or the Hague-Visby Rules and the Hamburg Rules, whilst in other jurisdictions legislation on the carriage of goods by sea is, by and large, modeled after the Hague Rules 1924, the Hague-Visby Rules or the Hamburg Rules. Thus, if Thailand elects to pursue this approach, such incompatibility will simply continue to exist. If in the future other countries choose to adopt the Rotterdam Rules, the law on carriage of goods by sea of Thailand will even contain greater dissimilarities to foreign legislation.

Now, in terms of modernity, although the *Carriage of Goods by Sea Act* , B. E. 2534(1991) as shall be amended by the *Carriage of Goods by Sea*

---

[1] Transport and Maritime Law Institute Project, Proceedings of the seminar on "The Carriage of Goods by Sea Bill(No. ...), B. E. ... ", held on 9th August, 2007 at Conference Room 222, Faculty of Law, Thammasat University.

Bill(No. ...), B. E. ... may, to some extent, provide solutions to problems plaguing the law on carriage of goods by sea of Thailand, the act has now appeared outmoded on account of its lack of mechanisms accommodating the use of electronic records—a bill of lading under the *Carriage of Goods by Sea Act*, B. E. 2534(1991) as shall be amended by the *Carriage of Goods by Sea Bill*(No. ...), B. E. ... is to be in a paper form whilst, by way of comparison, provisions in the Rotterdam Rules take recognition of electronic transport records in response to the trend, in the business world today, towards the use of electronic documents in lieu of traditional paper-based documentation. Furthermore, the Rotterdam Rules is more modern in the light of several new principles in various matters including those concerning performing parties, maritime performing parties or a "volume contract"(i. e. a contract of carriage that provides for the carriage of a specified quantity of goods in a series of shipments during an agreed period of time).

As far as the application of law is concerned, the *Carriage of Goods by Sea Act*, B. E. 2534(1991) as shall be amended by the *Carriage of Goods by Sea Bill* (No. ...), B. E. ... shall apply only to an international carriage of goods by sea whilst the application of the Rotterdam Rules covers both an international carriage of goods by sea and an international carriage of goods by sea which involves any other mode of carriage as well. In the author's view, if Thailand becomes a State Party to the Rotterdam Rules and needs to proceed with specific legislation to implement the principles in the Rotterdam Rules, such decision will nonetheless produce certain effects on the *Carriage of Goods by Sea Bill*(No. ...), B. E. ... regardless of whether such bill passes parliamentary muster or not.

Apart from impacts on the *Carriage of Goods by Sea Bill* (No. ...), *B. E. ...* Thailand's becoming a State Party to the Rotterdam Rules will also generate certain effects on the *Civil Liability of Port Operators in International Carriage Bill*, *B. E. ...* as a port operator is also regarded as a maritime performing party. Thus, when the Rotterdam Rules provides obligations and liability of the maritime performing party, the decision to become a State Party to the Rotterdam Rules and enact implementing legislation will result in some overlapping with the above-mentioned draft law. At this point, the author is of the opinion that as long as various countries have not yet enacted specific legislation on liability of port operators and the *Convention on the Liability of Operators of Transport Terminals in International Trade* has not yet come into force, a decision by Thailand, if any, to become a State party to the Rotterdam Rules will give rise to legal rules which shall be applicable to port operators and in line with international principles recognized by other countries, provided that those countries and Thailand become State Parties to the Rotterdam Rules alike. Such consequences seem more welcome than those flowing from any enactment of such specific legislation as now contained in the *Civil Liability of Port Operators in International Carriage Bill*, B. E. ... It is therefore recommended by the author that, if Thailand elects to become a State Party to the Rotterdam Rules when the *Civil Liability of Port Operators in International Carriage Bill*, B. E. ... has not yet been approved by the legislature in its legislative process, such bill should be discontinued and withdrawn. But, if the *Civil Liability of Port Operators in International Carriage Bill*, B. E. ... becomes a statute in force, such sui generis legislation should be repealed upon enactment of new legislation on carriage of goods by sea.

Indeed, Thailand has long been carrying on trade transactions with other countries up till present, with important revenues generated from international trade. International trade, whether in the form of sale or exchange of goods, is usually followed by payment and delivery. Delivery in a sale made with a trader in a neighboring country may involve a carriage by road whilst a sale concluded with a trader in a country with no adjacent border may involve a carriage by sea or, in case of expensive goods requiring speedy delivery, a carriage by air. However, 90 percent of Thailand's imported and exported goods rely on the sea carriage as this mode of transport allows bulky goods or a large quality of goods to be carried in comparison with other modes of transport. Despite such reality, Thailand has a limited number of our own vessels, with the result therefore that foreign fleets of vessels are used for sea carriage. In spite of measures put forth by Thailand over ten years in promoting Thai vessels with a view to enlarging

Thai fleets, such dependence on foreign fleets seems to continue its long life in Thailand. With such on-going reliance, Thailand is classified as a "shippers country". As such, national interests are generated by shippers and consignees making use of the services provided by foreign fleets. All this truism needs to be taken into account in our decision to enact legislation on carriage of goods by sea of Thailand or to become a State Party to an international convention on the carriage of goods by sea, because if Thailand enacts legislation or become a State Party to a convention with provisions much favorable to the carriers, then shippers and consignees will simply be disadvantaged. Such being the case, any action by Thailand should be taken in manner guarding national interests, in particular, those of shippers and consignees. Despite consistent attempts made by Thailand in promoting Thai fleets of vessels, it must be realized that introduction of legal principles of a civil and commercial nature in the form of legislation on carriage of goods by sea in a fashion principally benefiting carriers most of which own foreign ships will trigger national detriment simply because Thai shippers will reap incomparable benefits. It is, indeed, believed that Thai shippers pay too little attention to statutory position and dedicate more interests in other measures beneficial to owner-shippers. In effect, this option, which contributes to greater efficiency in the promotion of Thai fleets of ships, appears more apposite than trading off national interests. Also, despite an opposing view that enactment of law favorable to carriers are unlike to place shippers or consignees at a disadvantage as in practice such parties have an insurance over the goods whilst carriers are also insured against their liability. In the event of loss of or damage to the goods, insurers of respective parties make compensation for such loss or damage. In fact, most meticulous considerations must be made. It must not be overlooked that sometimes insurers of the goods carried by sea do not provide compensation against loss or damage, as envisioned in the case where the insured chooses a lower coverage of protection in view of lower premiums(for instance, where the Institute Cargo Clause C is chosen) or where the loss is occasioned by delay of delivery. In such cases, the shipper or consignee is left with a claim against the carrier. If legal principles concerning liability are allowed to be framed in a fashion too favorable to carriers, then shippers, consignees and Thailand as a whole will just be disadvantaged.

Our revisit of the *Carriage of Goods by Sea Act*, B. E. 2534(1991) as well as the *Carriage of Goods by Sea Bill* (No. ...), B. E. ... in the entirety, in particular, in the light of exclusions and limitations of liability which are principally based upon the Hague Rules 1924 and the Hague-Visby Rules and which have failed to receive support from developing countries dependent on foreign fleets of vessels in the carriage of imported and exported goods, reveals that Thai law on carriage of goods by sea is in favor of marine carriers, most of which are foreign carriers. However, in putting forth revision, it is rather difficult to secure proper understanding from stakeholders despite current attempts to do so.

Our analysis of modern characters and several new principles inherent and contained in the Rotterdam Rules, leaving aside the interest amongst the shipper, the consignee and the carrier, reveals that the principles enshrined in the Rotterdam Rules remain favorable to the carrier. Although the rules, as far as the limitation of liability is concerned, fix a higher amount of compensation payable by the carrier and allow a longer limitation period for a lawsuit, the defenses relieving the carrier from liability are in the main along the line of the Hague Rules 1924 and the Hague-Visby Rules, albeit little modification. In this connection, our comparison of this matter with the position in Thai law on carriage of goods by sea in the past and the legislation currently in force [i. e. the *Carriage of Goods by Sea Act*, B. E. 2534 (1991) as shall in the future be amended by the *Carriage of Goods by Sea Bill* (No. ...), B. E. ...] reveals that the provisions of the Rotterdam Rules are tailored in a manner more beneficial to shippers and consignees as well as Thailand as a whole than the position flowing from the principles enshrined in the *Carriage of Goods by Sea Act*, B. E. 2534 (1991) and the *Carriage of Goods by Sea Bill*, B. E. ... for the following reasons. First, the Rotterdam Rules lays down fewer defenses relieving the carrier's liability, with the result that the carrier shall assume more liability. Second, when the carrier is liable, the amount of limitation of liability of the carrier is higher than that laid down by the *Carriage of Goods by Sea Act*, B,E.

2534 (1991) and the *Carriage of Goods by Sea Bill* (No. ...), *B. E.* ... and, as such, in the event of loss of or damage to the goods, the shipper and the consignee will be entitled to a higher amount of compensation. Finally, a two-year limitation period for a suit as prescribed by the Rotterdam Rules is longer than the one-year statutory prescription under the *Carriage of Goods by Sea Act*, *B. E.* 2534 (1991). With such longer period, the shipper and the consignee need not hurriedly institute a lawsuit and will not suffer loss of rights by reason that the action is barred by the prescription as is the case in the current legislation. Therefore, if Thailand becomes a State Party to the Rotterdam Rules, Thailand will perceivably be more benefited by the ensuing effects.

There exists a view that becoming a State party to the Rotterdam Rules will simply result in adverse effects in terms of emerging complications plaguing working mechanisms of the legislation or draft legislation in Thailand, namely, the *Carriage of Goods by Sea Act*, B. E. 2534 (1991), the *Multimodal Transport Act*, *B. E.* 2548 (2005), the *Carriage of Goods by Sea Bill* (No. ...), B. E. ... and the *Civil Liability of Port Operators in International Transport Bill*, *B. E.* ... Those addressing such a view cast doubt as to the desirability of Thailand becoming a State Party to the Rotterdam Rules. But, it can be remonstrated that ensuing complications are indeed normal. Indeed, even at time when Thailand has not become a State Party to the Rotterdam Rules, certain difficulties have already arisen, in litigation ex casu, in relation to the application of the *Carriage of Goods by Sea Act*, B. E. 2534 (1991) and the *Multimodal Transport Act*, B. E. 2548. Those involved in the law need to, and indeed can do so, study and properly apply the law rather than form a mindset objecting the decision to become a State Party to the Rotterdam Rules on account of such complications arising from. Such opposing conclusion is too little justifiable and simplistic, having regard to the benefits flowing from becoming a State Party to the Rotterdam Rules as earlier discussed.

It is since 1991 that Thailand has promulgated sui generis legislation on carriage of goods by sea. Yet, Thailand has never become a State Party to any international convention related to international carriage of goods, be it the Hague Rules 1924/Hague-Visby Rules or the Hamburg Rules, simply because Thailand has chosen to frame such specific law on carriage of goods by sea in a manner balancing interests of shippers, consignees and carriers. Although such perception might, in principle, appear well suited to Thailand at that time, the transfer of principles embodied in the Hague Rules 1924 and Hague-Visby Rules or the Hamburg Rules into the enacted law was carried out in an incomplete manner, thereby providing one of the reasons for amending the *Carriage of Goods by Sea Act*, B. E. 2534 (1991), as envisioned in the *Carriage of Goods by Sea Bill* (No. ...), B. E. ... To date, no one has witnessed Thailand's positive position towards becoming a State Party to the Hague Rules 1924/Hague-Visby Rules or the Hamburg Rules although the Hamburg Rules, subsequent to the entry into force of the *Carriage of Goods by Sea Act*, B. E. 2534 (1991), has come into force with over 30 State Parties. As earlier explained, Thailand has always contended that at the time of drafting the *Carriage of Goods by Sea Act*, B. E. 2534 (1991), the Hamburg Rules, albeit well suited to the interests of Thailand, had not yet come into force, and framing legal principles along the line of the Hamburg Rules would simply result in our legislation on carriage of goods by sea being dissimilar to parallel laws of our trading countries from which ships would be used for carriage of goods to and from Thailand. However, given that the Hamburg Rules has now come into force, the contention pursued by Thailand above seems to have lost its merit. Yet, no action has been taken for desirable amendment of the law on carriage of goods by sea of Thailand along the line of the Hamburg Rules. Also, no decision has been made for becoming a State Party to these rules.

Thailand has indeed dedicated attention to the Rotterdam Rules since its early conception. At the stage of its drafting by the UNCITRAL, of which Thailand is a member, the Ministry of Foreign Affairs requested opinions from state agencies concerned, private bodies and those with proper knowledge of the Rotterdam Rules for the purpose of setting Thailand's position throughout the meetings held twice a year in New York and Vienna, for considering the draft. Those well-equipped with relevant knowledge in this matter attended some of these meetings as delegates from

Thailand. In effect, the Transport and Maritime Law Institute (of the Faculty of Law, Thammasat University) consistently organized seminars for brainstorming on and disseminating key principles of the draft convention with a view to educating the Thai public on this matter and suggesting to the Ministry of Foreign Affairs positions to be pursued by Thailand towards the draft rules.

Given that the Rotterdam Rules emerge as the world's third convention on carriage of goods by sea and as a product of blending, whether deliberately or inadvertently, due interests of shippers, consignees and carriers [indeed, an approach pursued at the time of drafting our *Carriage of Goods by Sea Act*, B. E. 2534 (1991)], any decision by Thailand to become a State Party to the Hague Rules 1924 and the Hague-Visby Rules or the Hamburg Rules will simply appear outmoded and no longer appropriate. It is thus more apposite to consider whether to become a State Party to the Rotterdam Rules. In this connection, it is hereby submitted that, for the reasons herebelow brought out, the time is ripe to Thailand to become a State Party to the Rotterdam Rules although these rules await their entry into force upon ratification by 20 Signatory States.

a) The Rotterdam Rules contains principles more beneficial to shippers and consignees as well as the nation as a whole than the principles encapsulated in the *Carriage of Goods by Sea Act*, B. E. 2534 (1991) and the *Carriage of Goods by Sea Bill* (No. ...), B. E. ..., in that the Rotterdam Rules provides fewer defenses or limitations of liability, higher amount of compensation and a longer period for lawsuit.

b) The Rotterdam Rules introduces several new principles not found in Thai law on carriage of goods by sea, including the principles concerning performing parties, maritime performing parties, a "volume contract" (i. e. a contract of carriage that provides the carriage of a specified quantity of goods in a series of shipments during an agreed period of time), documentary shippers, the right of control, controlling parties, and in particular, the principles dedicated to the use of electronic transport records in response to the world's new technological advancements in marine transport.

c) The Rotterdam Rules yields more benefits to Thailand than those stemming from the application of the legislation on international carriage of goods by sea currently in force as well as the *Carriage of Goods by Sea Bill* (No. ...), B. E. ... and provides solutions to several difficulties under the *Carriage of Goods by Sea Act*, B. E. 2534 (1991), including the difficulty in connection with institution of a lawsuit in tort, the limitation period, a lawsuit against agents or employees of the carrier, low amount of compensation, a charter party and the identification of the carrier.

d) A decision to become a State Party to the Rotterdam Rules will bring Thai legal principles applicable to international carriage of goods by sea in harmony with internationally recognized rules and also in line with laws of other jurisdictions, given that other countries elect to adopt the principles embodied in only one particular convention on carriage of goods by sea rather than blending principles contained in two conventions as witnessed in Thailand.

e) By becoming a State Party to the Rotterdam Rules, Thailand will be listed as such, with the result therefore that Thailand will be recognized by other countries as having legal principles compatible with internationally re cognized rules, thereby generating good national reputation and image in an international arena in place of our negative image in the past.

A related question lies in the manner in which new legislation is to be drafted in the implementation of the Rotterdam Rules. In this regard, different modes are available. For instance, the text of the Rotterdam Rules should, in the interest of expediency, be translated into the Thai language so as to form the Thai text strictly corresponding to the original text of the rules rather than couching the Thai text in a manner roughly reflecting the concepts enshrined in the Rotterdam Rules. Such latter manner appears to be time-consuming and runs the risk of having the contents departing from the intention or spirit of the rules in respective matters and possibly with certain missing points. Alternatively, the draft legislation intended to be enacted may contain merely short sections or articles with a reference that the text of the Rotterdam Rules annexed to the legislation shall be an integral part as well—indeed an approach pursued by certain countries including the United Kingdom. This approach is meritorious in terms of ex- pediency but may produce shortcomings not merely in terms of difficulty encountered in the interpretation of the English text but also in terms of resistance by Parliament as well as the Office of the Council of State. It is thus recommended that, as practical solution, enactment with merely short sections and with an annex of the text of the Rotterdam Rules should be preferable provided that experts in the translation as well as those concerned should be hired for this legislative task. The budget required for this important task does not seem to be excessive when compared with expenses incurred in payment of meeting allowances, meals and refreshments, phone bills and travel allowances.

泰国税制研究

Sumet Sirikunchoat[*]
闫　晴　译

摘要　泰国税制体系是泰国税制发展水平的重要体现,其为泰国税收具体立法、泰国税收征管、泰国税收司法建设均提供了明确指向,且一国税制体系的完善程度亦在很大程度上影响了一国经济的健康快速发展水平。本文在简要说明泰国税制功能、泰国中央税与其他税区别的前提下具体分析《税收法典》中涉及的个人所得税、企业所得税、增值税、营业税、印花税的纳税人、征税对象、税基、税率、纳税期限、纳税地点、豁免条件等,进而提出泰国税制建设存在问题需多方面优化。

关键词　税制;中央税;泰国税制

一、引言

一般而言,税收法律、税收政策与税收征管是任何税制的重要组成部分。泰国的税制与诸多国家相似,不仅致力于提高税收,也通过税收促进经济增长、控制消耗、有效配置资源、维护经济稳定、进行收入再分配。地方政府每年征收的税额约为 GDP 的 2％～3％,而中央政府每年征收税额约为 GDP 的 20％。中央税分为直接税形式与间接税形式,虽然间接税额与直接税额的比例为 3∶2,但泰国政府从间接税中获取更多的共享税额。

本文讨论泰国税收体系,尤其是由税务部门执行的《税收法典》的结构。泰国税务部门承担着税务管理的职责,每年征收中央全部税额的 60％。税收在筹集国家收入方面发挥重要作用,但除了中央税,其他机关亦可征收其他税赋。例如,海关征收关税,地方政府征收地方税。对于《税收法典》未涉及的其他税种,本文不予讨论。

---

*　Professor of Tax Law at the Faculty of Law, Thammasat University.

二、基于《税收法典》的税制概述

《税收法典》规定了多种税种,包括所得税、增值税、营业税、印花税。所得税属于直接税,分为个人所得税与企业所得税。而其他税种则是建立在消费基础上的间接税。所得税的征收基于收入,法律则尽量整合上述税种避免双重征税。所得税税基为纳税期间内的纯收入或纯利润,纳税人只有在年末可以精确计算其收入总额进行纳税申报,因此,所得税转嫁税负是非常困难的。而增值税、消费税、印花税属于间接消费税,经营者只是为享受商品或服务的消费者进行税务代理,并向政府缴税。通常,税基为消费的商品和服务的价值,因此,更容易将税负转嫁给消费者。

(一)个人所得税

个人所得税是一种重要的直接税,其作用在于为公共支出筹集税款和在纳税人收入与财富方面进行再分配。个人所得税纳税人分为自然人、普通合伙、非法人组织与不可分割遗产四类,需要依据收入在纳税年度次年 3 月最后一天之内计算应纳税款,进行纳税申报并缴纳税。纳税人收入均属应纳税款,但对于国外所得,只有纳税人于纳税年度内在泰国连续或累计居住满 180 日且该国外所得流入泰国境内才具有可税性。泰国个人所得税法律规定 8 种可税收入与 4 种扣除项目,其中特定津贴①允许扣除。泰国个人所得税实行累

---

① 特定津贴包括个人津贴、配偶津贴、抚育津贴、赡养津贴、人寿保险费、纳税人或其配偶的社会保险与慈善捐款。

进税率,纳税人需全额缴纳税款①。

泰国法律亦明确了个人所得税的特殊规定。泰国法律中存在阻止对个人收入与企业收入造成经济双重征税的股息税收抵免的规定,因此,在计算应纳税额时,纳税人可通过信用卡信息计算其已缴股息,并在最终纳税额中扣除;对于法律特殊规定的情况,纳税人收入的支付人可到税务机关进行源泉扣除,已扣除税款可在纳税人最终税额中扣除;在纳税年度内前六个月获得特定收入②的纳税人也需上交半年报告并于该纳税年度9月最后一天内向税务机关缴纳税款;自2012年开始实行的夫妻收入税的新修正案始,已婚夫妻可自行选择纳税申报方式③。

---

① 目前实现的个人所得税2013年、2014年纳税年度税率如下:

可税收入	税率(%)
(1)0～150000	5(豁免)
(2)150000～300000	5
(3)300000～500000	10
(4)500000～750000	15
(5)750000～1000000	20
(6)1000000～2000000	25
(7)2000400～4000000	30
(8)4000000以上	35

此外,依据《税收法典》第40条,收入种类属于(2)～(8)且每年收入达60000泰铢,纳税人必须以可得收入乘以0.5%计算最低税额,并与通过累进税率计算的应纳税额相比较。纳税人更易选择缴纳较高的税额。然而,如果最低税额不足5000泰铢则可豁免。

② 此处的特定收入包括租金、职业收入与商业收入。

③ 已婚夫妻纳税申报方式包括:(1)夫妻双方分开进行纳税申报;(2)夫妻共同进行纳税申报,夫妻收入合并计算并以丈夫名义进行纳税申报;(3)夫妻共同进行纳税申报,夫妻收入合并计算并以妻子名义进行纳税申报;(4)夫妻共同进行纳税申报,但丈夫因劳务雇佣获取的收入单独列出;(5)夫妻共同进行纳税申报,但妻子因劳务雇佣获取的收入单独列出。

(二)企业所得税

企业所得税是一种基于公司或合伙①而征收的直接税。一般而言,个人所得与企业所得的概念是相似的,但是对于收入来源、豁免与税收计算的规定是非常不同的。此外,在某些情况写关于企业净利润计算的规定也可直接应用于个人所得税的计算,如对日常必需花费扣除方式的规定。

在泰国从事商业活动的泰国或他国的公司或合伙被要求在距会计期间期满150天内进行纳税申报,且应纳税额与纳税申报一起上交。企业或合伙有义务明确其纯利润与应纳税额,并于会计年度上半年结束后的2个月内缴纳一半税款,预付税可抵免年终应纳税额。至于向不在泰国进行商业活动的公司或合伙支出的费用,该合法公司或合伙需通过支付者在付费时扣留的方式缴纳正常税费,支付者必须在支付次月的7日内向税务部门提交纳税申报并缴纳税款。在计算在泰国从事商业活动的公司或合伙的 CIT 时,应在权责发生基础上计算该公司或合伙的纯利润。公司或企业应将会计年度内来源于商业活动的所有收入考虑在内,并将与《税收法典》规定条件相符合的花费扣除。过去五年至目前会计年度的纯损失也允许作为一个扣除项目。

依据 2013 年、2014 年规定,泰国企业所得税税率为 20%,然而税率依据

---

① 文中"公司或合伙"可分为:

(1)依泰国法律注册成立的公司或合伙。

(2)依他国法律注册成立的公司或合伙,可能为:(a)依他国法律注册成立的公司或合伙在泰国进行商业活动;(b)依他国法律注册成立的公司或合伙在包括泰国在内的国家进行商业活动;(c)在货运或客运领域依他国法律成立并在包括泰国在内的国家进行商业活动;(d)依他国法律注册成立的公司或合伙,为在泰国进行商业活动设置一名雇工、一个代理或一个中间人并最终于泰国取得收入或利润;(e)依他国法律成立的公司或合伙,虽不在泰国进行商业活动但依据税收法典 40 条(2)～(6)规定存在来源于泰国的收入。

该条款也经再三扩展包含:

(c)由外国政府、外国政府组织或任何法人依他国法律注册成立以商业或盈利方式运作的商事主体;

(d)一方面为在公司或合伙间以商业或盈利方式运作合资企业,另一方面可能为公司、自然人、普通合伙等;

(e)基金会或协会从事创收业务,但不包括符合《税收法典》第 47 条 7b 规定的那些基金会或协会。

纳税人的种类有所不同①。向公司支付的特定种类的收入需在源头上扣留税款,扣留税款的税率取决于收入类型与接受者的情况。收入支付者需要在支出次月的 7 日内向区税务机关进行纳税申报并缴纳扣留税款,扣留税款可在该纳税人的应纳税额中抵免。

(三)增值税

增值税于 1992 年取代商业税开始实施。增值税是一种以生产、分配、服务等各阶段的价值增加额为计税依据的间接税。任何在泰国经常提供商品或服务的个人或组织都需缴纳增值税。如果服务在泰国提供而无论在哪使用或服务在泰国使用而无论在哪提供,服务都视为在泰国提供。货物进口时由海关征收增值税。某些商品免征增值税,而以特定营业税替代。特定的免税情形包括:年度成交量不足 18 万泰铢的小企业家;进口并销售未加工的农产品或相关产品;进口并销售报纸、杂志或教材等。

一般而言,增值税的税基为从商品或服务的提供而得到或可得的总价值。税基也包括与供货有关的任何增长的货物税。目前增值税的税率为 7%,而出口商品等特种活动的增值税税率可为 0%。增值税登记的个人或团体每次交易都需要保留发票,并在发票上注明销售商品或提供服务的价值与增值税

---

① 纳税人与计税基数	税率(%)
小型或中型合法企业或合伙	
纯利润不足 100000 泰铢	15
纯利润超过 100000 泰铢	
(2013 年、2014 会计年度内)	20
银行从世界银行机构获取的纯利润	10
从事全球运输的外国合法公司或合伙总收入	3
不在泰国从事商业活动但存在来源于泰国的特殊种类收入的	
外国合法公司或合伙股息	
除股息外其他种类的收入	15
外国公司或合伙在泰国外处置利润处置数额	10
有利润的社团或基金会总收入	2 或 10

税额。增值税用纳税额为销项税额与进项税额的差值①。在增值税中，特定进项税是不能抵免的，如与娱乐开支有关的进项税。

任何有增值税义务的个人或实体在开业之前或其营业额超过小企业标准30天内必须进行增值税登记的申请。注册申请地应为其营业地属于其管辖领域的地方税务局。如果纳税人有几个地方的企业或分支机构，那么其总部所在地视为其营业地。

增值税的纳税期限是1个月，因此增值税退税必须按月申请。如果有增值税退税和纳税，必须于次月的15日前提交区税务分局办公室。如果纳税人有多个经营场所，每个营业点必须分开申报付款，除非有税务局局长的批准。

(四)营业税

营业税是另一种自1992年实施的取代商业税的间接消费税，不征增值税

---

① "销项税额"意味着登记人向产品或服务的提供者收集或有义务收集增值税发票。"进项税额"意味着登记人要向其他登记人转交增值税发票。如果进项税额超过销项税额，纳税人可以提出退税的要求，可以在随后几个月以现金或税收抵免的形式使用。因此，如果零税率，纳税人将享受增值税退税。对于未使用的进项税，它可以在未来6个月内抵免销项税。

的特定企业需缴纳营业税①。任何应缴纳营业税的运营商都需要在开业日期30日内到当地税务局进行企业税务登记。如纳税人有几个商业活动点或分支机构,登记申请须提交商业总部地点所属的当地税务局。营业税按月缴纳,无论是否赢利,营业税按月提交。营业税必须于次月15日前向当地税务局申报并缴税。如果纳税人有多个经营场所,每个营业点必须分开申报并纳税,除非有特别批准。

---

① 以下在泰国进行的商业活动需缴纳营业税:(1)依据商业银行治理法规或任何其他特别法进行的银行活动;(2)依据商业治理类法规进行的金融活动、证券业务和信用管理业务;(3)依据人寿保险治理法规进行的人寿保险活动;(4)依据典当类法规进行的典当活动;(5)类似于商业银行的交易活动,比如发放贷款、提供担保、货币交换、发行债券、购买或销售票据、国外资金转移;(6)为追求利润以商业模式销售不动产的行为,但程序和条件需由法令规定;(7)依据泰国规制证券交易行为的法律在证券交易所出售证券的行为;(8)由法令规定的其他业务,如卖空证券许可、保理业务。

以下企业免征营业税:(1)泰国银行、政府储蓄银行、房屋银行、农业银行、农业合作组织的业务;(2)泰国金融公司的商业活动;(3)在提供给其成员或其他储蓄合作人的贷款情形下储蓄合作社的商业活动;(4)依据公积金治理法律从事公积金业务活动;(5)全国房管局的业务活动,仅限不动产的出售或出租;(6)地方政府机构的典当业务活动;(7)由法律规定的其他活动。

营业税的计税依据应为下列由负有纳税义务的个人从事商业活动已获得或可获得的全部收入:

特定商业活动与计税依据	税率(%)
银行、金融、证券与信贷业务活动,类似商业银行活动的交易活动。利润、折扣、服务费、其他费用与外汇利润	3.0
人寿保险 利润、服务费与其他费用	2.5
典当业务 利息、费用、销售没收货物的报酬	2.5
为利润以商业模式销售不动产 总收入	3.0
在证券交易所出售证券 总收入	0.1(可豁免)

备注:地方税在营业税最高税率上加10%。

(五)印花税

印花税是一种特定税收,只有属于《税收法典》第 6 章印花税目录规定的28 种情形之一时才需缴纳印花税。除非属于上述情况,否则不会发生印花税,如匿名转移合同或租赁股份而没有执行任何文件将不会发生印花税。印花税需在提前支付或当时支付,除非存在税收豁免。为了追回拖欠税款,局长有权下令没收或查封,由责任人在法院出具传票或命令拍卖前缴纳或解缴。此外,还有两种间接作用,即履行税款后具有民事案件的证据功能与付清税款后官方予以签字、允许执行或进行记录。

三、小结

泰国税制与大多数发展中国家的税制存在相似之处,且泰国在税收收入与支出方面基本保持平衡。由于政治上的限制、意识的缺乏与有经验人员的缺乏,泰国税法存在一定漏洞。这些漏洞使避税成为可能,泰国附加税问题出现与税法过时、税法关系复杂、税法不成体系有关,这造成了纳税人的困惑并导致违规。这些问题的解决需要废除模棱两可的条款,明确反避税规则,改变不公正的实体法规定,并在税收政策制定程序、解决税务争议与税收管理效率方面进行提高。泰国在通过改革建立更好的税制体系中还有诸多工作要做。

Taxation System in Thailand

Sumet Sirikunchoat[*]

Introduction

In general, tax policy, tax law, and tax administration are the key components of any tax system. Thailand maintains a tax policy similar to many other countries. Its tax policy aims not only to raise revenues, but also to foster social unity by enhancing economic growth, controlling consumption, allocating resources efficiently, fostering economic stability, and redistributing income.

The amount of tax levied yearly by the central government of Thailand is nearly 20% of its GDP value as compared with the 2% ~ 3% of GDP value imposed by the local government. Of the direct and indirect forms of central tax, Thailand gains its greatest share of tax revenues from indirect taxes. The ratio between the amounts of indirect tax to direct tax is 3 : 2[①].

This article discusses the taxation system of Thailand, and in particular, the substantive structure of the *Revenue Code* as administered by the Revenue Department of Thailand. This department bears responsibility and accountability for tax administration, and its efforts generate nearly

---

* Professor of Tax Law at the Faculty of Law, Thammasat University.

① (Bureau of the Budget, Ministry of Finance) (2014 Summary of Yearly Budget), retrievable from: http://www. bb. go. th/budget _ book/e-Book2557/FILEROOM/% 202557%20. PDF, on October. 1, 2014.

60% of all central tax revenues levied within a given year. Taxes play a significant role in raising revenues for public expenditures. In addition to the central tax revenues, a variety of taxes may be levied and controlled by different authorities. For instance, the controlling authority for excise taxes is the Excise Department, for custom duties is the Customs Department, and for local taxes is the local administrative governments. Other taxes that are not included in the *Revenue Code* will not be discussed here.

Overview of taxation according to the *Revenue Code* [1]

The *Revenue Code* provides a variety of taxes that include the income tax, value-added tax, specific business tax, and stamp duty. Income tax is a kind of direct tax that is subdivided into personal income tax and corporate income tax. The remaining taxes are classified as indirect taxes based on consumption. The Revenue Department of the Ministry of Finance supervises and controls all of these taxes.

Income taxes are based on the direction of the flow of income, where personal income taxes go to personal income and corporate income taxes pass to corporate income. Existing law integrates these taxes as much as possible to avoid the problem of economic double taxation. The tax base represents the income flow during the calendar year or 12 month accounting period. In general, the tax base is the net income or net profit accrued during these periods. Thus, if the taxpayer does not derive or realize an income during the tax year or accounting period, then no income tax liability is incurred. Because the amount of tax liability cannot be calculated exactly at any given moment of deriving or realizing income, unless it reaches the end of the year, when it is the time to decide the final tax liability and file a tax return. Thus, it is difficult to shift income tax burdens, the tax burden falls on the taxpayer.

---

[1] The *Revenue Code* and useful information are downloadable from: http://www. rd. go. th.

Unlike the income tax, the value-added tax, specific business tax, and stamp duty are classified as indirect consumption taxes. Taxpayers become tax agents who collect taxes from consumers of general goods and services. Collections are then transferred to the government. Normally, the tax base consists of the value of goods and services consumed. In this case, it may be easier to shift the tax burden to the consumer, because taxes are easily calculated and the amount of tax liability is known precisely prior to transactions.

Personal income tax

Personal income tax according to the *Revenue Code* is an important direct tax. Its role is not only to generate large revenue for public expenditures, but also an efficient fiscal measure in redistribution of income and wealth among taxpayers.

Personal income taxpayers can be divided into four categories, i. e. individual, an ordinary partnership, a non-juristic body of person and an undivided estate. Normally, income taxpayers have to compute their tax liability, file tax return and pay tax, depending on the income derived in each calendar year, within the last day of March following the taxable year. Such income, no matter in what type or form it appears, unless exempt by law, will be fallen within the scope of and liable for personal income tax. However, income from foreign sources shall be liable only if the taxpayer is residing in Thailand for a period or periods aggregating up to 180 days in relevant tax (calendar) year and only if such portion of foreign income is brought into Thailand in such period.

Assessable income is divided into 8 categories and 4 different ways of deduction may be applied. Then certain allowances (e. g. personal allowance, spouse allowance, child allowance, parents allowance, life insurance premium, social insurance contributions paid by taxpayer or spouse, charitable contributions) are allowed to be deducted in the calculation of the taxable income. Finally, progressive tax rates will be applied to taxable income and result in the tax amount having to be paid. The reduced rates to be implemented currently for the 2013 and 2014 tax years are as follows:

Taxable Income(baht)	Tax Rate(%)
(1)Over 0 but not over 150,000	5(Exempt)
(2)Over 150,000 but not over 300,000	5
(3)Over 300,000 but not over 500,000	10
(4)Over 500,000 but not over 750,000	15
(5)Over 750,000 but not over 1,000,000	20
(6)Over 1,000,000 but not over 2,000,000	25
(7)Over 2,000,000 but not over 4,000,000	30
(8)Over 4,000,000	35

In the case where income categories(2)—(8), according to Section 40 of the *Revenue Code*, amounts up to 60,000 baht per year, taxpayer has to calculate the minimum tax amount by multiplying 0.5% to such assessable income and compare with the tax amount calculated by progressive tax rates. The taxpayer is liable to the tax amount whichever is greater. However, the minimum tax amount will be exempt if it is not over 5,000 baht.

As there is the provision of dividend tax credit, aimed at preventing economic double taxation between personal and corporate income tax, therefore in computing assessable income, the taxpayer shall gross up his dividends by the amount of the tax credit received and the amount of tax credit is creditable against his final tax liability.

There are also certain types of income(e. g. interest income, dividend, income from sales of immovable property acquired by bequest or by way of gift)that the taxpayers are able to calculate tax amount separately from global income by selectively excluding such incomes with other types of income in computing the tax amount liable.

For certain cases specified by law, the payers of assessable income has the duty to withhold tax at source and remit such amount to the Revenue Department, the tax withheld shall then be credited against final tax liability of the taxpayer. Payers who do not conform to the law shall be sanctioned.

The taxpayer who derives certain types of income (e. g. rental, profession income, business income)during the first six months of the tax year is also required to file half-yearly return and make a payment to the

Revenue Department within the last day of September of that taxable year. Any withholding tax or half-yearly tax which has been paid to the Revenue Department shall be treated as a credit against the tax liability at the end of the year.

As to the new amendment of the income tax provisions on husband and wife since 2012, married couples now have 5 options in filing (either separately or jointly) their tax returns:

1) Each spouse files his/her tax return separately;

2) The couple files their return jointly, combining the wife's income with the husband's income and filing a return by the husband's name;

3) The couple files their return jointly, combining the husband's income with the wife's income and filing a return by the wife's name;

4) The couple files their return jointly, but the husband files his income derived by virtue of hire of service separately;

5) The couple files their return jointly, but the wife files her income derived by virtue of hire of service separately.

Corporate income tax

Corporate income tax(CIT)is a kind of direct tax levied on income of a juristic company and partnership while personal income tax is levied on income of a person. The term "a juristic company or partnership" is defined as:(1)a juristic company or partnership incorporated under Thai law, or(2)a juristic company or partnership incorporated under foreign law, it maybe:(a)a juristic company or partnership incorporated under foreign laws and carrying on business in Thailand, or(b)a juristic company or partnership incorporated under foreign laws and carrying on business in other places including Thailand, or(c)a juristic company or partnership incorporated under foreign laws and carrying on business in other places including Thailand, in case of carriage of goods or carriage of passengers, or(d)a company or juristic partnership incorporated under foreign laws which has an employee, an agent or a go-between for carrying on business in Thailand and as a result receives income or profits in Thailand, or(e)a company or juristic partnership incorporated under foreign laws and not carrying on business in Thailand but receiving assessable income under Section 40(2)～(6)which is paid from or in Thailand. The term is also extended repeatedly to include: (3)a business operating in a commercial or profitable manner by a foreign government, organization of a foreign government or any other juristic person established under a foreign law,(4)a joint venture, operating in a commercial or profitable manner, between a juristic company or partnership on the one hand and companies, juristic partnerships, individuals, non-juristic body of persons, ordinary partnerships on the other hand,(5)a foundation or association carrying on revenue generating business, but does not include the foundation or association as prescribed by the Minister in accordance with Section 47(7)(b)under *Revenue Code*.

In general, the concept of personal income and corporate income is similar but the rules related to income source, exemption and tax computing are quite different. Moreover, certain rules related to computing of the corporation's net profit are also applied to the computing of personal taxable income in some cases, i. e. the rule on method of deducting the ordinary and necessary expenses.

Thai and foreign juristic company or partnership carrying on business in Thailand are required to file their tax returns within 150 days from the closing date of their accounting periods. Tax payment shall be submitted together with the tax returns. Any juristic company or partnership disposing funds representing profits out of Thailand is also required to pay tax on the sum so disposed within seven days of the following month in which the disposal is made[①].

In addition to the annual(final)tax payment, any juristic company or partnership subject to CIT on net profits is also required to make tax prepayment. A juristic company or partnership is obliged to estimate its

---

① According to Section 70 *bis*. , it is required to pay tax within seven days from the date of disposal, however this date has been extended by the Ministerial Notification, dated Jul. 24, 2001.

annual net profit as well as its tax liability and pay half of the estimated tax amount within two months after the end of the first six months of its accounting period. The prepaid tax is creditable against its annual tax liability.

As regards to income paid to foreign juristic company or partnership not carrying on business in Thailand, the foreign juristic company or partnership is subject to tax at a flat rate in which the payer shall withhold tax at source at the time of payment. The payer must file the return and make the payment to the Revenue Department within seven days of the following month in which the payment is made.

In computing CIT of a juristic company or partnership carrying on business in Thailand, it is calculated from the juristic company or partnership's net profit on the accrual basis. A juristic company or partnership shall take into account all income arising from or in consequence of the business carried on in an accounting period and deducting them from all expenses in accordance with the condition prescribed by the *Revenue Code*. Net losses carried forward from the last five years up to the present accounting period are also allowed as a deductible expense. As for dividend income, one-half of the dividends received by Thai companies from any other Thai companies may be excluded from the taxable income. However, the full amount may be excluded from taxable income if the recipient is either a registered company in the Stock Exchange of Thailand or any limited company that owns at least 25% of the distributing company's capital interest, provided that the distributing company does not hold any share in the recipient company directly or indirectly. The exclusion of dividends is applied only if the shares are acquired not less than three months before obtaining the dividends and are not transferred within three months after obtaining the dividends.

The corporate income tax rate in Thailand is 20% on net profit (accounting periods 2013—2014). However, the rates vary depending on types of taxpayers.

Taxpayer and Tax Base	Rate(%)
1. Small or medium juristic company or partnership[①]	
—Net profit not over 1 million baht	15
—Net profit over 1 million baht	20
(accounting periods from 2013-2014[②])	
2. Bank deriving profits from International Banking Facilities(IBF)	
—Net Profit	10
3. Foreign juristic company or partnership engaging in international transportation	
—Gross receipts	3
4. Foreign juristic company or partnership not carrying on business in Thailand but receiving specific types of income from or in Thailand	
—Dividends	10
—Other specific types of income apart from dividends	15
5. Foreign juristic company or partnership disposing profit out of Thailand	
—Amount disposed	10
6. Profitable associations or foundations	
—Gross receipts	2 or 10

Certain types of income paid to companies are subject to withholding tax at source. The withholding tax rates depend on the types of income and the tax status of the recipient. The payer of income is required to file the return and submit the amount of tax withheld to the District Revenue Offices within seven days of the following month in which the payment is made. The tax withheld will be credited against final tax liability of the tax payer.

As to double taxation treaties, Thailand has concluded 58 double tax treaties (as to November, 2014), i. e. Armenia, Australia, Austria, Bangladesh, Bahrain, Belalus, Belgium, Bulgaria, Burma, Canada, Chile, China P. R., Cyprus, Czech Republic, Denmark, Estonia, Finland, France,

---

① A small juristic company or partnership is referred to as any juristic company or partnership with paid-up capital less than 5 million baht at the end of each accounting period and the assessable income in such accounting period is not over 30 million baht.

② Net profit not over 300,000 baht in the accounting period is also exempt. Moreover as to the currentnews from the Cabinet on Nov. 24, 2014, a reduced tax rate of 15% will be applied for up to 3 million baht of net profit in the accounting periods from 2015.

Germany, Hong Kong(China), Hungary, India, Indonesia, Israel, Italy, Japan, Korea, Kuwait, Laos, Luxembourg, Malaysia, Mauritius, Nepal, the Netherlands, New Zealand, Norway, Oman, Pakistan, the Philippines, Poland, Romania, Russia, Seychelles, Singapore, Slovenia, South Africa, Spain, Srilanka, Sweden, Switzerland, Taiwan(China), Turkey, Vietnam, Ukraine, United Arab Emirates, United Kingdom of Great Britain and Northern Ireland, United States of America and Uzbekistan.

Value-Added tax

Value-Added tax(VAT) has been implemented in Thailand since 1992 replacing the out-of-date business tax (BT). VAT is kind of indirect consumption tax imposed on the value added of each stage of production, distribution and service.

Any person or entity who regularly supplies goods or provides services in Thailand is subject to VAT. Service is deemed to be provided in Thailand if the service is performed in Thailand regardless of where it is utilized or if it is utilized in Thailand regardless of where it is performed.

An importer is also subject to VAT in Thailand no matter he is a registered person or not. VAT will be collected by the Customs Department at the time goods are imported. Certain businesses are excluded from VAT and will instead be subjected to specific business tax(SBT). Under VAT, taxable goods mean all types of property, tangible or intangible, whether they are available for sales, for own use, or for any other purposes. It also includes any types of articles imported into Thailand. Services refer to any activities conducted for the benefits of a person or an entity, which are not the supply in terms of goods. Certain basic exemptions include: small entrepreneur whose annual turnover is not over 1.8 million baht; sales and import of unprocessed agricultural products and related goods such as fertilizers, animal feeds, pesticides, etc. ; sales and import of newspapers, magazines, and textbooks; certain basic services such as domestic transportation and international transportation by way of land, healthcare services and clinics, educational services provided educational institutions, professional services, i. e. medical, auditing, lawyer services in court and other similar professional services that have laws regulating such professions, cultural services such as amateur sports, services of libraries, museums and zoos, services in the nature of employment of labor, research and technical services and services of public entertainers, other services such as religious and charitable services, services of government agencies and local authorities.

In general, the tax base of VAT is the total value received or receivable from the supply of goods or services. Value means money, property, consideration, service fees, or any other benefits which is ascertainable in terms of money. Tax base will also include any excise tax arising in connection with such supply. However, tax base is exclusive of the value-added tax itself and does not include trade discounts or allowances, penalties and certain subsidies.

General rate of VAT currently is 7 percent. Certain activities are liable to VAT at the rate of zero percent. Those activities include: export of goods; services rendered in Thailand and utilized outside Thailand in accordance with the rule, procedure and condition prescribed by the Director-General; aircraft or sea-vessels engaging in international transportation; supply of goods and services to government agencies or state-owned enterprises under foreign-aid program; supply of goods and services to the United Nations and its agencies as well as embassies, consulate-general and consulates; supply of goods and services between bonded warehouses or between enterprises located in EPZs.

VAT registered person or entity is required to issue tax invoices every time the transactions are made showing details of nature and value of goods sold or services provided and also amount of VAT due. Tax invoice is used as an important tool and as an evidence for claiming input tax credit.

VAT liability = Output Tax-Input Tax

"Output Tax" means VAT which a registrant collects or is liable to collect from a purchaser of goods or a recipient of services.

"Input Tax" means VAT which a registrant is called upon to pay to other registrant. The term also includes VAT paid by a registrant at the time of import.

In each month, if input tax exceeds output tax, the taxpayer can claim for the refund, either in form of cash or tax credit to be used in the following months. Therefore, in case of zero-rated, the taxpayer will be entitled to VAT refund. As for unused input tax, it may be creditable against output tax within the next six months. However, the refund can only be claimed within three years from the expiry time for filing tax return or from the date of paying tax in some cases.

Certain input taxes are not creditable under VAT, e. g., input tax related to entertaining expenses. However, those non-creditable input taxes can instead be used as deductible expenses under corporate income tax.

Any person or entity liable to VAT must file an application for VAT registration before the date of commencing business or within 30 days after its tax base (turnover) exceeds that of small business threshold. The registration application shall be filed at the local Revenue Office in whose jurisdiction a place of business is located. Should the taxpayer have several places of businesses or branches, the place of business is the place where the taxpayer's head office is located.

VAT taxable period is a calendar month. VAT return therefore must be filed on a monthly basis. VAT return together with tax payment, if any, must be submitted to Area Revenue Branch Office within 15 days of the following month. If taxpayer has more than one place of business, each place of business must file the return and make a payment separately unless there is an approval from the Director-General of the Revenue Department. Services utilized in Thailand supplied by service providers in other countries are also subject to VAT in Thailand. In such cases, the service recipient in Thailand is obliged to file VAT return and pay tax, if any, on behalf of the service providers.

In the case where supply of goods or services is also subject to excise tax, VAT returns and tax payment, if any, shall be filed and paid to the Excise Department within 15 days of the following month. In cases of imported goods, VAT returns and tax payment shall be filed and paid to the Customs Department at the point of import.

Specific business tax

Specific business tax(SBT)is another kind of indirect consumption tax implemented in 1992 replacing business tax. Certain businesses that are excluded from VAT will instead be subject to SBT.

The following businesses carried on in Thailand are subject to SBT:

(1)Banking under the law governing commercial banking or any other specific law;

(2) Undertaking of finance business, securities business and credit foncier business under the law governing such businesses;

(3)Life insurance under the law governing life insurance;

(4)Pawn broking under the law governing pawnshops;

(5)Business with regular transactions similar to commercial banking, such as extending loans, furnishing guarantees, exchange of currencies, issuance, purchase or sale of negotiable instrument or transfer of money abroad by any means;

(6)Sale of immovable properties in a commercial manner or for profit, irrespective of the manner in which such property is acquired, only in accordance with the rules, procedures and conditions prescribed by a royal decree;

(7) Sale of securities in a stock exchange under the law governing securities exchange of Thailand;

(8)Any other businesses as specified by a royal decree, e. g. , licensed short sale of securities, factoring business.

Certain businesses are exempted from SBT such as:

(1)Business of the Bank of Thailand, the Government Savings Bank, the Government Housing Bank, and the Bank for Agriculture and Agricultural Cooperatives;

(2)Business of the Industrial Financial Corporation of Thailand;

(3)Business of a savings cooperative, only in respect of loans provided to its members or to another savings cooperative;

(4) Business of a provident fund under the law governing provident

funds;

(5)Business of the National Housing Authority, only in respect of sale or hire-purchase of an immovable property;

(6)Pawn broking business of a ministry, sub-ministry, department or a local government authority;

(7)Any other businesses as specified by a royal decree.

The tax base for computing SBT shall be the following gross receipts received or receivable from the business carried on by a person liable to tax:

Specific Business and Tax Base	Tax Rate(%)
1. Banking, finance business, securities and credit foncier business, business with regular transactions similar business to commercial banking. Interest, discounts, service fees, other fees, profits from foreign exchange	3.0
2. Life Insurance	
Interest, service fees and other fees	2.5
3. Pawn Brokerage	
Interest, fees, remuneration from selling of forfeited pawned goods	2.5
4. Sale of immovable properties in a commercial manner or for profit	
Gross receipts	3.0
5. Sale of securities in a stock exchange	
Gross receipts	0.1(exempt)

Remark: Local tax at the rate of 10 % is imposed on top of SBT

Any operator of a business subject to SBT is required to be recorded for specific business tax registration within 30 days from the date of commencing business at the local Revenue Office. Should taxpayer have several places of business or branches, registration application must be filed to local Revenue Office where the head office is located.

SBT taxable period is a calendar month. SBT return must be filed on a monthly basis regardless of the receipt. SBT return and payment must be filed and paid to the local Revenue Office within 15 days of the following month. If taxpayer has more than one place of business, each place of business must file its return and make the payment separately unless there is an approval from the Director-General.

247

Stamp duty

Stamp duty is a kind of tax revenue collected on instrument base. Twenty-eight natures of instrument prescribed in the stamp duty schedule of the *Revenue Code* Chapter Ⅵ are charged with stamp duty on the execution of such instruments. The normal meaning of such execution is to sign in the instrument as defined by Section 9 according to the *Civil and Commercial Code*. There will be no stamp duty liability incurred unless there is such exe cution. For instance, the contract on transfer of anonymous shares or hire of work without execution of any document will not incurred stamp duty liability.

Stamp duty has to be paid duly before or immediately at the time when such instrument is executed unless it is tax exempt. Exemptions are those prescribed in Section 121 of the *Revenue Code*, stamp duty schedule, certain royal decrees or in other specific laws. Any person liable to duty or liable to cancel stamps who neglects or refuses to pay the duty or to cancel the stamps shall be punished with a fine according to the provision of the law. In order to recover tax arrears, the Director-General shall have the power to seize or attach and sale by auction assets of a person liable to pay or remit tax throughout Thailand without the court's summon or order. Besides, there are also another two ways of indirect enforcements. Firstly, when an instrument is not duty stamped, its original, duplicate, counterfoil or copy shall not be used as evidence in any civil case until the duty has been paid by stamping and by canceling at the full amount at the rate specified in the schedule. (Section 118) Secondly, with respect to an instrument which a government or municipal official has to give a signature to or acknowledgement, or has to be done before the government or municipal official, or is required to be recorded by the government or municipal official, the official shall not give a signature in acknowledgement, allow its execution or recording until the full duty thereon has been paid by stamping at the rates specified in the schedule. (Section 119)

Twenty-eight natures of instrument and the rates liable to stamp duty are as follows:

Natures of instrument stamp duty

(1) Lease of land, building, other construction or floating house 1 baht

For every 1,000 Baht or fraction thereof of the rent or key money or both for the entire lease period.

(2) Transfer of share, debenture, bond and certificate of debt issued by any company, association, body of persons or organization   1 baht

For every 1,000 Baht or fraction thereof of the paid-up value of shares, or of the nominal value of the instrument, whichever is greater.

(3) Hire-purchase of property   1 baht

For every 1,000 baht or fraction thereof of the total value.

(4) Hire of work   1 baht

For every 1,000 Baht or fraction thereof of the remuneration prescribed.

(5) Loan of money or agreement for bank overdraft   1 baht

For every 2,000 Baht or fraction thereof of the total amount of loan or the amount of bank overdraft agreed upon. Duty on the instrument of this nature calculating into an amount exceeding 10,000 Baht shall be payable only in the amount of 10,000 Baht.

(6) Insurance policy

(a) Insurance policy against loss   1 baht

For every 250 baht or fraction thereof of the insurance premium.

(b) Life insurance policy[1]   1 baht

For every 2,000 baht or fraction thereof of the amount insured.

(c) Any other insurance policy   1 baht

For every 2,000 baht or fraction thereof of the amount insured.

(d) Annuity policy   1 baht

For every 2,000 baht or fraction thereof of the principal amount, or, if there is no principal amount, for every 2,000 baht or fraction thereof of 33 1/3 times the annual income.

---

[1]   The amount of duty on the instrument of this nature, if exceeding 20 baht, shall be reduced to 20 baht. See *Revolutionary Party's Decree* No. 155.

（e）Insurance policy where reinsurance is affected. 1 baht for the original policy

（f）Renewal of insurance policy. 1 baht half the rate

（7）Authorization letter，i. e. a letter，not executed as a formal contract，for appointing an agent，including a letter appointing arbitrators：

（a）authorizing one or more persons to perform an act once only

10 baht

（b）authorizing one or more persons to jointly perform acts more than once. 30 baht

（c）authorizing to perform acts more than once by authorizing several persons to perform acts separately；the instrument will be charged on the basis of each individual who is authorized 30 baht

（8）Proxy letter for voting at a meeting of a company

（a）Authorized for one meeting only 20 baht

（b）Authorized for more than one meeting 100 baht

（9）（a）Bill of exchange or similar instrument used like bill of exchange for each bill or instrument 3 baht

（b）Promissory note or similar instrument used like promissory note for each note or instrument 3 baht

（10）Bill of lading 2 baht

（11）（a）Share or debenture certificate，or certificate of debt issued by any company，association，body of persons or organization

5 baht

（b）Bond of any government sold in Thailand 1 baht

For every 100 baht or fraction thereof.

（12）Cheque or any written order used in lieu of cheque for each instrument 3 baht

（13）Receipt for interest bearing fixed deposit in a bank 5 baht

（14）Letter of credit

（a）Issued in Thailand

—For value less than 10,000 Baht 20 baht

—For value of 10,000 Baht or over   30 baht

(b)Issued abroad and payable in Thailand for each payment   20 baht

(15) Traveler's cheque

(a)For each cheque issued in Thailand   3 baht

(b)For each cheque issued abroad but payable in Thailand   3 baht

(16)Carriers' goods receipt issued in connection with carriage of goods by waterway, land and air, namely, an instrument signed by an official or cargo master of a transport vehicle which carries goods as specified in that receipt upon issuing the bill of lading   1 baht

(17) Suretyship

(a)For an unlimited amount of money   10 baht

(b)For an amount exceeding 1,000 baht   1 baht

(c)For an amount exceeding1,000 baht but not exceeding 10,000 baht

       5 baht

(d)For an amount exceeding 10,000 baht   10 baht

(18)Pawn broking

For every 2,000 baht or fraction thereof of the debt.   1 baht

If the pawn broking does not limit the amount of debt.   1 baht

(19)Warehouse receipt   1 baht

(20)Delivery order   1 baht

(21)Agency

(a)Specific authorization   10 baht

(b)General authorization   30 baht

(22)Decision given by an arbitrator

(a)In the case where the dispute is concerned with the amount of money or price for every 1,000 baht or fraction there of   1 baht

(b)In the case where no amount of money or price is mentioned

       10 baht

(23) Duplicate or counterfoil of an instrument, namely an instrument having the same contents as the original document or contract and signed by the person executing the instrument in the same manner as the original

(a)If the duty payable for the original does not exceed 5 baht   1 baht (b)If the duty exceeds 5 baht   5 baht

(24)Memorandum of association of a limited company submitted to the
registrar   200 baht

(25)Articles of association of a limited company submitted to the
registrar   200 baht

(26) New articles of association, copy of amended memorandum of
association or articles of association submitted to the registrar

50 baht

(27)Partnership contract

(a)Contract on the establishment of a partnership   100 baht

(b)Amendment of the contract on the establishmentof a partnership

50 baht

(28)Receipt only as specified below:

(a)Receipt issued for government lottery prizes;

(b)Receipt issued in connection with a transfer of, or creation of any
right in, an immovable property, if the juristic act which gives rise
to such receipt is registered under the law;

(c) Receipt issued in connection with a sale, sale with right of
redemption, hire-purchase or transfer of ownership in a vehicle,
only if the vehicle is registered under the law governing such
vehicle. If the receipt under(a),(b) or (c)has an amount of 200
baht or more: for every 200 baht or fraction thereof   1 baht

Conclusion

Based on the foregoing discussion, the tax structures in Thailand appear
much similar to those present in most developing countries. Thailand
possesses a good balance between either revenues and public expenditures or
taxes based on income and consumption. Occasionally, certain tax loop
holes arise from amendments to tax laws due to political constraints and a
lack of sufficient awareness, experienced personnel with adequate knowledge
or cooperative academics. These loop holes enable tax avoidance through the
tax law. Additional tax problems in Thailand arise related to antiquated tax

laws, multiple complex tax laws, and unsystematic tax laws that confuse taxpayers and lead to noncompliance. These problems call for an attitude in tax reform that addresses the ambiguous provisions, anti-tax avoidance rules, and other unjust provisions in substantive law. Thailand also requires improvements in its tax policy making procedures, audit processes, standards for resolving tax disputes, and inefficiencies in tax administration. Thus, Thailand has much work ahead before it arrives at ideal, systematic tax reforms that result in a better taxation system.

外国国民在泰国从事贸易业务的相关立法

Article written by Dr. Ratchaneekorn Larpvanichar
王垚丹　译

　　泰国是东盟共同体的创始成员之一,可以说在国内和全球的自由贸易方面都有一个明确的支持政策。除了 6700 万的消费者外,2013 年还有26735583 名外国游客进入泰国,相比 2012 年增加了 19.6%。虽然很大部分的游客都来自中国①,但也有相当多数量的游客来自东盟成员国,这也是一种购买力的证明,这种购买力不仅打开了泰国的消费市场,同时也创造了泰国服务运作的商业市场。然而,除了消费者、风险和市场的问题外,法律也是投资方必须要考虑的问题。外国人应该对将要从事的商业活动之相关立法有一个基本了解,这对于是否继续相关商业行为是很重要的。本文将会讨论两个重要的相关立法,即《外商经营法》B. E. 2542(1992)和《境外就业法案》B. E. 2551(2008),这两部法律相互关联且不可避免地被引用。然而,泰国仍然保留了很多仅仅适用于本国国民的行业,因此外国投资商需要参考哪些行业类型是他们可以从事的。最后,由于商业的运作不能没有劳动力,因而又引出了劳动力雇佣的问题。

一、有关经营者的法律

　　关于经营业务的法律有很多,也就是说,商人从开始经营就会遇到很多不同的问题。而相比国内商人,外国商人会遇到更多的问题,因此对于外国商人来说,认真研究某国允许外来投资者运作的商业类型以及出于立法者主观目的而作出的限制很有必要。除此之外,还包括外国商人雇佣员工的问题,涉及很多相关法律。本章节将集中研究上述两部法律中所规定的外国商人在泰国

① http://tourism. go. th/index. php? mod=WebTourism accessed on 1 May 2014.

从事商业活动的问题,这当然也会影响各个行业中外国投资者雇佣劳动力的问题。

(一)《外商经营法》B.E.2542(1999)①

该法的关键在于对"外国人"一词的定义,即需要在泰国开展商业业务并且该活动被认为是外国业务的投资者。换言之,其他具有外国性质的商业活动有其他法律后果。该法律的规定附录于该法允许外国人投资的企业类别中,但是泰国仍然制定了相关政策,保留了只为本国国民提供的就业机会,从而保护本国国民的利益。因此,该法是有兴趣在泰国投资的外国人要学习的第一件事。当投资者来到泰国,他可能很欣赏泰国的传统纺织,从外商经营法中就可知作为一个外国人是否可以以出口蚕品种和编织为业。

在审查法律框架之后,我们可以观察到该法的禁止类别是基于两个标准的:(1)禁止的就业类型;(2)禁止的商业类型。

1.对"外国人"的禁止

法律明确规定了严禁在泰国从事商业的外国人类型,即:(1)外国人被驱逐出境或者未决的驱逐出境;(2)未经移民法或其他法律的允许留在泰国的外国人(第6条)。

尽管如此,泰国法律只为特定的情形提供规定,即一旦外商获得允许就可以从事商业活动;泰国法律也会检查业务类别和营业场所(第7条)。这包括(1)根据国籍法或其他法律规定出生在泰国但并非具有泰国国籍的外国人;(2)根据国籍法或其他法律退出泰国国籍的外国人。

虽然该法第4条对"外国人"进行了定义,但是这并不意味着"一个人是否可以从事一项特定的商业"仅仅由该法决定,还应该由其他法律决定,例如与国际和移民相关的法律。

对"外国人"因素的审查标准根据《外国企业法》第4条的规定:

(1)第4条第3款:要确定一个法人属于外国国籍还是本国国籍,应该审查其资本股份。例如,一个在泰国注册的法人,其一半或一半以上的资本由外国人持有,那么该法人非泰国法人。在外国注册的法人当然也不属于泰国法人。在有限合伙企业或普通合伙注册公司的情形下,如果管理的合伙人或者管理人不具有泰国国籍,则该企业属于外国人。

---

① B.E.是佛教时代的缩写,是泰国使用的编年系统。

(2)第4条第4款:法人在泰国注册,但是一半及以上的资本由非泰国国籍的人持有,或者在泰国国外注册的法人,或者50%及以上的股份由外国人持有的法人,都被认定是外国法人。他们如果在泰国从事商业活动就应该受该法的约束。

2.禁止的商业类型

泰国法律将禁止的商业类型规定在该法律的3个附录部分中,将禁止外国人就业的类型规定在该法第8条。

(1)附录1概述了外国人由于某些特殊原因不准从事的就业类型,比如畜牧业、园艺、农业、林业、木业和限于泰领海和专属经济区内捕捉海洋动物的渔业。

(2)附录2概述了涉及国家安全或影响文化艺术、传统、民俗工艺品或国家资源和环境的企业。

(3)附录3概述了泰国不准备与外商竞争的行业,如农产品生产、水产动物、造林业、会计服务业、法律服务业、建筑服务业、工程技术服务业、经纪或代理业、广告业务、酒店业务但酒店管理服务、旅游服务除外,即外国人不被允许在泰国当导游,出售食物或饮料,提供种植或宣传等服务。我们可以看出,从附录3的清单中随机选择一个都是涉及服务行业的企业,这可能会引出一个问题,即在旅游区外国人的餐饮企业应该如何设置。在现实中,真正的酒店运营商或所有者可能并不是泰国人而是泰国人的配偶;也有可能该餐厅并没有注册为法人,这就要求投资者自己管理投资,自负盈亏、自担风险;或者该真正的运营商或所有者只持有少数股权(49%)。

该法律还规定了不允许外国人就业的类型。

附录2第15条:除非有其他原因,否则一个外国人不能从事这些行业,必须有一个泰国国民或在该法定义下,有持有不低于40%的资本的非外国法人。有内阁授权的大臣可以在上述情况下放松股权要求,但还是不得低于25%,并且至少五分之二的股东是泰国国民。

附录3:虽然外国企业法规定,附录3清单里泰国不准备与外国人竞争的行业不允许外国人从事,但附录3中仍然包含一些特定的范畴,例如:

(1)建筑业,只包括那些呈现基本服务的,涉及公共事业和需要特殊工具、机械、技术或专业知识结构的交通运输业务,最少500亿泰铢以上的外资。

(2)由部门规章规定的其他类别的建筑业务。

(3)经纪人或代理商承销证券,提供与农产品相关的期货交易服务,金融票据或者安全方面贸易的代理。

（4）经纪人或代理人为了销售泰国制造或进口的产品而进行交易、购买、分发或寻求国内或国外市场，其中由外国人持有最低 100 亿泰铢资本的国际运营业务。

（5）部门规章规定的其他经纪人或代理人类别。

（6）包括国际招标在内的拍卖会，不是古玩、历史文物或艺术品的拍卖会而是艺术、工艺品或古董或具有历史价值的泰国作品的拍卖会。

（7）部门规章规定的其他拍卖类别。

（8）最低总资本超过 100 亿泰铢的零售类别。

（9）资本最少超过 100 亿泰铢的各出口批发类别。

由此可以得出结论，外国企业法的原则是禁止外国人从事经营活动。允许外国人开展的业务必须得到明确的规定。

（二）境外就业法 B. E. 2551（2008）

如果你参观普吉府，你可能会遇到这样一家法国餐厅，它是由法国人运营的，除了一个意大利厨师还雇用了一个在泰国居住了一段时间的法国厨师，有来自缅甸的招待人员，而收银员是泰国人。这怎么可能呢？在现实中，这是可能的，也就是企业会雇用外国人作为服务员或经理或其他，泰国法律不会强迫你在你的企业仅仅雇用泰国人。正是出于这个原因，某些类别的企业还可以在非经营者的职位上聘用外国人。

该法案的目标是控制泰国的外国工人数量，它规定进入泰国工作的外国工人必须得到许可，以便正常工作。这有助于政府清楚系统内的职工人数，包括进入本国工作的职工人数。因此，该法律只关注"非泰国国籍的自然人"。

（三）外国经营法和境外就业法的联系

当外国企业向泰国寻求经营业务的许可时这两部法律就联系在一起了。在泰国，自然人经营者或者进入该国经营业务的相关人员都需要寻求工作许可。

二、可以由外国投资者从事的业务类别

如前所述，泰国的法律仍然限制外国投资者可以从事的业务类型。因此，投资前，投资者必须预先审查他们所感兴趣的业务是否是泰国法律所禁止的。如果他们感兴趣的业务被允许投资，他们才需要进行后续的步骤，即是否该企业需要获得泰国政府机构的许可。

(一)无须许可的业务

部门规章中关于服务性企业的条款规定,外国人不需要运行的权限,3月11日的 B.E.2556(2013)也规定外国经营者投资某些类型的企业有无须寻求国家许可的自由。这些业务如下:

1.依据证券交易法规定的证券公司和其他企业

(1)证券交易

(2)投资咨询服务

(3)证券承销

(4)证券借贷

(5)共同基金管理

(6)私募基金管理

(7)创业投资管理

(8)提供贷款证券业务

(9)金融咨询服务

(10)证券的政策服务

(11)证券或衍生工具的公司客户托管服务

(12)私募基金资产托管服务

(13)基金托管人服务

(14)债券持有人代表

2.依照法律衍生品的衍生工具企业

(1)衍生品交易

(2)衍生产品咨询服务

(3)衍生品基金管理

3.依据法律对资本市场中的信托交易的规定的信托服务

(二)需要许可的业务

指外国人可以从事但仍需获得许可的业务,即:

1.存在泰国作为当事国或受约束国的国际条约

这种情形是泰国已经与其他国家签订协议,允许该国家国民正常运行一般外国人被禁止的业务。这是给予相应国家国民的特殊权利,即那些国家的国民享有各种法律条款限制的豁免(第5条、第8条、第15条、第17条和第18

条），只受到相关条约的限制。通常该协议是互惠协议。

然而，在承接上述业务的时候，外国人在申请许可和证书的过程中有义务通知总干事业务发展部。原则上，总干事应该从接到通知之日起及时处理，最晚不超过 30 日。但如果总干事确定该通知不符合部门规章的规定和程序，或者未依照本法第 10 条，也存在例外情形。在这种情况下，总干事应该及时通知该外国人，必须在收到通知之日起 30 日内通知完毕。

2. 依据有关投资促进法获得特权的业务

该情形是一个外国人已经依据法律规定获得了经营某业务的投资鼓励。这必须属于附录 2 或附录 3 中的业务类型。外国投资者应该向总干事业务发展部申请证书。在外国人需要得到总干事的验证而提交投资促进卡的情况下，将得到该法规定下的豁免（但仍然受第 21 条、第 22 条、第 39 条、第 40 条和第 42 条的约束）。

3. 依据泰国的工业遗产管理法获得特权的业务

这种情形是从已经获得投资鼓励的情形中引申的，除了总干事应该得到通知并确认可以颁发投资许可证的业务的情形以外。当然，这些企业必须是附录 2 或附录 3 中的业务。

4. 接受业务经营许可证的程序

依据《外国企业法》第 17 条，申请业务许可证可以按业务类别和授予者分为以下几种：

一般业务，外国人应该依据部门规章中列出的规则和程序，向部长或总干事提交许可经营证书申请。

附录 2 中的业务，外国人应该向部长会议提交许可证申请。

附录 3 中的业务，外国人应该向总干事提交许可证申请。

由此，权威人士必须从收到申请之日起 60 日内完成审查。当部长会议需要考虑或者在合理期间内无法考虑清楚，审议期可以延长，但是不能超过自截止日期起 60 日。当根据第 1 款部长会议已经批准或总干事已经允许，那他们必须自允许之日起 15 日内发出许可证。

当然，许可证要受部门规章的约束，即：

(1)自然人情形

1)提供护照或外国人证书复印件。

2)提供房产登记证明，居住在泰国的证明或者有证据证明其是依据移民法，凭借暂住证进入泰国的。

3)具有持证人资格的证明并且没有第 16 条所列的禁止情形。

4）提供有关允许外国人从事的业务类别的文件，包括以下内容：

①业务许可类别，包括整个过程。

②估算许可证持有人3年内每年或经营不足3年的经营期限内，在泰国所获得永久资产和业务运营的支出。

③企业的规模。

④许可证持有人在泰国雇用工人的数量。

⑤如果有进口和传播外国技术的计划，也应该附加。

⑥如果有列出研究和发展计划，也同样应该附加。

⑦业务持续时间。

⑧此项业务能给泰国带来的经济利益。

5）简明显示有关业务经营地的计划

（2）未在泰国注册的法人情形

1）提供法人证书的复印件，表明名称、资本、目标、公司地址、董事名单和被授权法人代表的签名。

2）提供包括授权法人签名在内的委托书，授权泰国的法人代表承担经营责任。

3）提供护照，外国人证书或在（2）情形下指定代理证的复印件。

4）提供房产登记证明，居住在泰国的证明，或者有证据证明其是依据（2）情形下约定的代理和移民法，凭借暂住证进入泰国的。

5）许可证持有人保证该持有人、董事、经理或指定代理人具有资格条件，并且没有被 B. E. 2542（1999）第16条所禁止。

6）提供有关许可证持有者在泰国雇用工人的数量的证明文件，以及进口和传播国外技术计划的证明文件（如果存在这种情形）。

（3）在泰国注册的法人情形

1）提供有关许可证持有者在泰国雇用工人的数量的证明文件，以及进口和传播国外技术计划的证明文件（如果存在这种情形）。

2）提供法人证书的复印件，表明名称、资本、目标、公司地址、董事名单和被授权法人代表的签名。

3）许可证持有人保证该持有人、董事、经理或指定代理人具有资格条件，并且没有被 B. E. 2542（1999）第16条所禁止。

4）证明泰国国民和外国人之间的股权所有，股权份额和外国人所持有的股票种类。

许可证申请应该在以下地点提交：

①曼谷：业务发展部门、商务部或总干事通知的其他地点。

②其他省份：业务发展省委办公厅或总干事通知的其他地点。

三、为了支持业务雇用外国劳工

投资时，除了经营者，劳动者也可以推动业务的发展。为了确保泰国工人和外国工人的就业是合法的，经营者应该关注劳动法。除了泰国劳工，这个领域的外国劳工可以分为两类：合法入境的外国劳动者和非法入境的外国劳动者。一些泰国律师认为，雇主和非法入境的劳动者之间的雇佣合同是无效和非法的，这也是《民商法》第 150 条规定所禁止的。①

正如前文所述，没有泰国国籍的自然人必须按照《外国就业法》的规定申请工作。该法第 27 条规定："禁止任何人雇用外国工人，除非外国工人根据地方相关规定持有工作许可证而开展工作。"

该法的要点在于，经营者应该知道：

（1）申请许可的外国人必须居住在泰国，或者根据移民法获准暂住。很重要的一点是，如果一个外国人不是以游客或过境的身份进入泰国，就不会受制于部门规章（第 10 条）的任何禁止规定。

（2）如果一个经营者打算雇用一个从外国进入泰国工作的外国人，该经营者必须申请许可，并代表该外国人支付一定的费用（第 11 条第 1 款）。

（3）在外国人已经根据投资促进法进入泰国工作的时候，仍然需要依据本法申请工作许可。但在等待获取许可的期间，《外国就业法》第 12 条允许该外国人工作，因为他们享有对第 24 条的豁免权。②

四、总结

在泰国投资经营并不是一件困难的事情，但这仍然需要足够的法律知识

---

① 即使其他律师认为这样的合同是有效的，其推理也并不清晰。另外，最高法院也尚未对此作出判断。这意味着经营者在这个问题上应该非常小心，否则会承担很高的风险。泰国政府无意推动外国非法劳工的就业，因为这对泰国没有任何好处，甚至会鼓励更多的人潜入泰国以获取工作。

② 第 24 条规定："被许可的收件人必须携带许可证并在工作期间保管在工作地，确保在任何时候都能呈现给主管官员。"

作为前提。笔者承认,在外国人开展业务方面,泰国的法律规定非常复杂。但是困难程度依旧取决于经营者自身。即使经营者的法律顾问可以处理此类事务,掌握基本的法律知识对经营者而言还是很有益的。外国经营法在未来很可能出现修正案,因为判断一个经营者是否为外国人的评判标准相对复杂,容易导致法律漏洞。但是很显然,在该法明显成为外商投资的阻碍之前,泰国是不会主动修改法律的。目前泰国已经减少了对本国国民的业务保留,因为泰国商人也越来越具有竞争力。当然,除此之外,泰国还需要外国资本。

Undertaking Business in Thailand by Foreign Nationals: Related Legislation

Article written by Dr. Ratchaneekorn Larpvanichar[*]
Translated by Dr. Jaruprapa Rakpong[**]

Introduction

Thailand is one of the founding members of the ASEAN Community and can be said to have a clear policy of supporting free trade, both domestically and internationally. In addition to 67 million consumers, in B. E. 2556(2013) a further 26,735,583 foreign tourists flowed into Thailand, representing a 19.6% increase compared with B. E. 2555(2012). Although the largest number of tourists originated from China,[③] there were a similar number of tourists from ASEAN member states, which is indicative of the purchasing power that will create a market for business to operate in Thailand serving not only the Thai consumer market. Nevertheless, apart

---

[*] LLB(2nd Class Honors)Thammasat University, Barrister at Law, the Thai Bar Association, LLM(International Law)Lille 2 University, PhD(Private Law)(Droit Privé)(specialized in Private International Law) Lille 2 University(Mention Honorable), Full-Time Lecturer, the Faculty of Law, Thammasat University.

[**] LLB(1st Class Honors), King's College London; LLM(2nd Class Honors), University of Cambridge; PhD(European and International Trade Laws),University College London.

③ Statistical information from the Department of Tourism, Ministry of Tourism&Sports, http://tourism. go. th/index. php? mod = WebTourismaccessed on 1 May 2014.

from the issues of consumer, risk and marketing, legal issues are an important and unavoidable consideration in investment. A basic understanding of the laws of the undertaking business by foreigners is therefore essential for those deciding to undertake such business. This article discusses two important pieces of legislation, namely the *Foreign Business Act B. E.* 2542(1999)and the *Foreign Employment Act B. E.* 2551 (2008), as they are interlinked and it is not possible to avoid quoting these (Part 1). However, Thailand still reserves many types of professions solely for its own nationals. Therefore it is necessary to refer to the types of professions in which foreign investors can undertake business(Part 2). Finally, there is the issue of employment of foreign nationals to support the business (Part 3) since business is unlikely to be able to operate without labor.

Laws concerning business operators

Inevitably there are many inter-related laws concerning operating the business. It can be said that from starting up the business, businessmen are sure to encounter many different problems. In the case of foreign businessmen, there will be additional problems compared to native businessmen. It is necessary to study the types of business a particular country allows foreign nationals to operate, the limitations of which are likely to vary from country to country and be dependent on the objectives of the lawmakers. After that there is the matter of the legal structure of the business to be founded, a limited company or a type of partnership. There is then the matter of employing staff, all of which, irrespective of position, has related laws, especially if the employment of foreign nationals is required. The scope of this article is limited to the study of the law concerning undertaking business by foreign nationals defined in the act and the law concerning work undertaken by foreign nationals, which affects the employment of foreign nationals to various positions within the respective business.

Foreign Business Act B.E. 2542(1999)[①]

The key point in this law is the definition of the term "foreigner" who needs to undertake business in Thailand and the activity is considered to be foreign business. In other words, those that having foreign characteristics which would have legal implications elsewhere. This law specifies in the appendix to the act the business categories in which foreigners are able to invest, as Thailand still has a policy of protecting its nationals by reserving many categories of employment solely for its own nationals. This law is therefore the first thing that foreigners interested in investing in Thailand should study. When you come to Thailand, you might admire the Thai knowledge in weaving silk or "Sin Teen Jok," the traditional Thai textile. As a foreigner, the answer to whether or not you can set up a business breeding silkworms and weaving for export lies in the contents of the *Foreign Business Act B.E. 2542(1999)*.

After examining its legal framework, one can observe that this law outlines the prohibited categories based on two criteria, namely (1) categories of prohibited employment and (2) categories of prohibited business.

1. Categories of prohibited foreigners

The cases where the law clearly prescribes which categories of foreigners are strictly prohibited from undertaking business in Thailand are namely (1) foreigners deported or pending deportation and (2) foreigners staying in Thailand without permission under immigration law or other laws. (Article 6)

Nevertheless, the Thai law only provides categories in which foreigners are allowed to undertake business once they have received a permit and are subject to examination of the category of business and the place of business. (Article 7) This includes (1) foreigners born in the kingdom but are not Thai nationals under

---

① B. E. is the abbreviation for Buddhist era, the system of year numbering used in Thailand. The corresponding B. E. year is mostly 543 greater than the equivalent A. D. year.

nationality law, ①or other laws and (2) foreigners as a result of withdrawal of nationality in accordance with nationality law or other laws.

It can be seen that even though this law defines "foreigner" in Article 4, it does not mean that the determination of whether a person can or cannot undertake the particular business solely depends on this act, it is also determined by other laws, for example the laws concerning nationality and laws concerning immigration.

Examination criteria of the elements of a "foreigner".

In accordance with the provisions of Article 4 of the *Foreign Business Act*:

(1) When determining whether a juristic person is foreign or not, the number of capital shares shall be examined. For example, a juristic person registered in Thailand will be a foreign juristic person, if of half or more of the capital shares are held by natural persons who are not Thai nationals. Also the juristic person is foreign if he has registered abroad. In the case of a limited partnership or registered ordinary partnership, a juristic person will be a foreigner if the managing partner or manager does not have Thai nationality. [Article 4(3)]

(2) Juristic persons registered in Thailand having half or more of its capital shares held by a person who is not a Thai national or a juristic person registered abroad or a juristic person registered in Thailand with foreigners holding 50% or more of the shares are considered to be foreigner juristic persons. Those undertaking business must comply with this act. [Article 4(4)]

2. Categories of prohibited business

The prohibited business under the Thai law is specified in a total of three appendixes of the act. The list of business prohibited to foreigners is prescribed in Article 8 of this act.

(1) Appendix 1 outlines the business in which foreigners are not allowed to undertake for special reasons, for example animal husbandry, rice cultivation, gardening, farming, forestry, carpentry, fisheries limited to catching marine animals

---

① In cases where persons born in Thailand but presumed to be foreign national for illegally entering the country as per Article 7 *Bis* Paragraph 3 of the *Nationality Act B. E.* 2508(1965)as a-mended by Act No. 2 B. E. 2535(1992).

in Thai territorial waters and Thailand's Exclusive Economic Zone. ①

(2) Appendix 2 outlines the business relating to national safety or security or affecting arts and culture, traditions, folk handicraft or national resources and the environment.

(3) Appendix 3 outlines the business which Thais are not ready to compete with foreigners, for example rice milling, flour production from rice and farm products, raising aquatic animals, forestry, accounting services business, legal services business, architectural services business, engineering services business, brokering or agency business for all types of goods with minimum capital for each retail venue of less than 100 million Baht, advertising business, hotel business except for hotel management services, tourism services, that is foreigners are not allowed to be tour guides in Thailand, selling food or beverages, plant cultivation or propagation services. It can be seen in a random selection from these three appendixes that it largely concerns business in the service sector. This may give rise to the question of how restaurant business of foreigners encountered in tourist areas can be set up. In reality, it is possible that the real operator or owner of the business is not a Thai national but is the spouse of a Thai national or it is possible that the restaurant does not register as a juristic person, which would require the investor to manage investment, profitability and risk themself, or is a foreigner who has invested in such business holds a minority investment stake(49%).

Regardless, this law also specifies the business which foreigners are excluded from undertaking, namely:

(1) Businesses under Appendix 2

If a foreigner is going to undertake one of these business categories it is necessary to have a Thai national or non-foreign juristic person defined by the act

---

① Deepwater fisheries, plant cultivation and propagation, forestry not less than 500 Rai(a Thai measurement unit, 1 Rai equals to approximately 1600 square meter). Plant cultivation and propagation are business in which foreigners are allowed to invest in accordance with Thai laws on investment promotion or the Board of Investment(BoI). But in the case of local Thai plants, there must be a Thai shareholder with a shareholding of not less than 51% of the registered capital. From these reasons, it can be seen that even where foreigners are limited by the *Foreign Business Act* in organizing business they may be allowed to invest in the same business under the *Investment Promotion Act B.E.* 2520(1977).

holding shares not less than 40% of the capital held by that foreign juristic person, except where there is a valid reason. A minister authorized by the Cabinet may relax the shareholding in the aforementioned situation, but it shall not be less than 25% and at least two fifths of the total number of directors must be Thai nationals. (Article 15)

(2)Businesses under Appendix 3

Although the *Foreign Business Act* prescribes that foreign nationals are prohibited from undertaking business listed in Appendix 3 as Thai nationals are not ready to compete with foreigners, Appendix 3 contains exceptions in certain categories, namely:

①Construction business, only those rendering basic services to the public in the areas of public utilities and transportation that require special tools, machinery, technology or construction expertise, with minimum foreign capital of 500 million Baht or more.

②Other categories of construction, as prescribed by the ministerial regulations.

③Brokers or agents underwriting securities or providing services connected with futures trading of agricultural commodities or an agent trading in financial instruments or securities.

④ Brokers or agents trading, purchasing or distributing or seeking both domestic and foreign markets for selling Thai-manufactured or imported goods, which have international business operations, with a minimum capital held by foreigners of 100 million Baht or more.

⑤ Other categories of brokers or agents prescribed by the ministerial regulations.

⑥Auctions that contain international bidding and are not auctions of antiques, historical artefacts or art objects that are Thai works of arts, handicraft or antiques or objects of national historical value.

⑦Other categories of auction prescribed by the ministerial regulations.

⑧All categories of retailing with a total minimum capital of more than 100 million baht.

⑨ All categories of wholesaling with a minimum capital for each outlet of more than 100 million Baht.

It can be concluded that the principle of the *Foreign Business Act* is to prohibit foreigners from undertaking business operations. Business allowed to be undertaken by foreigners must be clearly prescribed and considered to be exceptions.

Foreign Employment Act B.E. 2551(2008)

If you were to visit Phuket Province, you might encounter a French restaurant being run by a French person, employing a French chef who has resided already for a period in Thailand, in addition an Italian chef, but with waiting staff from Myanmar, and when you come to pay you encounter a Thai cashier. How is this possible? In reality, it is probable that the business employs foreigners as labor or the manager or other positions in the business, as the Thai law does not compel you to employ only Thai staff in your business. It is for this reason that certain categories of business may also employ foreigners in positions other than the business operator.

The objective of this act is to control the number of foreign workers in Thailand, as it specifies that foreign workers entering Thailand to work must seek permission and receive a work permit. This assists the government in knowing the number of workers in the system, including the number of people entering the country to work. This law is therefore only concerned with "natural persons who are not of Thai nationality. "

The link between the Foreign Business Act B.E. 2542(1999) and the Foreign Employment Act B.E. 2551(2008)

Both laws are linked in that the Foreign Business Act concerns seeking permission from the Thai state to operate business, whereas the business operator who is an natural person or related persons who have to enter the country to operate the business must also seek permission to work in Thailand.

Business categories which can be undertaken by foreign investors

As stated previously, Thai laws still restrict the types of business that foreign investors may undertake. Therefore, before investing investors must check beforehand whether or not the business they are interested in is the business prohibited by Thai foreign business laws. If it is a permitted business then of course they should check in the subsequent step whether or not it is a business requiring permission from a Thai government agency.

Business not requiring permission

If one examines the ministerial regulations specifying the service business that foreigners do not require permission to operate[11 March B. E. 2556(2013)], one will see that there is freedom for foreigner business operators to invest certain types of business without seeking permission from the state. These are as follows:

(1)Securities business and other business in accordance with the securities and exchange law

①Securities dealing

②Investment advisory services

③ Securities underwriting

④Securities borrowing and lending

⑤Mutual fund management

⑥Private fund management

⑦Venture capital management

⑧Providing loans for securities business

⑨Financial advisory services

⑩Securities registrar services

⑪Securities or derivatives companies client depository services

⑫Private fund asset depository services

⑬Mutual fund trustee services

⑭Bondholder representative

(2)Derivatives business in accordance with the derivatives law

①Derivatives dealing

②Derivatives advisory services

③Derivatives fund management

(3)Trustee services in accordance with the law for the trust for transactions in the capital market

Business requiring permission

This refers to the business that foreigners can undertake, but requires permission, namely:

(1)Where there is an international treaty to which Thailand is a party or is bound by

This is where Thailand has reached an agreement with another country to allow nationals of that country to normally operate a business which is prohibited in general to foreigners. This is a special right for nationals of the relevant foreign country, whereby those foreign nationals are exempted from the restrictions of various legal articles, namely Articles 5, 8, 15, 17 and 18, and are subject to the restrictions of the relevant treaty. Usually this is a reciprocal agreement.

Nevertheless, when undertaking business under the aforementioned, the foreigner is obliged to notify the Director-General of the Department of Business Development in order to apply for permission and a certificate. In principle, the Director-General is obliged to promptly process the issuing of the certificate to the foreigner in not more than 30 days from the date when the notification is received from the foreigner. There is an exception that the Director-General determines that the notification is not in accordance with the rules and procedures prescribed in the ministerial regulations or is not in accordance with Article 10 of this act. In these cases, the Director-General shall promptly notify the foreigner concerned within 30 days from the date of receipt of the letter of notice from the foreigner.

(2) Where the business has received a privilege in accordance with the law concerning investment promotion

This is where a foreigner operates the business that has received investment promotion in accordance with the law. It must be a type of business in Appendix 2 or Appendix 3. The foreigner shall notify the Director-General of the Department of Business Development to apply for a certificate. In cases where the foreigner needs to submit the Investment Promotion Card for verification by the Director-General, the foreigner will receive an exemption from this act (but still continues to be bound by Articles 21, 22, 39, 40 and 42).

(3) Where the business has received a privilege in accordance with the law concerning the industrial estates authority of Thailand

This is as per the case for the business that has received investment promotion, except that Director-General shall be notified and verify the investment permit to issue the certificate. These business categories must also be under Appendix 2 or Appendix 3.

Procedure for receiving a business operation license

Upon examination of Article 17 of the *Foreign Business Act*, one will see that application for a business permit can be divided by business category and the person granting approval as follows:

(1)General business

The foreigner shall submit the permit application for the business operation certificate to the Minister or the Director-General in accordance with the rules and procedures outlined in the ministerial regulations.

(2)Business in Appendix 2

The foreigner shall submit the permit application to the Council of Ministers.

(3)Business in Appendix 3

The foreigner shall submit the permit application to the Director-General.

Whereby the person in authority must complete the review within 60 days from the date when the application was submitted. In cases where the Council of Ministers needs more time to consider and the Council is unable to consider this within the pre-scribed period, the period for consideration shall be extended as necessary but must not exceed 60 days from the prescribed deadline. When the Council has given approval or the Director-General has given permission under Paragraph 1, the Council or Director-General must issue the permit within 15 days from the date of the Council's approval or Director-General's permission. The Minister shall specify the conditions stipulated by the Council or prescribed in the ministerial regulations under Article 18 for cases of business under Appendix 2 or the Director-General shall prescribe the conditions stipulated by the ministerial regulations and issued under Article 18 for business under Appendix 3.

Receipt of the permit will of course be subject to the ministerial regulations, [1] namely:

(1)Case of natural persons

1)Copy of the passport or alien certificate.

2) House registration, certificate of residence in the Kingdom or evidence showing permission to temporarily enter the Kingdom in accordance with immigration law.

---

[1] Ministerial regulations prescribing the rules and regulations applying for a Business Operation License in accordance with Article 17 B. E. 2546(2003)dated 1st November B. E. 2546 (2003).

3)Guaranteed that the permit holder has the qualifications and has no prohibited characteristics outlined in Article 16.

4)Document detailing the category of business permitted, comprising the followings:

①Category of business permitted, including the entire procedure.

②Estimate of the expenditure that the permit holder will use in Thailand for business to acquire permanent assets and for business operations for each year of 3 years or in accordance for the period of the business undertaking for cases where the business undertaking is less than 3 years.

③Size of the business.

④Number of workers in Thailand employed by the permit holder.

⑤If there is a plan to import and disseminate foreign technology, this shall also be attached.

⑥ If there is a research and development plan outlining a research and development program, this shall likewise be attached.

⑦Intended duration of business undertaking.

⑧ Expected general economic benefits to Thailand from the business undertaking.

5)Plan of showing in brief the place of business undertaking in Thailand.

(2)Case of juristic persons not registered in Thailand

1)Copy of certificate or evidence of juristic persons, showing the name, capital, objective, office address, list of directors and authorized juristic person's signature.

2)Letter appointing an agent containing the authorized juristic person's signature in accordance with the previous record granting responsibility to the agent to operate the business in Thailand on behalf of the juristic person.

3)Copy of the passport, alien certificate or Thai identification card of the agent appointed under 2).

4) House registration, certificate of residence in the Kingdom or evidence showing permission to temporarily enter the Kingdom in accordance with immigration laws of the agent appointed under 2).

5)Guarantee from the permit holder that the permit holder, directors, managers or appointed agent has the qualifications and no prohibited characteristics outlined in Article 16 of the *Foreign Business Act B. E.* 2542 (1999).

6)Evidence or documents relating to the number of workers in Thailand employed by the permit holder and plans of importing and disseminating foreign technology(if there is one).

(3)Case of juristic persons registered in Thailand

1)Evidence or documents relating to the number of workers in Thailand employed by the permit holder and plans of importing and disseminating foreign technology(if there is one).

2)Copy of the certificate or evidence of juristic persons, showing the name, capital, objective, office address, list of directors and authorized juristic person's signature.

3)Guarantee from the permit holder that the permit holder, directors, managers or appointed agent has the qualifications and no prohibited characteristics outlined in Article 16 of the *Foreign Business Act B. E.* 2542 (1999).

4)Letter notifying the share of ownership between Thai nationals and foreigners, the number of shares, the category or type of shares held by foreigners.

The permit application should be submitted at the following locations:

1) Bangkok: the Department of Business Development, Ministry of Commerce or other locations notified by the Director-General.

2) Other provinces: the Provincial Office of Business Development or other locations notified by the Director-General.

Employing foreign labor to support the business

When investing in a business, apart from the business operator, labor is also required to drive the business. To ensure that the employment of labor is legal, the business operator should pay attention to labor laws, for both Thai workers and foreigner workers. The complexity in this area does not relate to Thai workers, but to foreign workers who can be divided into two categories: foreign workers who have entered the country legally and foreign workers who have entered illegally. Some Thai lawyers believe that employment contracts between employers and foreign workers who have entered the country illegally are null and void as this is clearly forbidden in the law, in accordance with Article 150 of the *Civil and Commercial Code.* [①]

Work permit for foreign workers

As mentioned previously, natural persons who are not of Thai nationality must apply for a work permit in Thailand as prescribed in the *Foreign Employment Act B. E.* 2551 (2008). Article 27 lays down the principle that "it is prohibited for any person to employ foreign workers, unless the foreign worker is in possession of a work permit and to undertake work in accordance with the category or type of work specified in the work permit, at the place of work specified in the work permit."

The key points of this law that the business operator should be aware of are:

(1) The foreigner applying for the permit must have a place of residence in the Kingdom or have been given permission to temporarily enter the Kingdom in accordance with immigration law. It is important that the person does not enter as a tourist or in transit and does not have any prohibited characteristics specified in the ministerial regulations. (Article 10)

(2) If a business operator intends to employ a foreigner who enters the Kingdom of Thailand to work in his business, the business operator is able to apply for permission and pay a fee on behalf of that foreigner. (Article 11, Paragraph 1)

[①] Even though other lawyers are of the opinion that such employment contracts are valid, the reasoning is unclear. Furthermore, the Supreme Court has not yet made a judgment on this matter. This means that business operators should be very careful in this matter as employing illegal labor carries high risks in other areas. The Thai government has no intention of promoting the employment of illegal foreign workers as this brings no benefits to Thailand as it would encourage more foreigners to attempt to slip into the country in the hope of getting work.

(3)In the case of a foreigner who has entered Thailand to work under the laws concerning investment promotion, it is also necessary to apply for a work permit in accordance with this law. However, whilst waiting to receive the work permit, Article 12 of the *Foreign Employment Act* permits that foreigner to work in the meantime as he is exempted from complying with Article 24 until the registrar notifies him to come to pick up the permit. ①

Summary

Investing in Thailand is not a difficult matter, although it relies on having sufficient legal knowledge. The author accepts that Thai laws relating to foreigners undertaking business may be more complicated than other countries in the matter of defining a foreign business discussed previously. However, it is not too difficult for business operators to understand this themselves. Even if they have a legal advisor looking after this matter, it would be beneficial to have a basic level of understanding. As for amending the foreign business law, it is likely that there will be a future amendment since the criteria used to define whether or not a business is foreign are somewhat complicated and have led to loopholes in the law. However, it is clear that Thailand naturally will not amend the law until it becomes a significant obstacle to foreign investors. There has been a reduction in the idea of professions reserved for Thais because Thai businessmen are increasingly competitive. In addition, Thailand still requires foreign capital.

---

① Article 24 states that "the recipient of the permit must carry the permit on them or keep it at their place of employment during working hours in order to present it to a competent official or registrar at all times."

对泰国私人公司法的理解

Nilubol Lertnuwat

徐梦静　译

在泰国,商业组织形式包括个人独资、合伙企业、私人公司和上市公司;而私人公司(18世纪泰国对英国公司法的采纳使现在的私人公司极具西方公司的特征)是最常见的。而对私人公司作出规定的基本法律是《民商法》12篇"合伙与公司"("CCC" Title 12 "Partnership and Company")。本文旨在探讨对泰国私人公司的基本理解以及CCC 08修正案对泰国私人公司的影响。首先,从私人公司的6个方面入手初步谈及对泰国私人公司的理解:泰国私人公司的本质与形成、股份与股东、私人有限公司的管理、股东大会、股息和储备基金、资金。然后再分别谈及修正案在对泰国私人公司规定上的四大修改以及影响。

一、基本了解

(一)泰国私人公司的本质与形成

私人公司是根据《民商法》条款由至少3个公司发起人发起创立且把公司资本划分为等价的股票而股东依其所持股份对企业承担有限责任而设立的公司。

私人公司的组建与形成一般需要5步:首先,依据法规标准预定公司名称;其次,董事需要向商业登记部门提交公司章程;再次,发起人须使全部股票份额得到认购且该股票不能向公众发行,股票的发行价格相对于其票面价值只能高不能低;复次,认购完成之后,发起人须按时召开法定大会(全体大会),通过的决议须交由董事执行并将会议报告送往当地登记机关。最后,会议结束3个月内,董事须申请注册公司。

(二)股份与股东

一份股的票价最低额度不得少于 5 泰铢且不可分割,而且股价一般都以金钱的方式认购,为保护债权人利益,股东不得以抵销的方式认购且一个公司不能自己认购自己的股份。

就股东而言,每一位股东都有权取得所持股权的凭证,股权凭证分记名与不记名两种形式,这也决定了股票流转的不同要求,记名股票在流转程序与要求上较不记名股票而言要繁杂和严格得多。另外,值得注意的是股东须注册,以详细表明股东的情况,股票的数量,每个股东所持有的股权,所付的数额等。

(三)私人有限公司的管理

私人公司由一名或多名董事依据公司组织大纲和公司章程在股东大会的支配下管理该公司,而公司组织大纲或章程的修改需要由绝大多数股东同意然后由董事在 14 之内作出登记。董事的数量、薪水、任命与罢免均由股东大会决定,决定一旦生效,公司将会对董事的行为负责,即使股东的某些行为是不当的,董事、公司以及第三人的关系也应依据法律进行。

CCC 也规定了董事会的一般权利和义务。董事会有权决定董事的人数,但至少 3 人,且任一董事可以随时要求召开董事大会,会议由董事长主持。董事必须履行注意义务与忠实义务(与普通法系中的信赖义务相似)。当一名董事违反其义务时,泰国公司法认可派生诉讼即公司、股东、债权人均有权就股东的不当行为造成的损失提起诉讼要求赔偿。

(四)股东大会

股东大会分为全体大会和特殊会议,是汇聚股东和董事意见的重要场所。全体股东大会在公司注册登记六个月内第一次举行后,每年举行一次,而特殊会议则是在董事会觉得必要时提起的(在公司财产损失一半时董事会必须提起)或由拥有 1/5 股权的股东提出书面申请提起的等。

并非每一位股东都有表决权,参与表决权的股东的股权必须达到一定数额,其他未达数额的股东可以联合推出一名代理人行使表决权,而没有支付要求应付的股票额的股东不得参加所有会议,与该次会议有特殊利益的股东不得参加此次会议;会议开始前的不记名股东,向公司提交股权证明的股东有权参加此次会议。每一位有权表决的股东都应出席表决或由其代理代为之,表决方式可以是举手表决或投票。除非两个及以上股东提出要求,否则全体股东大会均以举手表决的方式进行。某代理人可以基于附详细信息的代理信代表不能出席的股东行使表决权,且该代理信须在会议开始前提交给会议主席。值得注意的是,不管投票方式如何,会议主席都有决定性的一票。

股东大会的决议一般需大多数在场的股东同意,而特殊的重大决定则需要至少持 3/4 股权的股东出席会议且出席者全票通过。若股东大会的决议违反法律相关规定,股东或董事可以申请取消此项决议,但该申请须在会议结束后一个月内提出。

(五)股息和储备基金

股东有权就其对股份的投资按比例获得股息,而持优先股的股东根据公司章程明文规定获取的股息是不一样的。只要公司认为公正股息可以 分年终股息和期中股息。从资金中抽离出的股息,在公司遭受损失时不会发放。一个公司必须要保证适当的储备基金,每次的股息分配都应该将利润的 1/20 留作储备基金直至储备基金达到公司总资产的 1/10。公司股息的分配不得损害债权人的利益,否则债权人有权要求非善意股东返还股息。

(六)资金

公司的资本数额应该出现在公司章程中,且为保证其能够支付债务对资本的保护也作出了许多相关规定。公司可以增加或减少其资本。公司可以依据股东大会的重大决议通过发行新股增加其资金,所有新股都是由现有股东按份提供的;也可以依据股东大会的重大决议通过减少股票数量或降低股价来减少资金,但是减少的股票数量不能少于每一股数量的 1/4 且受债权人的异议权影响。值得注意的是,不论是通过增加还是减少资金的重大决议,公司都须在决议日期起 14 天内注册登记。

二、CCC 08 修正案对泰国私人公司的影响

与 CCC 的其他部分相比,对私人公司的规定看起来是最有活力的,因为它们经常依据公司运营和实践的变化而被不时地修订。最近的也可能是最突出的便是第 18 次修订的 08 修正案。这些修订使公司的操作灵活,这增加了泰国公司在国际上的竞争力。

(一)允许注册和开办公司在一天内完成

08 修正案允许一天之内成立一个公司,在修改之前,公司的创建过程大约需要两个星期。一天之内创立公司的政策是政府鼓励泰国商业发展的结果,也是激励公司创立的表现。

(二)股东最小数量为 3 人

私人公司的建立必须要有发起人,而 08 修正案对发起人的最小数量要求从 7 人减少至 3 人,因此,维持公司状态的股东的数量要求也从至少 7 人减至至少 3 人。这是鼓励在泰国建立中小型企业组织。

(三)允许在一次会议内批准特殊的重大决议

08 修正案之前通过了一项特别决议,公司必须召开两个连续股东会议,第一次会议,决议须由全部股东 3/4 人数一致同意;第二次会议,决议须由全部股东 2/3 人数一致同意;两次会议时间间隔须大于 14 天。而 08 修正案允许在一次会议内批准特殊的重大决议,该重大决定需要至少持 3/4 股权的股东出席会议且出席者全票通过。该修正,有利于对公司的管理,使公司运营更加灵活快捷。

(四)为促进股东大会召开的通知可以只在当地报纸出版一次

在 08 修正案之前,法律规定至少在公司股东大会召开的 7 天前,公司须在当地报纸至少发布两次通知或在会议召开的 7 天前通过邮寄通知到每一个股东。而 08 修正案则规定开会通知至少须在会前 7 天刊登在当地报纸上 1 次且开会通知也应在 7 天前投递给相应股东,该修正案为公司增加了一个额外的义务,即既要发布通知又要发送通知;然而,它在当地报纸发布通知的次数从至少两次减少为一次且通知必须包含此次会议地点、具体日期与时间和已拟制在会议上将讨论的事项。此修正有利于股东大会及时有效地进行。

The Understanding of Thai Private Company Law

Nilubol Lertnuwat[*]

Introduction

Forms of business organizations in Thailand include sole proprietorship, partnership, private company, and public company. Setting up branches or representative offices of foreign corporations is also possible. The most common form of business structures in Thailand is the private company. The fundamental law which governs incorporation and management of the private company is the *Civil and Commercial Code* ("CCC") Title 12 "Partnership and Company." The characters of Thai private companies are similar to those of western corporations. This is a consequence of adaptation of the English company law occurring in the 18th century.

This article is intended to provide the fundamental understanding of Thai private company law rather than detailing its complicated legal issues. [②] Besides, the article points out some significant changes in Thai private company law as a result of the amendment of the CCC in 2008. Such changes are to facilitate the incorporation and to revise the provisions that impose undue burdens on private companies. The amendment coheres with the need of the government to grow trade and business of small and medium-sized

---

[*] Faculty of Law, Thammasat University.

[②] For those who are interested in Thai public company, please further consider the *Public Limited Company Act B. E.* 2535.

companies. Together with the nature and scope of Thai company law, the details of such changes are discussed below.

Nature and formation of Thai private company

Under the CCC, a private company is a business organization having the capital divided into shares, all of which have equal value. The liability of shareholders is limited to the amount unpaid on the shares respectively held by them, if any. The shareholders in a general meeting are entitled to elect and remove the directors and to make a decision on important matters such as the election and removal of directors, the increase or reduction of company's capital, and the amendment of the memorandum of association. The directors are responsible for managing the company and implementing the decision made by the shareholders' meeting. It is necessary to have at least three persons—the promoters—to promote and form a private company. The requirement on the number of promoters was changed from seven to three persons in 2008. As a result, the number of shareholders for maintaining the status of the company is reduced from at least seven to three persons. This is to encourage the establishment of the small and medium-sized organizations in Thailand.

To incorporate a private company, the first step is to reserve a company name following the regulations and guidelines of the Business Development Office in the Ministry of Commerce. This can be done online. Certain names associated with the royal family, ministries or close to those of other companies are not allowed to be used. The approval from the authority is generally given within 3 days after submitting the reservation and valid for 30 days. The promoters then file a memorandum of association with the Commercial Registration Department.

The memorandum of association includes the proposed name of the company, which must always end with the word "limited," the address in the Kingdom where the registered office of the company is situated, the objects of the company, a declaration that the liability of the shareholders is limited, the amount of share capital with which the company proposes to be registered, and the divisions thereof into shares of a fixed amount, the names, addresses, occupations and signatures of the promoters, and the number of shares subscribed to each of them. The memorandum of association must be made in at least two original copies and signed by the promoters, and the signatures must be certified by two witnesses. One of the copies of the memorandum of association must be deposited and registered at the local registration office whose jurisdiction covers the company's registered office.

After registering the memorandum of association, the promoters must have entire registered shares subscribed. However, the invitation to subscribe for shares must not be made to the public. This is to prevent fraud. Issuing shares at a higher price than their par value is allowed but issuing shares at a lower price than their par value is prohibited. The excess amount of payment must be paid with the first payment. The excess will be added in the company's reserve fund. [1] At least 25 percent of par value of share price is required to be paid prior to the registration of the company. The CCC requires each promoter to subscribe at least one share.

Once the entire registered shares are subscribed, the promoters must hold a general meeting of subscribers with no delay. This meeting is called the statutory meeting. At least seven days before the meeting date, the promoters must forward a statutory report, certified by them, to all subscribers. After sending the report to subscribers, the promoters must file a copy of the statutory report certified by them with the local registrar office.

At the statutory meeting, the matters to be discussed are the adoption of the articles of association of the company, the ratification of any contracts entered into and any expenses incurred by the promoters in promoting the company if any, the amount of payment if any to be paid to the promoters, the number of preference shares if any to be issued and the nature and extent of the preferential rights accruing to them, the number of ordinary shares or

---

[1] The details of the reserved funds is discussed in Section Ⅵ.

preference shares to be allotted as fully or partly paid-up otherwise than in money if any and the amount up to which they shall be considered as paid-up, the appointment of the first board of directors and auditors and the scope of their respective powers. The law prohibits the promoters who have a special interest in a resolution to cast their votes in order to prevent a conflict of interests. To pass a resolution, it must be approved by at least half of subscribers who are entitled to vote and whose shares equal not less than a half of total shares. After the meeting, the promoters must render the company's business to the directors. If the statutory meeting does not approve a contract or payment incurred by the promoters, they are jointly and unlimitedly liable for such a contract or payment.

When at least 25 percent of share price is paid as required, the directors must apply for the registration of the company. The CCC imposes that the registration must be completed within three months after the statutory meeting. If the company is not registered within the period of three months, the directors must return all the collected money to the subscribers without deduction. The directors who fail to do so are liable for the full payment and interest from the expiration of the three months unless they could prove that the delay is not due to their fault.

In 2008, the CCC was significantly amended. In addition to reducing the number of promoters from seven to three persons, such amendment allows the establishment of a company in one day. Before the amendment, the incorporation process took approximately two weeks. The one-day incorporation policy is from the incentive of the government to encourage business establishment in Thailand.

Shares and shareholders

The CCC imposes the minimal amount of a share—not less than five baht. Each share is indivisible and if the share is owned by two or more persons, they must appoint one of them to exercise their rights as a shareholder. However, they are jointly liable for payment of the share price. Generally, the whole amount of every share must be paid in money.

The meeting of shareholders may decide to allot shares to be fully or partly paid otherwise than in money. The shareholders cannot avail themselves of a set-off against the company as to share payments. Besides, a company is prohibited to own its own shares or to take them in pledge. Such prohibitions are to ensure that the company's capital is well preserved for its creditors.

The directors are entitled to call upon the shareholders to collect wholly or partly residual share payment. In each call, 21-day prior to notification, including the details of the amount and payment date of such call fixed by the directors, must be given. If the shareholders fail to make a payment, the directors are required to send another notification requesting the shareholders to pay the share price with an interest at the rate of 7.5 percent per annum from the due date to the date of complete payment received within a given reasonable time. Importantly, it must be clearly stated in the second notification that non-payment shares may be forfeited. If the payment is not received, the directors are able to declare the shares to be forfeited any time. The forfeited shares must be sold without delay by public auction. The surplus after the payment of the call and interest due for the forfeited shares, if any, must be returned to the shareholders.

Each shareholder is entitled to obtain a certificate of shares held by them. There are two types of the certificates: registered and bearer. The company is able to issue bearer certificates to shareholders only if authorized by the articles of association and for shares which are fully paid up. The details appeared on the certificate of shares are the name of the company, the number of shares to which it applies, the amount of each share, the amount paid on each share, the name of the shareholder or a statement that the certificate is to bearer. A signature of at least one director and the seal of the company are also required.

Transfer of registered shares must be made in writing and signed by the transferor and the transferee whose signatures are certified by one witness at least. Share transfer is allowed without the consent of the company unless it is stated otherwise by the articles of association. The transfer of shares is invalid against the company and the third party until the transfer together with the name and address of the transferee are recorded in the register of shareholders.

The company may refuse to record any share transfer under two circumstances, firstly, when the shareholders fail to make a payment on outstanding share price, and secondly during 14 days preceding the ordinary general meeting. The transferor of a share not fully paid up is continually to be liable for the full amount unpaid for two years after the register of the transfer. The exceptions are, firstly, the obligations of the company occurred after the transfer and, secondly, when the existing shareholders are able to satisfy the contributions required. Comparatively speaking, transfer of bearer shares is less complicated. The transfer can be made by the mere delivery of a bearer certificate. The company is not allowed to impose any limitation on bearer-certificate share transfer.

The register of shareholders is a very important document. It includes the details of the shareholders, the number of shares, the amount of shares held by each shareholder, and the amount paid on the shares. The register must be kept at the registered office of the company from the date of the registration of the company. Shareholders are entitled to inspect the register subject to reasonable restrictions imposed by the directors. The details appearing on the register are presumed to be correct evidence of any matters imposed by law to be inserted in it.

Management of Thai private limited company

A private company is managed by a director or directors according to the memorandum of association and the articles of association and under the control of the meeting of shareholders. To amend the contents of the memorandum of association or the articles of association, the super majority vote of the shareholders' meeting is required. The alteration on such documents must be registered by the directors within 14 days after the date of the resolution.

The meeting of shareholders imposes the number and remuneration of the directors. The shareholders' meeting is also empowered to appoint and remove the directors. Even though afterwards it is discovered that there was some defects in the appointment or the disqualification of a director, any act done by him is valid as if he had been duly appointed and was qualified to be a director. The relations among the directors, the company and third persons are governed by the provisions of the law on agency.

Unless stated otherwise, at the first ordinary meeting after the registration of the company and at every annual meeting, one-third of the directors must retire their office. If their number is not a multiple of three, the number is nearest to one-third of the directors. To resign from the post, a director must tender his resignation letter to the company. The effect of the resignation takes place from the date when resignation letter reaches the company. If a director becomes bankrupt or incapacitated, his office is vacated. The board of directors may appoint a director to replace a vacated post occurring in the board otherwise than by rotation. The appointed director can retain his office during such time only as the vacating director was entitled to retain the same. The general meeting of shareholders may remove a director before the expiration of his period of office, and appoint another person in his place. The appointed person can retain his office during such time only as the removed director was entitled to retain the same. The company is obliged to register the change of a director within 14 days from the date of such change.

Unless otherwise specified in the articles of association, the CCC imposes the general powers on the directors. The directors may fix the quorum of the directors' meeting, unless so fixed the quorum is constituted when there are at least three directors. If the number of directors is reduced, the existing directors are still able to manage the company. However, if the remaining directors are not sufficient to form a quorum, the subsisting directors are able to only act for the purposes of increasing the number of directors to that number, or of summoning a general meeting of shareholders. They are prohibited to act for other purposes.

A director can call a meeting of directors anytime. To pass a resolution in a directors' meeting, a majority of votes are required. If the votes are equal, the chairman has a casting vote. The chairman of the board of directors is elected by the directors. The period for which he is to hold office is as well specified by the directors. If the directors do not elect the chairman or if the chairman is not present at the meeting, the directors present may choose one of the remaining directors to be chairman for such meeting.

The CCC prescribes the scope of the duty of directors. Similar to the fiduciary duty of directors in the common law system, the duty of directors is divided into two categories—duty of care and duty of loyalty. To discharge from the duty of care, a director must apply the diligence of a careful businessman in conducting the business. In particular, the directors are jointly responsible for the collection of share payments made by shareholders, the existence and regular keeping of books and documents prescribed by law, the proper distribution of the dividend or interest, the proper enforcement of the resolutions of the general meetings of shareholders. Regarding the duty of loyalty, the director is not generally allowed to be involved in commercial transactions of the same nature as or competitive with those of the company either on his own account or that of a third person. Besides, the director must not be a partner with unlimited liability in another commercial organization carrying a business of the same nature as and competitive with that of the company. The only exception is that the shareholders in a general meeting give consent to such director.

Thai company law recognizes the concept of derivative actions. If a director breaches his duties, the company may bring a claim against the such director for compensation for injury caused by him to the company. If the company refuses to sue the director, any of the shareholders is entitled to do so. The creditors of the company are also entitled to bring a claim against the mismanaging director so far as their claims against the company remain unsatisfied. However, if an act of the director is approved by a general meeting of shareholders, such director is no longer liable for the said act to the shareholders who have approved it or to the company. The shareholders who have not given approval to the director are still able to bring a case against such director within six months after the date of the general meeting in which such act was approved.

Shareholders' meeting

Shareholders' meeting is a very significant venue where all shareholders gather and have their opinions heard by other shareholders and directors. A shareholders' general meeting must be held within six months after the re gistration and at least once every 12 months. All other general meetings are called extraordinary meetings. The directors are entitled to summon extraordinary meetings whenever they think fit. Besides, if the company has lost a half of the amount of its capital, the directors must summon such meeting without delay to inform the shareholders of such loss. Alternatively, shareholders can also call an extraordinary meeting. The shareholders holding not less than one-fifth of the shares of the company may make a request in writing to demand the directors to summon such a meeting. Together with the written request, the shareholders must include the objectives for which the meeting is required to be summoned.

The directors must call an extraordinary meeting whenever the above shareholders request without delay. If the meeting is not summoned within 30 days after the date of the requisition, the shareholders submitting the demand to the directors or any other shareholders amounting to the required number may summon the meeting themselves.

In order to inform shareholders of the meeting, the notification of the summoning of every shareholder's meeting must be published at least once in a local paper not later than seven days before the meeting date. Besides, the notification could be sent by post not later than seven days before the meeting date to every shareholder whose name appears in the register of shareholders. Prior to the amendment of the CCC in 2008, the law requires the company to either publish the notification in a local paper at least twice not later than seven days before the meeting date or send the notification by post to every shareholder not later than seven days before the meeting date. Such amendment creates an extra obligation as the company must both publish and send the notification; however, it facilitates a meeting call as reducing the number of publishing the notification in a local paper from at least twice to once. The notification must include the place, the day and the hour of meeting, and the nature of the business to be discussed at the meeting.

Every shareholder has the right to be present at any general meeting. The company is not allowed to impose any limitation on this. Unless specified otherwise in the articles of association, a quorum of a shareholders' meeting represents at least one-fourth of the capital of the company. If the quorum is not formed within an hour and such meeting is summoned by shareholders, the meeting must be dissolved. However, if the meeting is summoned by the directors, the directors may call another meeting held within 14 days after the prior meeting date and at such meeting no quorum is necessary.

The chairman of the board of directors is the chairman at every general meeting of shareholders. If there is no such chairman or if he is not present within 15 minutes after the scheduled meeting time, the shareholders elect one of their members to be chairman. The chairman is empowered to adjourn any meeting with the consent of the meeting. At an adjourned meeting, shareholders cannot transact any business apart from the business left unfinished at the original meeting.

To vote, a shareholder must present at the meeting or give his proxy to a representative. Under Thai law, there are two means to vote. Firstly, every shareholder shows his hand and each of the shareholders has one vote. Secondly, to vote by a poll, every shareholder has one vote for each share of which he holds. At any general meeting, a resolution put to the vote must be decided on a show of hands. Alternatively, two shareholders may demand to vote by a poll before or on the declaration of the result of the show of hands. If there is such demand, the chairman will decide how the poll is taken.

The company may specify in its regulations prohibiting a shareholder from voting unless he is in possession of a certain number of shares. The shareholder who does not possess such number of shares may join with other shareholders to form the said number of shares and appoint one of them as proxy to represent them and vote at any general meeting. There are few exceptions of the shareholders' right to vote. The shareholders who fail to pay the calls due are not entitled to vote in any resolution. A shareholder who has a special interest in a resolution cannot vote on such resolution. Holders of bearer certificates are able to vote if they deposit their bearer certificates with the company before the meeting.

A shareholder who is not able to be present at the meeting may vote by proxy. A proxy letter must be done in writing with the details of the number of shares held by the shareholder, the name of the proxy, the meeting or meetings or the period for which the proxy is appointed. The proxy must submit the document to the chairman of the meeting at or before the beginning of the meeting at which the proxy named in such document proposed to vote. In the case of an equality of votes, whether on a show of hands or on a poll, the chairman of the meeting is entitled to a casting vote.

The matters which most considered and approved in the meeting of shareholders include director election and removal, auditor appointment and removal, capital reduction and amendment of the memorandum of association. To pass a resolution on a general matter such as director election and removal, the majority of votes of the total number of shareholders presenting at the meeting are required. For particular matters such as capital reduction or amendment of the memorandum of association, the votes of total number of shareholders holding three-fourth of total shares presenting at the meeting are necessary. Prior to the amendment of the CCC in 2008, to pass a resolution with a special resolution, a company must convene two consecutive shareholders' meetings and the resolution had to be passed by votes of three-fourth of the total number of shareholders in the first meeting and votes of two-third of the total number of shareholders in the second meeting. The second meeting must be convened not less than 14 days after the first meeting. As a result of the change, the shareholders' meeting can approve a special solution within one meeting. This facilitates the management of the company.

If a general meeting or a resolution passed is against the provisions of the law or the articles of association of the company, a shareholder or director may request the court to cancel such meeting or resolution. Such a shareholder or director must apply for the cancellation within one month after the meeting date.

Dividends and reserve funds

In return for their investments, shareholders are entitled to receive dividend. The distribution of the dividend must be made in proportion to the amount paid upon each share. Those who hold preference shares may receive the dividend differently. Such difference must be clearly specified in the articles of association. The annual general meeting of shareholders is entitled to declare whether and how much dividend will be paid. Alternatively the directors can from time to time pay to the shareholders interim dividends if it appears to the directors that the profit of the company justifies to do so. The dividend must not be paid from the company's capital. If the company has incurred losses, it is not allowed to pay the dividend unless such losses have been recovered. If the company fails to pay the dividend, the shareholders are not authorized to receive interest on the outstanding dividend.

The company must ensure that a reserve fund is appropriately set up. At each distribution of dividend, the company must take at least one-twentieth of the profits for the reserve fund until the reserve fund reaches one-tenth of the capital of the company. In the articles of association, the company may specify a higher proportion. In addition, if the company issues shares at a value higher than the par value, it must add the excess to the reserve fund until the fund has reached one-tenth of the company capital or higher as specified in the articles of association.

If the company does not distribute the dividend properly; for instance, the company pays the dividend even though it incurs losses, the company's creditors are entitle to request the dividend to be returned from the shareholders to the company. However, if the shareholders receive the dividend in good faith, they do not have to return such dividend.

Capital

The amount of the company's capital appears in the memorandum of association. There are number of provisions aiming to preserve the company's capital to ensure that its debts will be paid. For instance, the shareholders cannot avail themselves of a set-off against the company as to share payments. In addition, the company is prohibited from owning its own shares or to take them in pledge.

A company can increase its capital by issuing new shares with a special resolution of the meeting of shareholders. All new shares must be offered to the existing shareholders in proportion to the shares held by them. To offer such shares, the company must send the notification to shareholders specifying the number of shares to which the shareholders are entitled and the date, after which the offer, if not accepted, is considered to be declined. After such date or on the receipt of the shareholders that they declined to accept the shares offered, the director then offers such shares for subscription to other shareholders or may subscribe the shares to himself.

If a company wishes to reduce its capital, it has to obtain a special resolution from the meeting of shareholders. The reduction can be done by reducing the number of shares or lowering the price of each share. However, such reduction cannot be less than one-fourth of the amount of each share. After the share reduction proposal is approved by the shareholders' meeting, the company must publish a notification at least once in a local paper and submit to all creditors known to the company a notification of the share reduction proposal. Such notification must require the creditors to present any objection they may have to such reduction within 30 days from the date of knowing such notice. If the company does not receive any objection within such period of time, none is deemed to exist. If a creditor raises an objection, the company cannot proceed the reduction unless the company has satisfied the claim or given security for such claim. If a creditor has not given the notice of raising objection within 30 days and such delay is not his fault, the shareholders who receive the refunded shares remain personally liable to such creditor to the extent of the amount refunded. The liability remains for a period of two years from the date of registration of such reduction. The special resolution by which any increase or reduction of capital has been authorized must be registered by the company within 14 days after the resolution date.

Conclusion

Compared with other parts of the CCC, the provisions on a private company seem to be the most dynamic as they have been frequently amended to follow changes in business operation and practice. The most recent and possibly most prominent amendment was the 18th amendment in 2008. Such amendment allows the establishment of a company in one day, decreases the minimum number of shareholders to three persons, allows approval of a special resolution within one meeting, and facilitates a call for a general meeting by publishing in a local paper only once(originally twice). Making operation of a company more flexible, this increases competitiveness of Thai companies at an international level.

泰国与东盟共同体[*]

杨丽艳　万　强　阮氏河[**]

东盟共同体将要于 2015 年年底建成。东盟各成员国都在为之积极地努力。泰国地处中南半岛中心位置,作为东盟老六国成员,充分意识到建设东盟经济共同体是大势所趋,是区域合作的重要机制,对于本国是利大于弊。因此泰国利用自身优势,在东盟共同体建设中发挥着重要作用。那么,东盟共同体究竟为何物? 对于泰国来说,有哪些利弊和意义? 在泰国专篇里笔者试图做一个抛砖论述,或许可引出大家对东盟共同体的作用、意义及其对亚太区域的影响等一系列问题的思考。

一、东盟共同体的由来

(一)东盟共同体是由东盟发展而来

东盟(The Association of Southeast Asian Nations,or ASEAN)是一个封闭的区域性组织,它于 1967 年在泰国曼谷建立,以曼谷宣言的签署作为标志,当时的 5 个成员国有印度尼西亚、马来西亚、菲律宾、新加坡和泰国,它们被合称为东盟建立之父。[①]

建立东盟的主要目的是维护地区安全。原因是冷战时期,大国在东南亚

　＊　该论文为广西民族大学东盟研究中心课题(20120134)、西南政法大学国际法学院院级项目(33113204002)广西文科中心中国—东盟法律制度团队(TD2011014)项目系列的成果之一。

　＊＊　杨丽艳,西南政法大学国际法学院教授;万强、阮氏河为西南政法大学国际法学院研究生。

　①　http://www.asean.org/asean/about-asean,下载日期:2015 年 1 月 20 日。

角逐，国际组织发展迅速。成立伊始，它的实质性合作措施不多，但在近 20 年里，却紧跟世界经济一体化的步伐，在其区域组织内部采取了一系列一体化的法律措施，同时，在外交、军事、政治等方面也有区域组织的方针和政策，并取得了一定的效果。这一事实证明了，东盟作为一个区域性国际经济组织，在区域一体化方面采取了法律的形式，极其有效地促进了东盟的一体化。在经历了 1967—1975 年初步发展时期；1976—1991 年东盟一体化开始阶段；1992—1997 年东盟进入一体化快速发展时期；1997—2003 年金融危机减速恢复时期[1]以及 2003 年至今这 5 个阶段，东盟进入了一个平稳发展阶段。而 2003 年，在金融危机仍然还有一定影响的情况下，各国领导在 2003 年第九届东盟峰会上表决应该建立东盟共同体（ASEAN Community）。2007 年第 12 届东盟峰会上各国领导再次肯定要加速东盟共同体的建立，并且将时间明确写在了塞布宣言（the Cebu Declaration）里，确定建立的时间为 2015 年。

（二）东盟共同体的构成

东盟共同体由三大支柱（three pillars）构成：东盟政治安全共同体（the ASEAN Political-Security Community，APSC）；东盟经济共同体（ASEAN Economic Community，AEC）以及东盟社会文化共同体（ASEAN Socio-Cultural Community，ASCC）。每个支柱都有自己的发展蓝图（blueprint），与东盟一体化战略框架倡议［the Initiative for ASEAN Integration（IAI）Strategic Framework］以及东盟一体化倡议工作计划阶段［IAI Work Plan Phase II（2009-2015）］一起，构成了东盟共同体（2009—2015）的路线图。

二、东盟共同体的 3 根支柱设计及其理念分析

（一）东盟政治安全共同体（APSC）[2]

强调 3 个主要的原则或者 3 个特性：一是价值和规则分享的以规则为导向的共同体（a rules-based community of shared values and norms）；二是一个

---

① 杨丽艳：《东盟的法律和政策与现代国际法》，广西师范大学出版社 2000 年版，第 5 页。

② http://www.asean.org/images/resources/2014/Jul/ASEANAnnualReport20132014.pdf，下载日期：2015 年 1 月 28 日、29 日。

有凝聚力的、和平的、顺应的共同分担全面安全的责任的共同体（a cohesive, peaceful and resilient region with shared responsibility for comprehensive security)；三是一个在日益一体化和相互依存的世界里的动态和外向型地区（a dynamic and outward-looking regionin an increasingly integrated and interdependent world)。[①]

APSC 旨在确保东盟成员国及其人民能够生活在彼此之间和平共处以及世界范围内的公正、民主、和谐的环境中。为了做到这一点，APSC 要促进与民主、法治和良治挂钩的政治发展，并且尊重写在东盟宪章里的促进和保护人权与基本自由的原则。与此同时，APSC 寻求旨在加强东盟与对话伙伴和朋友之间的互利关系。

(二)东盟经济共同体(AEC)[②]

强调 4 个主要的支柱：一是建立单一市场（single marketand production base)；二是建立竞争经济区域（competitive economic region)；三是公平地发展经济；四是要融进世界经济一体化（integrating into the global economy)。具体目标是通过促进货物、服务、投资和熟练劳动力以及资本的自由流动增加机构、人民对人民的联系，以降低经商成本；通过制订有针对性的方案缩小各国国内和东盟成员国之间的发展差距；并通过以参与双边自由贸易协定和东盟自由贸易区去建成区域全面经济伙伴关系（RCEP)以达到协同的结果。此外，通过 AEC 的记分卡机制（the AEC scorecard mechanism)去跟进我们的进步和既定目标。为了达到这些目的：设计了 AEC 的记分卡机制（the AEC Scorecard mechanism)，这些机制围绕上述四个支柱的实现而进行，即以消除关税，促进货物、服务、技术工人、投资、资本的自由流动，促进重点整合行业、食品、农业和森林的发展等措施达到货物的自由流动；以构建竞争政策、消费保护、知识产权保护以及基础设施的建设来加强竞争经济区域制度；以发展中小企业（SMEs)、促进一体化来达到公平的经济发展；以融进全球经济一体化。该记分卡机制启动于 2008 年，总共分 4 个阶段来实施：2008—2009，

---

① ASEAN Political-Security Community(APSC)http://www. asean. org，下载日期：2015 年 1 月 28 日；http://www. asean. org/images/resources/2014/Jul/ASEAN Annual Report20132014. pdf，下载日期：2015 年 1 月 28 日、29 日。

② http://www. asean. org/images/2013/factsheet/2013% 20（6. % 20Jun）% 20-% 20ASCC. pdf，下载日期：2015 年 1 月 28 日。

2010—2011,2012—2013,2014—2015。同时,东盟还采取了相应的法律和政策来落实,如实施了东盟全面投资协定(ASEAN Comprehensive Investment Agreement,ACIA),东盟便利货物贸易框架协议(ASEAN Framework Agreement on the Facilitation of Goods in Transit,AFAFGIT);东盟投资协定下的所有相关措施(all measures under the ASEAN Investment Agreement,AIA);东盟全面投资协定生效前的暂时例外和敏感清单(Temporary Exclusion Lists and Sensitive Lists under the ASEAN Comprehensive Investment Agreement,ACIA);促进和便利投资的行动(activities in support of promoting and facilitating the investment)等。

(三)东盟社会文化共同体(ASCC)

东盟社会文化共同体旨在促进东盟共同体以人为导向(people-oriented)和承担社会责任,追求建立一个拥有共同身份、充满爱心和共享的社会,这个社会对于人们来说是具有包容性、友善、充满活力、福利不断增强的。人类发展(Human Development);社会福利和保护(Social Welfare and Protection);社会公正和权利(Social Justice and Rights);确保环境的可持续性(Ensuring Environmental Sustainability);建立东盟身份(Building ASEAN Identity);缩小发展差距(Narrowing the Development Gap)。具体而言,就是要建立关爱性社会的共同体,以解决贫困、平等和人类发展的问题;通过建立以具有竞争力的人力资源为基础的和具有充分的社会保障体系因素的共同体来发展管理经济一体化的社会影响的能力;增强环境的可持续性和健全的环境治理;加强区域社会凝聚力迎接 2015 年到来的东盟共同体。

(四)三个共同体的建立成效

1.政治安全共同体的建设目标高远,东盟以其强调的保持和增进和平稳定对地区经济发展和繁荣的基础性作用作为其政治共同体的成效。即在瞬息万变的地区和国际形势下,各国领导人强调东盟在演变中的区域架构和大国关系中巩固其战略地位保证了东盟的主导性、公信力和重要性。

2.在经济共同体的建设上,表现出来的一是"东盟地区经济增长稳健,2013 年 GDP 增长率达 5.1%。预计 2014 年地区经济增长速度将减缓至 4.6%,预计 2015 年 GDP 增长速度上升为 5.3%。二是保持稳健的宏观经济基本要素和金融稳定,解决内部劣势,特别是基础设施方面的缺陷,深化经济一体化和自由化的重要性。这将保证并提升地区在贸易和投资方面的竞争力"。

3. 在社会文化共同体的建设上,在建设东盟社会文化共同体的重要方面取得许多进展,这些领域包括:气候变化、灾难管理和减轻灾难风险、减贫、保护和提高农民工权益等。

东盟秘书处负责社区和企业事务的副秘书长 AKP Mochtan 2015 年年初在雅加达代表东盟秘书长黎良明主持新闻发布会,向各国驻东盟使团介绍了本月中旬将要在内比都举行的第 25 届东盟峰会上讨论的东盟共同体建设的有关情况。他表示,东盟共同体的三大支柱的建设取得长足进展,实施率已达到约 88%。[①]

另外,在东盟共同体的身份认同上,东盟已经迈出了重要的步骤,如:在机场设立"东盟成员通道"。2014 年 12 月,马来西亚吉隆坡国际机场出入境口岸新设一条东盟专用通道,来自东盟成员国的游客可以享受作为"东盟公民"的特殊待遇,快速通关。在东盟共同体的建设方面,泰国的一些做法和意识一直比较超前。早在 1995 年,泰国就曾在廊曼国际机场开设一条东盟专用通道。而今年担任东盟轮值主席国的马来西亚也雄心勃勃,准备今年内在机场增设 5 个专用通道。

值得一提的是,"东盟成员通道"虽然事小,但是说明东盟在共同体建设上已经迈出步伐了。一条专用通道的开设,或许只是细节问题,但绝非无足轻重,这是东盟各国需要花点心思去提供的一项服务。东盟共同体的认同感,恰恰就是在这样点滴的细节中凝聚、累积而成。[②] 东盟专用通道是东盟各国领导人依据 2010 年在越南河内达成的共同协议,敦促各国设立的。设立专用通道的初衷是,当东盟各国的公民迈出国门时,首先能寻找到一个"专用区域",体验到"我来自东盟"的自豪感,从而建立起对共同体的契约观念和深切认同。[③]

东盟三个共同体的理念崇高、目标宏大,机构的配置也顺应了其设计。

就政治共同体(ASEAN Political-Security Community)来说,配套建立了东盟政府间人权委员会(ASEAN Intergovernmental Commission on Human

① 王珊:《东盟共同体建设实施率已达约 88% 各国承诺 2015 年完成》,http://gb.cri.cn/42071/2014/11/26/6071s4780205.htm,下载日期:2015 年 2 月 10 日。

② 李颖:《随笔:从细微处看"东盟共同体"建设》,http://news.xinhuanet.com/world/2015-02/04/c_1114257137.htm,下载日期:2015 年 2 月 10 日。

③ 李颖:《随笔:从细微处看"东盟共同体"建设》,http://news.xinhuanet.com/world/2015-02/04/c_1114257137.htm,下载日期:2015 年 2 月 10 日。

Rights,AICHR),东盟外交部长会议(ASEAN Foreign Ministers' Meeting,AMM),东盟地区论坛(ASEAN Regional Forum,ARF),东盟国防部长会议(ASEAN Defence Ministers Meeting,ADMM),东盟法律部长会议(ASEAN Law Ministers Meeting,ALAWMM),东盟跨境犯罪部长会议(ASEAN Ministerial Meeting on Transnational Crime,AMMTC)[1]等 6 个机构来进行合作。

就经济共同体(ASEAN Economic Community)来说,由东盟经济部长(ASEAN Economic Ministers,AEM),东盟自贸区(ASEAN Free Trade Area,AFTA Council),东盟能源部长会议(ASEAN Ministers on Energy Meeting,AMEM),东盟农林部长会议(ASEAN Ministerial Meeting on Agriculture and Forestry,AMAF),东盟金融部长会议(ASEAN Finance Ministers Meeting,AFMM),东盟投资区理事会(ASEAN Investment Area,AIA Council),东盟矿业部长会议(ASEAN Ministerial Meeting on Minerals,AMMin),东盟科技部长会议(ASEAN Ministerial Meeting on Science and Technology,AMMST),东盟湄公河发展合作(ASEAN Mekong Basin Development Cooperation,AMBDC),东盟交通部长会议(ASEAN Transport Ministers Meeting,ATM),东盟通信与计算机部长会议(ASEAN Telecommunications and IT Ministers Meeting,TELMIN),东盟旅游部长会议(ASEAN Tourism Ministers Meeting,M-ATM),东盟一体化启动及缩小发展距离机构[Initiative for ASEAN Integration(IAI)and Narrowing the Development Gap,NDG],在东盟经济部长会议管辖下的各部事项(Sectoral Bodies under the Purview of AEM)等 15 个机构构成。

就社会文化共同体来说,它也由下面 14 个机构组成:东盟负责文化艺术(ASEAN Ministers Responsible for Culture & Arts,AMCA),东盟体育部长会议(ASEAN Ministerial Meeting on Sports,AMMS),东盟灾难管理部长会议(ASEAN Ministerial Meeting on Disaster Management,AMMDM),东盟教育部长会议(ASEAN Education Ministers Meeting,ASED),东盟环境部长会议(ASEAN Ministerial Meeting on Environment,AMME),各方会议及东盟跨境雾霾污染协议(Conference of the Parties to the ASEAN Agreement

---

[1] http://www. asean. org/communities/asean-political-security-community,下载日期:2015 年 2 月 10 日。

on Transboundary Haze Pollution，COP to AATHP），东盟健康部长会议
（ASEAN Health Ministers Meeting，AHMM），东盟负责信息部长会议
（ASEAN Ministers Responsible for Information，AMRI），东盟劳工部长会议
（ASEAN Labor Ministers Meeting，ALMM），东盟郊区发展和根除贫困部长
会议（ASEAN Ministers Meeting on Rural Development and Poverty
Eradication，AMRDPE），东盟科技部长会议（ASEAN Ministerial Meeting on
Science and Technology，AMMST），东盟社会福利发展部长会议（ASEAN
Ministerial Meeting on Social Welfare and Development，AMMSWD），东盟
妇女部长会议（ASEAN Ministerial Meeting on Women，AMMW），东盟青年
人部长会议（ASEAN Ministerial Meeting on Youth，AMMY）。

综观上述 3 个共同体及其下属机构，不难看出，每个共同体都因为有着特
殊使命而设置了诸多下属机构，而这些机构几乎涉及了所有的国内事项，当然
也背负着实现重要目标的使命；如：政治共同体的终极目标是消除各国政治摩
擦、协调各国不同的政治体制、建立国内民主法治体制、维护地区安全、形成政
治共同体；而经济共同体要消除资本、劳动力、货物和服务的自由流动的障碍，
促进投资自由化，达到 4 个支柱的目标；至于社会文化共同体，则要建立一个
拥有共同身份、充满爱心和共享的社会，一个具有包容性、友善、充满活力、福
利不断增强的社会，这就要各国消除包括文化制度在内的文化隔阂和障碍，实
行宗教自由，确立公平、公正的价值观。这些目标显然具有高难度。而上述机
构具有的特点是合作性、拼凑性、缺乏一体性和超国家性。事实证明，国际组
织里的超国家因素的机构是提高该国际组织效率和效果的有利机制之一。因
为诸国的长期合作，利益冲突通常是会有的，而超国家因素机构在协调管理国
际组织的目标，法律、政策实施等方面会超越国家而行驶自己的职能，会促使
一体化产生更好的效果。因此，东盟共同体的机构设置要根据目标的完成来
进行必要的改进。

三、泰国在东盟共同体建设中的努力

(一)泰国是东盟的创始国

1967 年东盟的创立与泰国是分不开的。在创立和发展之初，泰国扮演了
一个积极的角色。成立时的会议以及宣言的签署都是于 1967 年 8 月 8 日在
泰国首都曼谷的萨兰柔姆宫（Saranrom Palace)进行的。

（二）泰国在东盟的发展中一直发挥积极的作用

一是泰国一直将东盟视为外交政策的基石（a cornerstone），强调在东盟的框架下与东盟其他各国家合作的重要性以及与东盟各国建立起信任，共同促进地区的和平稳定繁荣。二是泰国在促使东盟宪章具有法律效力以及使东盟成为以规则为导向的国际组织（rules-based organization）方面作出了积极的努力，如：2008—2009 年，泰国是东盟的轮值主席，其间泰国高度重视东盟的建设进程：致力于有效实施东盟宪章，认为这对于东盟建立程序式管理是重要的；另外一个重要的行动是，在泰国的主持下通过了一项重要的文件：东盟共同体路线图（2009—2015）[the Roadmap for the ASEAN Community (2009-2015)]，该路线图制定了一系列的行动来指导东盟政治安全共同体、经济共同体以及社会文化共同体的建设工作。因为泰国认为这三个支柱的建设在 2015 年之后将支持一个强大的东盟共同体的建设。

（三）泰国在三个支柱建设中发挥着位于前列的促进作用

在政治和安全领域，泰国正致力于与东盟各成员国一道，维护和平稳定的地区环境，认为这对于持续的经济发展至关重要。泰国一直积极促进东盟区域的建设，通过现有或建设各种机制和框架，如：1976 年的《东盟军事与合作条约》（Treaty of Amity and Cooperation，TAC）[①]，东亚峰会（East Asia Summit，the EAS），东盟各国防部长会议（ASEAN Defense Ministers' Meeting，ADMM）and ADMM Plus，东盟区域论坛（ASEAN Regional Forum，ARF），来保证区域和国家的安全，以及促进预防性外交和处理某些现有的区域争议，让东盟的争端解决机制真正发挥作用。泰国在区域的促进和保护人权方面也发挥了重要作用。如促进建立了该地区的东盟政府间人权委员会（AICHR），并且积极参加和支持利益相关者在该地区的《人权宣言》的起草过程，该宣言在第 21 届东盟领导人峰会上通过。

在经济领域，泰国认为区域经济一体化是一种方式或手段，即可以确保东盟区域经济的可持续和公平增长，加强东盟成员国的竞争力，将东盟的一体化

---

① 该条约于 1987 年修改，向世界各国开放。到目前为止，已经有中国（2003）、美国（2009）、欧盟（2012）等 16 个国家加入，http://en.wikipedia.org/wiki/Treaty_of_Amity_and_Cooperation_in_Southeast_Asia，下载日期：2015 年 2 月 16 日。

成效奉献于全球经济。自东盟自由贸易区于 1992 年成立到具有一定规模以来,泰国一直是一个强烈支持东盟区域经济一体化的成员国,并且泰国将在继续深化区域经济一体化中发挥积极作用。通过 RCEP 的发展【2011 年 11 月第 19 届东盟峰会启动了东南亚区域全面经济伙伴协定(the Regional Comprehensive Economic Partnership,RCEP)。主要是以东南亚国家联盟 10 国为主体,加上日本、中华人民共和国、韩国、印度、澳大利亚、新西兰等 6 国,由 16 个国家所构成,是更近一步的自由贸易协定(FTA)。在第 44 届东盟经济部长会议及相关会议上,10 个东盟国家和 6 个伙伴国的经济部长们一致同意在 2012 年年底之前开始 16 国间的一个自由贸易协定的谈判——东南亚区域全面经济伙伴协定(RCEP)。RCEP 的 16 个参与国的政府官员——10 个东盟成员国和它们的自由贸易伙伴(中国、澳大利亚、日本、韩国、印度及新西兰)在文莱的达鲁萨兰开始基于细节的谈判并且致力于在 2015 年年底之前结束谈判。其与在 2012 年 11 月份的 RCEP 领导关于开始谈判的联合声明和在 2012 年 8 月 30 日在部长级会议签署的谈判指导原则和目标一致。RCEP 谈判将以以下几点为目标:建立一个现代的、综合的、高质量的共同利益经济伙伴合作关系,在本区域建成一个开放型的贸易和投资环境以加快区域贸易和投资的扩展并且有利于全球经济增长和发展。以及基于本地区已有的经济纽带,促进经济增长以及经济均衡发展,加强先进的经济合作,通过 RCEP 扩大并且深化本区域的经济整合。2013 年 9 月 23—27 日在澳大利亚举行的第二轮 RCEP 谈判进展顺利。代表团主要专注于商品、服务和投资贸易。根据 RCEP 指导条款,他们也涉及经济和科技合作、竞争、知识产权、解决分歧以及其他事务。2014 年 1 月 20 日—24 日,在区域全面经济伙伴协定第三轮谈判期间,16 个参与国大量地交换了意见,希望能在 2015 年年底前达成结束谈判的目标。

参与国继续专注于商品、服务和投资贸易:在商品贸易方面,参与国就关税程序、免税措施、技术法规、标准与合格评定(STRACAP)、卫生与动物检疫措施(SPS)以及海关手续和贸易便利化(CPTF)和原产地规范(ROO)展开了建设性的讨论。在服务业方面,参与国讨论了 RCEP 服务章程的结构与组成,市场准入的利益方面和一系列特殊的事项。在投资方面,参与国交换了投资程序意见以及进一步商议了 RCEP 投资章程的细节问题。为了提前大范围领域事项的谈判,参与国建立了 4 个工作领域:知识产权保护、竞争经济、技术合作、分歧解决,一些代表在某些参与国感兴趣的特定领域做了表述。在回合谈判的同时,有两个研讨会展开。马来西亚和日本组织了一场知识产权保护的研讨会,对在知识产权保护方面的各领域事项和知识产权保护如何进一步支持贸易和投资进行了讨论。

澳大利亚组织了关于贯穿服务业和投资方面的研讨会。参与国在这些事项上进行了良好的谈判。http://zh.wikipedia.org/wiki/维基百科网2015年2月18日查。

2014年4月,各国代表在南宁举行了第4轮RCEP谈判。4月4日,为期5天的《区域全面经济伙伴关系协定》(RCEP)第4轮谈判在广西南宁圆满结束。在前3轮谈判的基础上,东盟10国、中国、澳大利亚、印度、日本、韩国、新西兰等16方在本轮谈判中继续就RCEP涉及的一系列议题进行了密集磋商,在货物、服务、投资及协议框架等广泛的问题上取得了积极进展。在货物贸易方面,重点讨论了关税、非关税措施,标准、技术法规和合格评定程序,卫生与植物卫生措施,海关程序与贸易便利化,原产地规则等议题。在服务贸易方面,就谈判范围、市场准入领域等议题充分交换了意见。在投资方面,就投资模式文件和投资章节要素进行了深入探讨。新成立的知识产权、竞争政策和经济技术合作工作组也就相关议题进行了讨论。会议取得了积极进展。谈判各方决定,第5轮谈判将于2014年6月在新加坡举行。RCEP谈判于2012年11月正式启动,目标是在2015年年底前达成一个现代、全面、高质量和互惠的经济伙伴关系协定。(http://www.mofcom.gov.cn/article/ae/ai/201404/20140400541040.shtml中国商务部网站,2015年2月20日查)2014年6月23日至27日,区域全面经济伙伴关系协定(RCEP)第5轮谈判在新加坡举行。中方代表团由商务部、发展改革委、工业和信息化部、财政部、农业部、海关总署、工商总局、质检总局、版权局、知识产权局等部门组成。东盟10国、澳大利亚、印度、日本、韩国和新西兰等派代表团出席。谈判期间,16方谈判代表就RCEP涉及的一系列议题进行了密集磋商,并对将于今年8月在缅甸举行的第二届RCEP贸易部长会进行筹备。在货物贸易方面,各方重点讨论了关税减让模式,贸易救济,原产地规则,海关程序与贸易便利化,标准、技术法规和合格评定程序,卫生与植物卫生措施等议题。在服务贸易方面,就谈判模式、章节要素等领域充分交换了意见。在投资方面,就投资模式文件和投资章节要素进行了深入探讨。新成立的知识产权、竞争政策、经济技术合作和法律问题工作组也就相关议题进行了讨论。http://www.mofcom.gov.cn/article/ae/ai/201407/20140700651613.shtml中国商务部网站,2015年2月20日查2014年12月5日,在印度新德里RECP结束了其第6轮谈判。根据印度媒体报道和评论,本轮谈判的关注重点包括统一的优惠关税安排、

RCEP 可能采用的 IPR 等标准、达成谈判成果的先后顺序等。http://world. chinadaily. com. cn/2014-12/17/content_19103164. htm 中国日报中文网 2015 年 2 月 23 日查,2015 年年末,RCEP 谈判计划在 2015 年年末结束。】,这个由东盟提出的将引领全球一半市场规模的合作,会进一步帮助提高东亚经济集体潜力。东盟 10 国成为一个整体,在其内外增强其整体性 (connectivity)是至关重要的。因此,泰国提议以全面的姿态、包括有形可视的,机构的以及人民与人民之间联系紧密而表现出来的整体性。实施东盟整体性的规划是东盟最重要的领域之一。

在社会文化领域,泰国全力支持由《东盟宪章》设想的以人为本的东盟共同体。泰国就任东盟主席期间,启动了东盟领导人会议以及东盟内部议会代表大会(AIPA),民间社会组织(CSO),以增加他们与东盟的互动,促进他们参与东盟共同体的建设过程。泰国也将继续与东盟同事密切合作,以进一步促进各种社会文化领域的发展,如灾害管理、教育区域合作、缩小发展差距、环境、公众健康以及建立东盟的共同身份,为了最终在东盟实现关爱和共享的社会。

泰国地处中南半岛的中心位置,2009 年以来,如上所述,积极促进东盟共同体建设;同时也一直致力于加快建设交通网络、培养服务人才、创造良好的投资环境、发挥地理优越性、努力参与建设东盟三个共同体。

2015 年已经到来,东盟共同体将于 2015 年 12 月 31 日建成。今年东盟要完成《2009－2015 年东盟共同体路线图》的剩余任务。目前东盟共同体建设计划尚有 10％没有完成,而且大多是共同体建设的难点。今年,东盟经济共同体建设面临着统一海关标准、贸易准则、金融部门自由化、确保投资受到保护、消除有关地区性的直接融资障碍等诸多任务。目前,东盟正努力通过执行《东盟一体化倡议》(IAI),缩小东盟各国之间以及东盟和世界之间的发展差距;通过实施《东盟互联互通总体规划》(MPAC)促进东盟民众积极互联互通。根据东盟经济共同体建设的要求,大多国家需要制定、修改和通过相关经济法律法规,以便互联互通。东盟各成员国的经济发展状况不同,经济发展依然存在较大差距,制约了东盟经济共同体的建设进程。对取消非关税障碍、熟练劳动力流动等方面的整合要到 2020 年才能完成。[①]

---

① 许宁宁:《2015 年东盟经济共同体面临大考》,http://world. people. com. cn/n/2015/0218/c157278-26581505. html,下载日期:2015 年 2 月 19 日。

2015 年之后,东南亚将面临更大的挑战。对于东南亚而言,东盟经济共同体是战略目标,东南亚推进区域融合、提高竞争力,期望形成 AEC(东盟经济共同体)实现经济达到 3% 的增长,但这并不是 AEC 的全部目标。我们知道泰国、马来西亚、文莱、老挝、越南、柬埔寨、印度尼西亚、缅甸、菲律宾、新加坡等 10 个国家正努力建立东盟共同体,这个共同体包括各个不同方面的合作。这是东盟国家合作的一个纬度,可以分成三方面,一是政治安全共同体;二是经济共同体;三是社会文化共同体。关于 AEC 的界定,东南亚希望将 10 个国家转变为统一的市场基地,把东南亚打造为具有高度竞争力的基地,使东盟成为经济发展较快的地区。东南亚希望能够实现东盟 10 国之间的充分融合,并且融入世界经济,尤其是与中国、日本、韩国、印度、澳大利亚以及新西兰的融合。相信在东盟国家的共同努力下,东盟共同体一定会达到自己的目的。

Thailand and the ASEAN Community

周　敏　译

The ASEAN Community shall be established by 2015, and all ASEAN member countries are making the greatest efforts. With the position in the middle of Indo-China Peninsula, Thailand, as an original member of ASEAN, has been fully aware of that the ASEAN Community will be an important regional cooperation mechanism, as the trend of the times. It will bring about more benefits than harm for Thailand. Hence, Thailand plays a vital role in the construction of the ASEAN Community with its advantages. What is the ASEAN Community? What does it bring about for Thailand? This paper tries to discuss about such questions and even turns to the topic of ASEAN Community's significance and effects on Asian-Pacific region.

The origin of the ASEAN Community

1. The ASEAN Community is developed from ASEAN

The Association of Southeast Asian Nations, or ASEAN, was established on 8 August 1967 in Bangkok, Thailand, with the signing of the Bangkok Declaration by the founding fathers of ASEAN, namely Indonesia, Malaysia, Philippines, Singapore and Thailand.

The original aim of ASEAN is to promote regional peace and stability. During the Cold War, lots of super countries staying at Southeast Asian made the international associations develop quickly. At the beginning, there was little substantial cooperation in ASEAN. However, it has kept up with the pace of world economic integration in the recent 20 years with many advanced legal, diplomatic, military and political policies. Such fact reveals that, as a regional economic organization, ASEAN greatly promotes the integration of Southeast Asian nations with legal measures.

2. The components of the ASEAN Community

The ASEAN Community consists of three pillars, ASEAN Political-Security Community (APSC), ASEAN Economic Community (AEC) and ASEAN Socio-Cultural Community (ASCC). Every pillar has its development blueprint, the Initiative for ASEAN Integration (IAI) Strategic Framework, IAI Work Plan Phase Ⅱ (2009-2015), all these make up the ASEAN Community's route map.

The design and principle of the three pillars

1. The ASEAN Political-Security Community(APSC)

APSC has three main principles. The first one is " a rules-based community of shared values and norms. " The second one is " a cohesive, peaceful and resilient region with shared responsibility for comprehensive security. " The third one is "a dynamic and outward-looking region in an increasingly integrated and Interdependent World. "

APSC aims to ensure a peaceful life between the ASEAN member countries and a fair, democratic and harmonious world. To achieve this, APSC needs to promote the political development concerning fairness, democracy and harmony. Also, it shall respect the basic principles of freedom and human rights written in the Charter of ASEAN. At the same time, APSC seeks to strengthen the communication of Southeast Asian countries and mutually beneficial relationship between such partners and friends.

2. The ASEAN Economic Community(AEC)

AEC has four main pillars. First, establishing a single market and production base; second, establishing a competitive economic region; third, making the economic development fairly; forth, Integrating into the global economy. The concrete goal is to promote the free flow of goods, services, investment, skilled labor, and capital and to increase connection between institutions and people. In addition, it aims to narrow the development gap between ASEAN member countries with some directed plans, and to build Regional Comprehensive Economic Partnership(RCEP)through participating the bilateral free trade agreements.

The AEC scorecard mechanism helps a lot to achieve such purposes. This mechanism started in 2008. Its plan has been divided into four periods, 2008-2009, 2010-2011, 2012-2013, and 2014-2015. Meanwhile, ASEAN sets out a lot of corresponding laws and policies for it, such as the ASEAN Comprehensive Investment Agreement(ACIA), Protocols 1, 2, 7 and 9 of the ASEAN Framework Agreement on the Facilitation of Goods in Transit (AFAFGIT), all measures under the ASEAN Investment Agreement (AIA), Temporary Exclusion Lists and Sensitive Lists under the ASEAN Comprehensive Investment Agreement (ACIA) activities in support of promoting and facilitating investment as scheduled, etc.

3. The ASEAN Socio-Cultural Community(ASCC)

The ASEAN Socio-Cultural Community aims to promote the ASEAN Community as a people-oriented society, and it will full of social responsibilities. It pursues a common identity, a caring and sharing society, and such society is inclusive, friendly, energetic. The main points are human development, social welfare and protection, social justice and rights, ensuring environmental sustainability, building ASEAN identity and narrowing the development gap.

In particular, it is to establish a caring social community, in order to solve problems concerning poverty, equality and human development. It is the establishment of competitive human resources, the social security system, great environmental sustainability, environmental management and regional social cohesion that makes the ASEAN community wonderful in 2015.

4. The effect of three communities

(1) As for the ASEAN Political-Security Community, the basic function of maintaining and promoting the peace and stability for the regional economic development and prosperity is its most obvious effect. Even in a rapidly changing world, the leaders emphasize that ASEAN needs

to consolidate its dominant strategic position to guarantee its dominance, credibility and significance.

(2) As for the ASEAN Economic Community, it firstly shows that ASEAN countries keep up with stable economic promotion. Every year, there is a rate of increase with more than 5%. Secondly, it maintains the stability of basic key elements of macroeconomic and financial to solve the internal weaknesses, especially the defect of infrastructure. This will ensure and improve the competitiveness of the region in terms of trade and investment.

(3) As for the ASEAN Socio-Cultural Community, it makes a lot of progress of the construction of the following areas: climate change, disaster management and disaster risk reduction, poverty reduction, protection and improvement of the rights and interests of migrant workers, etc.

The efforts of Thailand in the construction of the ASEAN Community

1. Thailand is a founding country of ASEAN

The establishment of ASEAN in 1967 has a close relationship with Thailand. At the beginning of the establishment and development, Thailand has played a very positive role. The founding meeting and the signing of the declaration happened on August 8, 1967 is in the Saranrom Palace of Thailand's capital.

2. Thailand plays a positive role in the development of ASEAN

Thailand regards ASEAN as a cornerstone of its diplomatic policy and it often emphasizes the importance of mutual trust between itself and other ASEAN countries to maintain the regional peace and stability. Moreover, Thailand helps to make the ASEAN Chapter have legal effects, and then make the ASEAN a rules-based organization. For example, in 2008-2009, when Thailand is the rotating chairman of the ASEAN, it attached great importance to the construction of ASEAN, and fully committed to start the effective implementation of the ASEAN Charter. Another effective action is the Roadmap for the ASEAN Community (2009-2015) that Thailand vigorously promotes. This roadmap provides a series of actions to guide the construction of ASEAN Political-Security Community, Economic Community and Socio-Cultural Community.

3. Thailand is located in the forefront in the construction of the three pillars

In terms of politics and security, Thailand is working with ASEAN member countries to maintain peace and stability in the region, and regards such work as the important part to sustain the ASEAN economic development. Thailand has been at the forefront of ASEAN countries to support various regional mechanisms to ensure the regional and national security. There are some main construction mechanisms. For example, Treaty of Amity and Cooperation(TAC)signed in 1976, East Asia Summit (EAS), ASEAN Defense Ministers' Meeting(ADMM), ADMM Plus and ASEAN Regional Forum(ARF). All these help to solve a lot of diplomatic problems and regional disputes.

In terms of economy, Thailand believes that regional economic integration is a powerful method, which can ensure sustainable and equitable growth of ASEAN countries. Also, it can strengthen the competitiveness of ASEAN countries and then contribute to the global economy. The ASEAN free trade area was established in 1992 and becomes an influential area gradually. During these years, Thailand has always been a strong supporter for the ASEAN regional economic integration of member countries, and Thailand will continue to play a positive role in deepening regional economic integration. Through the development of the RCEP, such cooperation proposed by the ASEAN will lead the half the size of the global market, and it will help further improve the collective potential of the East Asian economy. The 10 ASEAN countries as a whole, in inside and outside need to strength connectivity. Therefore, Thailand proposes that such connectivity should be in a comprehensive, tangible and visual way, which makes institutions and people closely linked. The implementation of the ASEAN integration is one of the most important plans among member countries.

In terms of Socio-Culture, Thailand fully supportsASEAN countries to be a people-oriented ASEAN Community that is put forward in the ASEAN Chapter. When Thailand was the chairman on duty for the ASEAN,

Thailand launched the ASEAN leaders' meeting, AIPA, civil society organizations(CSO) in order to increase their interaction with ASEAN and promote them to participate in the construction of the ASEAN Community. Thailand will continue the close cooperation among member countries, in order to further enhance the development in various social and cultural fields, such as disaster management, regional cooperation with education, public health, environment protection. It will help to establish the Southeast Asian countries common identity eventually realizing a caring and sharing society in ASEAN.

Conclusion

As we have discussed above, Thailand actively promotes the ASEAN Community construction. At the same time, it also has committed to speeding up the construction of transportation network, talents training service, to create a good investment environment for the three pillars of the ASEAN Community.

2015 has arrived, and the ASEAN Community would be completed on December 31, 2015. This year, ASEAN needs to complete the remaining tasks of "the ASEAN Community 2009-2015 road map. " There is still 10% of this plan remained to be finished, but most of them concern difficult problems of constructing the ASEAN Community. This year, the construction of the ASEAN Economic Community faces problems of unifing customs' standards, trade standards, the financial sector liberalization, investment protection, regional direct financing obstacles, and many other tasks. At present, ASEAN is trying to execute the ASEAN Integration Initiative(IAI) to narrow the development gap between ASEAN and world; to execute ASEAN interconnection master plan (MPAC) to promote the positive connectivity. According to the requirements of the construction of the ASEAN Community, most countries need to develop, modify the related economic laws and regulations to achieve connectivity. The situation of development is different in ASEAN member countries, so there is still a large gap to span.

ASEAN is facing more challenges now. For Southeast Asia, the ASEAN Economic Community is the strategic target to promote regional integration, enhance competitiveness. However, these are not the targets all. As we all know, Thailand, Malaysia, Brunei, Cambodia, Indonesia, Laos, Vietnam, Myanmar, Philippines, Singapore and other countries are trying to establish the ASEAN Community which includes various aspects of cooperation. This is a comprehensive cooperation which can be divided into three aspects as stated above. As for the definition of the ASEAN Community, Southeast Asia countries want to make themselves enter enter into a single market and then make ASEAN enter into the world economy. With all joint efforts of Thailand and other ASEAN countries, the ASEAN Community will reach the peak soon.

图书在版编目(CIP)数据

中国—东盟法律评论.第 4 卷/张晓君,纳隆·栽罕主编.—厦门:厦门大学
出版社,2015.9
ISBN 978-7-5615-5339-8

Ⅰ.①中…　Ⅱ.①张…②纳…　Ⅲ.①法律-中国、东南亚国家联盟-文集
Ⅳ.①D92-53②D933-53

中国版本图书馆 CIP 数据核字(2014)第 283164 号

官方合作网络销售商:　dangdang .com　亚马逊 amazon.cn　JD.COM 京东

厦门大学出版社出版发行

(地址:厦门市软件园二期望海路 39 号　邮编:361008)
总 编 办 电 话:0592-2182177　传真:0592-2181406
营销中心电话:0592-2184458　传真:0592-2181365
网址:http://www.xmupress.com
邮箱:xmup @ xmupress.com
厦门市明亮彩印有限公司印刷
2015 年 9 月第 1 版　2015 年 9 月第 1 次印刷
开本:720×970　1/16　印张:21　插页:2
字数:366 千字
定价:60.00 元
本书如有印装质量问题请直接寄承印厂调换